THE
SELF-REGULATION
HANDBOOK FOR TEENS & YOUNG ADULTS

THE
SELF-REGULATION
HANDBOOK FOR TEENS & YOUNG ADULTS

~~~~~

A Trauma-Informed Guide to Fostering Personal Resilience and Enhancing Interpersonal Skills

Kathy P. Wu, PhD

ULYSSES BOOKS
FOR YOUNG READERS

Published by

 ULYSSES BOOKS
FOR YOUNG READERS

an imprint of The Stable Book Group
32 Court Street, Suite 2109
Brooklyn, NY 11201
www.ulyssespress.com

Library of Congress Catalog Number: 2025930797
ISBN: 978-1-64604-757-4
eISBN: 978-1-64604-766-6

Acquisitions editor: Claire Sielaff
Managing editor: Claire Chun
Project editor: Renee Rutledge
Proofreader: Swetha Rao
Front cover design: Akangksha Sarmah
Layout: Abbey Gregory
Artwork: cover watercolor © nekotaro/Adobe Stock; cover and part pages © Анна Удод/ Adobe Stock; self-reflection header graphic © Goper Vector/Shutterstock.com; self-regulation, positive-change, and resources header graphics © bearsky23/Shutterstock.com

Printed in the United States
10 9 8 7 6 5 4 3 2 1

NOTE TO READERS: This book has been written and published strictly for informational and educational purposes. It is not intended to serve as medical advice or to be any form of medical treatment. You should always consult your physician before altering or changing any aspect of your medical treatment. Do not stop or change any prescription medications without the guidance and advice of your physician. Any use of the information in this book is made on the reader's good judgment after consulting with his or her physician and is the reader's sole responsibility. This book is not intended to diagnose or treat any medical condition and is not a substitute for a physician. This book is independently authored and published and no sponsorship or endorsement of this book by, and no affiliation with, any trademarked brands or other products mentioned within is claimed or suggested. All trademarks that appear in this book belong to their respective owners and are used here for informational purposes only. The author and publisher encourage readers to patronize the brands mentioned in this book.

For
Jaden, Adelyn, Chelsea, Maxwell & Winnie

CONTENTS

~~~~

INTRODUCTION

~~~~~

Do you remember when playtime was *everything*—the times when you felt like you could do anything, laugh forever, and never run out of energy? How do those memories make you feel now? For some, a trip down nostalgia lane brings back memories of simpler times. But for others, like me, it's a bittersweet journey.

You see, while I can generally look back on my childhood with fondness, I can't help but feel a twinge of regret and disappointment. Why? Because as I grew older, the promises of adulthood failed to materialize in the ways I'd expected. We're told that if we work hard and make the right choices, success and happiness will follow. Sadly, reality, for many, is often far more complex.

As I reflect on my own upbringing in Queens, New York, it's clear that life was anything but simple. Balancing academics, extracurriculars, and part-time jobs was a constant struggle. Also navigating social dynamics and expectations (aka "people drama") as a minority, 1.5 generation immigrant (I was born in China, but raised in the US), and working-class kid only added another layer of complexity to an already challenging equation.

What's most striking, perhaps, is how events beyond my immediate bubble constantly disrupted my transition into adulthood. From national tragedies like 9/11 and numerous deadly mass shootings, to economic crises such as the Great Recession of 2007 and international wars, each upheaval left a lasting mark on my development. Even though I have many positive memories of my youth, the extraordinary circumstances that my millennial peers and I faced often made it feel as though we were trying to build sturdy foundations on shifting sands.

While it's tempting to compare hardships across generations, it's important to acknowledge that each era faces its own unique challenges. Millennials and older generations have certainly experienced our share of difficulties, but the chronic trauma that you, *Gen Z* and *Gen Alpha*, are growing up with is truly unprecedented. The harsh realities of recent years—such as the COVID-19 pandemic, sociopolitical polarization, multiple wars, economic instability, and climate change, to name a few—serve as reminders that none of us exist in isolation. We're all navigating a world influenced by forces both large and small, and beyond our control.

As a psychologist specializing in the mental health of teens and young adults, I've had the privilege of witnessing the profound struggles many of my clients endure. From grappling with anxiety and depression to facing the debilitating effects of post-traumatic stress disorder (PTSD), they navigate a tumultuous landscape filled with insecurity and self-doubt. You, the young people of today, are emotional warriors, bravely confronting your private battles amid the chaos of adolescence and early adulthood.

Young people like you are indeed confronting significant mental health challenges. Here are some recent concerning statistics about the overall mental health and well-being of your peer group in the US:

✣ About one in six youth aged 6 to 17 experiences a mental health disorder each year.[1]

✣ In 2021, approximately 3.7 million young people aged 12 to 17 were affected by depression.[2]

✣ Around 31.9% of individuals between 13 to 18 struggle with anxiety disorders, such as excessive worrying, social anxiety, or panic attacks.[3]

✣ Suicide is a leading cause of death for teens and young adults, ranking as the second leading cause for those aged 10 to 14 and third among individuals between 15 to 24 in 2022.[4]

✣ In 2023, 10.9% of eighth graders, 19.8% of tenth graders, and 31.2% of twelfth graders reported illicit drug use in the past year.[5]

Many young people face challenges accessing mental health care, with only about two-thirds of children and adolescents with mental disorders receiving the services they need, highlighting a significant gap in care.[6]

While I recognize that this paints a bleak picture of the current state of mental health among teens and young adults, I want to assure you that I'm not a cynic. I consider myself an eternal optimist, a sunshine enthusiast, or even a hopeful hedonist. I believe we all have the power to change the circumstances that weigh us down. To make progress, we must take proactive steps to prioritize our mental health and well-being, refusing to let our circumstances define the lives we want to lead.

You are just as capable as—if not more so than—any established adult of empowering yourself to face life's challenges and avoid becoming another statistic. Consider yourself a river carving its path through rock; with persistence and determination, you can shape your own journey and overcome any obstacle in your way.

UNDERSTANDING CONTEXT IS CRUCIAL

The first step to taking control of a dreary circumstance is to acknowledge and accept that the environment we're exposed to growing up holds a significant influence on human development. The Adverse Childhood Experiences (ACES) studies, initiated in the mid-1990s, delved into people's childhood experiences and tracked their development over time. What they revealed was striking: The more adverse experiences someone faced during childhood—such as poverty, parental divorce, abuse, and neglect—the higher the likelihood of encountering problems later in life. These problems span from physical ailments like heart disease and diabetes to mental health issues and difficulties in forming healthy relationships.[7]

The studies further uncovered a *cumulative* effect of negative experiences. In essence, the more frequent or numerous these adversities were during childhood, the more daunting the path to a healthy adulthood becomes. It's akin to each challenging experience adding another weighty rock to life's backpack, leaving little space for carrying helpful and protective tools that you need to build a stronger foundation for your future.

Fortunately, follow-up studies have identified various tools or protective factors that promote resilience, or the ability to bounce back from challenges, setbacks, or difficult situations. These factors include supportive relationships with caregivers or other adults, positive social connections, access to mental health services and resources, and personal characteristics such as self-efficacy (this is the belief that you "got it" when faced with a problem), good problem-solving skills, and coping strategies. Especially heartening is that these protective factors, like adversities, are also cumulative. Developing resiliency reduces the negative effects of ACEs, and it prevents future harm to yourself and others.[8]

SELF-REGULATION IS A SUPERPOWER

In tricky situations, it can be comforting to imagine a superhero swooping in to save the day. While it's a charming thought, we all know there aren't any caped crusaders waiting in the wings. Instead of indulging that fantasy, we might invest our imagination dollars in more practical long-term pursuits—like creating innovative schools, designing a new video game series, concocting new skin care that will get rid of acne for good, building hospitals, developing community enrichment programs, or even inventing a teleportation device to get us into all of Taylor Swift's concerts.

My main goal for this book is to help you develop your own superhero power—specifically, your *self-regulation* skills. These tools will empower you to navigate our wild-wild world while enjoying your current youth and looking forward to tomorrow.

What is self-regulation anyway? Well, psychologists define self-regulation as the capacity to manage our thoughts, feelings, and actions to achieve our goals, adapt to changing circumstances, and maintain our overall well-being. It involves a dynamic interplay of cognitive, emotional, and behavioral processes that help individuals own their impulses, control their attention, and modulate their emotional reactions. To illustrate the application of these elements of self-regulation, visualize them in the context of a video game, where you are the protagonist or hero.

1. **Setting Goals:** Imagine yourself embarking on a quest to defeat a powerful enemy and save the world. Your goal is clearly defined: Don't die, and restore peace to the realm.

2. **Monitoring Progress:** Throughout your quest, you track your progress by completing objectives, collecting items, and leveling up your skills. You check your quest log and map to ensure you're moving closer to your goal.

3. **Adjusting Strategies:** As you encounter challenging enemies or obstacles, you adapt your strategies by learning new abilities, upgrading your equipment, or seeking help from allies. You experiment with different approaches until you find what works best.

4. **Managing Emotions:** The path is fraught with danger and uncertainty, but you remain focused and determined. You control your fear and frustration, channeling your emotions into motivation to overcome obstacles and continue your quest.

5. **Self-Reflection:** After completing a major objective or reaching a milestone, you take a moment to reflect on your trajectory. You consider your successes and failures, analyze your decisions, and plan your next steps accordingly.

Conversely, imagine what would happen if you didn't employ self-regulation strategies. Without setting clear goals, you might wander aimlessly in the game world, unsure of what you're supposed to accomplish. You could spend hours exploring without making any progress toward your objectives, leading to frustration and disengagement. If you neglect to monitor your progress, you may miss important clues, overlook side quests, or fail to notice when you're running low on resources. As a result, you might find yourself ill-prepared for upcoming challenges or unaware of how close you are to completing your mission.

When faced with difficult enemies or obstacles, lacking self-regulation skills could leave you stuck in repetitive patterns of gameplay, trying the same approach repeatedly without success. You might refuse to consider alternative strategies or seek help from in-game resources, prolonging your struggle unnecessarily. Without the ability to manage your emotions, you could easily become frustrated, angry, or discouraged when you encounter setbacks. You might lash out at other characters, blame external factors for your difficulties, or even rage quit the game, depriving yourself of having a fun and rewarding time.

Lastly, without engaging in self-reflection, you'd miss out on valuable opportunities for learning and improvement. You could repeat the same mistakes, overlook important lessons, and fail to recognize your own strengths and weaknesses as a player. As a result, you might struggle to progress in the game and ultimately feel unsatisfied with your experience.

As the hero and protagonist of your life, it's clear that self-regulation is essential for success and enjoyment. In fact, self-regulation isn't just about managing your time or controlling your impulses (though those are important too!), it's about *taking ownership* of your thoughts, emotions, and actions. Self-regulation is about using that awareness to navigate the complexities of whatever life stage you are in with intentionality and resilience. With self-regulation as your guide, you'll be better equipped to create the life you envision for yourself, one mindful choice at a time.

TRAUMA-INFORMED SKILLS

As mentioned in the subtitle of this book, the self-regulation strategies I'll discuss are *trauma-informed*. Let me clarify what that means.

Given the stormy state of our world, it's unrealistic to expect people to self-regulate without addressing the underlying chaos. It's like telling someone to "stop, drop, and roll" while they're in a burning building without also working to put out the fire. Similarly, a trauma-informed approach acknowledges the need for both a supportive environment and meaningful action to help people cope and heal.

As a trauma-informed therapist, I strive to create a space that fosters safety, choice, and empowerment for my clients who are in survival mode—when their mind and body are focused on just getting through each day, often because of stress, fear, or past experiences that make it hard to feel safe or in control. This therapeutic space understands how adverse experiences can affect the way you respond to problems and how you cope with challenges. It's important to clarify that this approach does not imply that you, the reader, should be diagnosed with PTSD; rather, the trauma-informed self-regulation strategies are for anyone facing our modern life's most common challenges. Ultimately, a trauma-informed approach emphasizes compassion, resilience, and a strengths-based perspective to facilitate healing and growth.

HOW THIS BOOK IS ORGANIZED

We will use the framework of trauma-informed self-regulation described above to address frequently occurring issues that teens and young adults deal with these days. Each chapter focuses on a "specific challenge" within three separate domains: self, others, and the world at large.

PART I: Increasing Personal Resilience. Chapter 1 presents key principles and base ingredients of self-regulation, and all subsequent chapters will build on top of these foundational skills. Chapters 2 to 9 explore challenges that arise at the self-level—from managing anxiety and depression to addressing anger, perfectionism, burnout, addiction, and neurodivergence. These chapters provide tools to help you better understand your thoughts, feelings, and how you can better manage them.

PART II: Enhancing Interpersonal Skills. Chapters 10 to 14 delve into the difficulties you may face as a social being, including loneliness, identity discrimination, relational abuse, familial discord, and grief and loss. You'll learn how to communicate more effectively, resolve conflicts, and build healthier connections.

PART III: Thriving in a Turbulent World. Chapters 15 to 19 address global issues that exist on the outside, such as climate anxiety, economic stress, mass trauma, political fatigue, and technological drawbacks. You'll discover ways to make a positive impact in your community and beyond, tackling larger-scale problems and fostering meaningful change.

SOME GROUNDING NOTES

1. Use What Speaks to You: First, the self-regulation strategies presented here were developed out of psychological treatment models, such as cognitive behavioral therapy (CBT), acceptance commitment therapy (ACT), and dialectical behavioral therapy (DBT). These are fancy treatment modalities that have been deemed clinically effective and gold standards of care in the therapy world. However, the specific techniques shared here have not themselves undergone "clinical effectiveness trials." Translation: I'm not here to promise they'll work for everyone, every time. Therapy isn't a one-size-fits-all deal, and requires some discernment on your end about what works and what doesn't work for you. Most importantly, these strategies aren't a replacement for actual therapy. Because let's be real: You can't bottle up the whole therapy experience in a book or fully replace an effective therapist with AI (artificial intelligence), yet! They're still pretty darn helpful. So, go ahead, explore, and find what vibes with you!

2. Not a Self-Diagnosis Manual: This guide outlines common psychological conditions, their symptoms, and potential causes, much like how one might recognize the general characteristics of a physical ailment such as the flu or a cold, along with its typical, evidence-based treatments. However, this information is intended as educational overviews and is not sufficient for self-diagnosis. To gain an accurate understanding of your mental health, it's important to seek a professional assessment by a qualified psychologist or psychiatrist. A trained clinician can provide a comprehensive evaluation and offer tailored recommendations, ensuring you receive the most appropriate care for your unique needs.

3. Case Examples: In each chapter, I've included composite stories of young people who've faced different challenges and hardships relevant to the topic. These stories are meant to illustrate the points discussed, but they aren't based on any one client or people I personally know. If any parts of these stories seem biographical, it's purely coincidental. I've used gender-neutral names and pronouns to make sure everyone can relate to the experiences shared.

4. Self-Reflection and Connection: I've crafted sets of questions to help you tune into your emotions and experiences related to each topic. These questions are designed to prompt personal reflection and encourage deeper connections with others. While they're meant for your own introspection, I suggest also using them as conversation starters with friends, family, or even strangers you meet to foster meaningful interpersonal relationships. It's highly recommended that you take out a pen, a notebook, and write away!

5. Overlap and Repetition of Skills: The self-regulation strategies I've outlined for you are designed to address the specific challenges of each chapter. While each chapter can be read independently, you might notice some overlap in the techniques presented. Start with Chapter 1, though, as I outline a basic set of skills for self-regulation, which you will build onto with each chapter. Like core ingredients in a recipe, certain tools—such as mindfulness and improved communication—are effective for a variety of mental health and wellness issues, from loneliness to familial conflict to political fatigue. These foundational techniques are versatile and can be applied across different situations to support overall well-being.

6. Positive-Change Kickstarter: Each chapter concludes with a call to action, because ideas and insights are like cookies—they're delightful to have around, but they're not much use if you can't eat them! I leave you with a few guiding questions to help you identify immediate action steps for igniting positive change. Consider your answers to these final questions as your starter kit for your hero's quest, empowering yourself to tackle the challenges you're facing with your shoulders back and head held high.

7. I Am Not a Teen: Finally, I am not a teenager or in my twenties anymore (I've already done my time!). I understand that I might not always get everything right about your lived experiences. In my writing, I've included quotations to illustrate how some of my clients have described their experiences with adversity, but these client perspectives may not capture your experiences precisely. These quotes aren't attributed to any specific situation but aim to capture the essence of those experiences. My goal is to empathize with what you may be going through, rather than claim to fully understand it *as* you. While I strive to be relatable, I recognize that my perspectives are shaped by my own limitations and biases as a millennial adult.

ONE LAST NOTE

I am looking forward to this centering experience with you. Before we proceed though, I want to say this to all former and present-day young people: thank you for doing your best today (period).

PART I
INCREASING PERSONAL RESILIENCE

"Knowing others is intelligence; knowing yourself is true wisdom. Mastering others is strength; mastering yourself is true power."

—Lao Tzu

CHAPTER 1

GENERAL PRINCIPLES OF TRAUMA-INFORMED SELF-REGULATION

~~~~

KEYS TO SAFETY, EMPOWERMENT, AND CHOICE

As I mentioned in the introduction, trauma-informed self-regulation skills prioritize safety, empowerment, and choice, while also recognizing the unique experiences and needs of those who've faced adversity. This approach isn't one-size-fits-all; it focuses on meeting you where you are and guiding you toward a place of growth. In my years of working with people like you, I've found that those who embrace three key elements—*openness*, *self-compassion*, and *restfulness* (yes, a good night's sleep)—tend to get the most out of therapy. These elements are not just helpful tools; I believe they are the foundation for lasting change and healing, allowing you to navigate life's challenges feeling safe with your emotions, empowered to solve problems, and secured in your choices.

Openness. When it comes to your mental health and happiness, remember there are many paths to feeling better. When things get overwhelming, it's easy to get tunnel vision—we start to believe there's no other way to feel or be. However, I've seen time and time again that being open-minded is one of our best defenses against suffering.

Let me share the story of "The Fox and the Grapes" with you. Imagine a hungry little fox who stumbles upon some delicious-looking grapes hanging high up on a vine. The fox tries and tries to reach them, but no luck. Frustrated, the fox walks away, telling itself, "Those grapes were probably sour anyway." The truth, though, is that the fox couldn't reach them because of its own perceived limitations—not because the grapes weren't sweet. It's like we sometimes convince ourselves something isn't worth it simply because it's out of reach right now.

When it comes to building self-regulation skills in this sometimes-intimidating world, keep an open mind. Explore different perspectives, try new ways to feel better. You never know—what seems out of reach today might just turn out to be your sweetest grape yet.

Self-Compassion. Self-compassion is another crucial part of handling bad days, especially when you're working on self-regulation. Practicing compassion is about offering yourself the same kindness, dignity, and understanding you'd offer your bestie who's struggling. Sadly, when things aren't going well or you're feeling overwhelmed, it's easy to turn on yourself. However, realize that nobody has it all figured out all the time (most of us are actually just faking it until we make it), and being hard on yourself won't help you move forward, be more competent, or be more acceptable in society.

Let's say you've been working hard on a project, like a TikTok or YouTube video, and it flops—maybe it doesn't get the views or engagement you were hoping for. Instead of spiraling into frustration or thinking you're not good enough, self-compassion would be taking a step back and reminding yourself that creating content is a process, and an art in itself. You might think, *"Okay, this video didn't perform how I wanted, but that doesn't define me. I'm learning with every upload, and I'll use what I've learned to refine my craft and make the next one better."*

When you are being self-compassionate, you are not making excuses for an undesired outcome, but recognizing that mistakes and setbacks don't mean you're not capable or worthy. It's instead focused on creating space to validate your pain, reset, keep going, and approach the next challenge without carrying the weight of self-doubt or negativity with you everywhere you go. Self-compassion is essentially the act of providing yourself unconditional love, which can come in handy when you're faced with moments in which the world sadly doesn't seem to be so open to what you have to say or what you have to offer.

Restfulness. When you've got the mindset down, it's just as important to keep your brain and body in optimal health. You've probably heard it all before from well-meaning older adults who've advised you about the importance of quality sleep, good nutrition, and exercise. But these ingredients really are foundational to our psychological well-being, when we are lucky enough to have access to them daily. You might have heard of Abraham Maslow, the psychologist who developed a theory of motivation, which focuses on how we meet our needs and ultimately reach our full potential, as shown in the following diagram:[9]

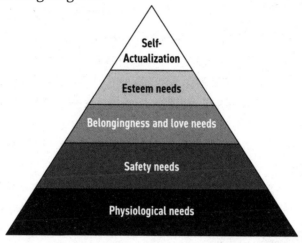

Maslow's Hierarchy of Needs

At the base of the pyramid are our physiological and safety needs, which include food, shelter, water, warmth, rest, and security from danger. The idea is simple: if we don't take care of the very container for our brain and vital organs, what good is it to focus on abstract concepts like belonging or self-actualization?

Experts recommend that teens and young people get between 8 to 10 hours of sleep each night for optimal health.[10] However, many fall short. According to the National Youth Risk Behavior Survey by the CDC, about 73% of high school students don't get enough sleep on school nights, averaging less than seven hours.[11] Think of your brain as a high-tech gadget. If it's running on just 3% battery like your phone, it won't function at its best. A quick power nap can't replace the need for a full recharge.

Young people often experience a natural shift in their sleep-wake cycle, making it harder to fall asleep early and wake up for school. When you add academic and extracurricular pressures to the mix, it can easily lead to chronic sleep deprivation.

Plus, using electronic devices before bed can interfere with sleep. The blue light from smartphones, tablets, and computers disrupts melatonin (hormone that regulates sleep) production, making it harder to fall asleep. The COVID-19 pandemic has only made this worse, with increased stress, anxiety, and changes in routine leading to irregular sleep patterns.

Chronic sleep deprivation can have serious consequences for physical health, mental well-being, and academic performance. Studies link insufficient sleep in young people to higher risks of obesity, diabetes, depression, anxiety, poor academic achievement, and even car accidents.[12]

If you are constantly sleep deprived, here are some tools to help you get better rest (modify these suggestions as your lifestyle, resources, and space allow):

1. Develop a Consistent Sleep Schedule: Try to go to bed and wake up at the same time each day, including weekends, holidays, and other days off from your usual schedule. If you can only focus on one, prioritize waking up at the same time each day, as this practice better anchors your sleep cycle and makes it easier to fall asleep at night.

2. Create a Relaxing Bedtime Routine: Start a relaxation routine 30 to 60 minutes before bed. This allows your body and mind to unwind, helping to boost melatonin production and prepare for restful sleep. Activities like reading, a warm bath, or deep breathing can reduce stress and lower your body temperature, making it easier to fall asleep. Starting early ensures you give yourself enough time to transition into a relaxed state before bed.

3. Limit Screen Time Before Bed: Avoid using electronic devices for at least an hour before bed. Activities like doom-scrolling or watching endless video reels can keep your brain active, making it harder to relax. Try using a separate alarm clock instead of your phone, and charge your device out of reach to minimize temptation and give your mind a chance to wind down before sleep.

4. Make Your Bed and Environment Sleep-Friendly: If possible, make sure your sleeping space is cool, dark, and quiet. Use blackout curtains, white noise machines, or earplugs to minimize distractions. Refrain from doing anything else, like studying, gaming, or any other activity that is not purely sleeping, in your bed. You want to have your brain associate your bed with sleep, and not wakefulness or a waiting room for sleep to arrive. If you are not tired yet, no need to be in bed; actually use your bed for sleep and nothing extra if you can help it.

5. Limit Caffeine and Stimulants: In addition to caffeine, other stimulants like nicotine and certain medications can interfere with your ability to fall asleep. It's best to avoid these, especially in the afternoon and evening, as they can keep your mind alert and disrupt your natural sleep rhythm. Similarly, energy drinks, sugary snacks, and even some over-the-counter cold medications may contain stimulants that can hinder your ability to unwind and get a restful night's sleep.

6. Regular Exercise: Engaging in regular physical activity can help you fall asleep faster and enjoy deeper sleep. Just make sure to avoid vigorous exercise close to bedtime.

7. Limit Naps: Short naps can be helpful, but keep them to 20 to 30 minutes (think kitten naps) and avoid napping late in the day to prevent interfering with nighttime sleep.

8. Seek a Sleep Specialist If Needed: If you're still struggling with sleep despite making lifestyle changes, talk to a healthcare provider or mental health professional. You might be dealing with underlying sleep disorders or other issues that need attention.

By prioritizing openness, self-compassion, and restfulness, you are already well on your way to creating a strong foundation for your healing and personal growth.

CHILL VIBES ONLY: WAYS TO FIND YOUR CALM

Now that you've got the base ingredients for a chill life, let's dive into some go-to self-regulation skills that'll make managing things like goals, progress monitoring, emotions, and self-reflection way easier. These skills will help you stay grounded, stay cool, and stay in control, even when life feels daunting. Think of laid-back, go-with-the-flow types like Bob Ross, Pharrell Williams, Matthew McConaughey, Keanu Reeves, and Zendaya. These people seem to have a natural chill vibe that reflects solid coping skills and ability to stay grounded.

GROUNDING AND MINDFULNESS

Being present and connected is crucial for feeling stable and in control during overwhelming moments. Grounding serves as an anchor, helping you navigate emotional storms and negative memories with clarity and resilience. It is no wonder that most evidence-based therapies, including CBT, DBT, and ACT, incorporate mindfulness practices because they are proven to help manage overwhelming emotions and improve mental health. These therapies emphasize staying present, observing your thoughts without judgment, and grounding yourself in the current moment—skills that are essential for building emotional chillness and gaining clarity during confusing times. By integrating mindfulness into your daily life, you can develop the ability to pause, reflect, and respond with intention, rather than reacting impulsively to big emotions. This foundation of mindfulness can help you regain control and reduce the impact of stress and adversity on your well-being.

- ☼ **5-4-3-2-1 Exercise:** Focus on your five senses to bring yourself into the present moment. For example, name five things you can see, four things you can touch, three things you can hear, two things you can smell, and one thing you can taste.

- ☼ **Deep Breathing:** Close your eyes and take a slow, deep breath in for four counts, hold for four counts, and exhale for four counts. Repeat for a few minutes to center your mind.

- ☼ **Mindful Walking:** Pay attention to each step you take as you walk. Focus on the feel of your feet against the ground, the rhythm of your movement, and the sounds around you. This brings your awareness to the present and helps clear your mind.

- ☼ **Visualization:** Imagine yourself in a peaceful place, whether it's a beach, a forest, or a quiet room. Picture every detail—the warmth of the sun, the sound of the waves, or the smell of the air. This visualization can act as a mental "reset" and offer a calm moment when you need it.

* **Body Scan Meditation:** Start at your feet and slowly work your way up your body, paying attention to how each part feels. Notice any tension, tightness, or discomfort, and then consciously relax each area as you go. This can help you become more aware of where you're holding stress and release it.

* **Breathing with Mantras:** Combine deep breathing with repeating a calming word or phrase to keep your focus. For example, as you breathe in, say "I am calm," and as you breathe out, say "I am at peace." This can deepen your sense of relaxation and bring you back to the present.

* **Mindful Eating:** Pay full attention to your food—look at it, smell it, and taste it slowly. Notice the textures and flavors as you chew. This practice not only enhances your appreciation for what you're eating but also encourages you to eat mindfully, helping with digestion and creating a sense of satisfaction.

* **Active Listening:** Choose a piece of music or sounds from your environment. Close your eyes and focus only on the sound—whether it's the rhythm of a song, the chirping of birds, or the hum of traffic. Let your attention be absorbed by the sound, letting go of any other thoughts or distractions.

EMOTIONAL MANAGEMENT

Managing intense emotions, whether from past or present experiences, is key to achieving a sense of chill. By identifying and naming your feelings and practicing relaxation techniques, you can gain more control over your mind and body, allowing you to respond in calm, thoughtful, and flexible ways.

❊ **Label Your Emotions:** If you're feeling anxious, angry, or sad, just naming it can make it feel more manageable. It's like turning the volume down on the emotional storm

happening in your head. For example, if you're feeling overwhelmed by everything going on, stop for a sec and say to yourself, *"I'm feeling really stressed right now."* This simple act can give you a little distance from the emotion, making it easier to cope. Read Chapter 2 for more information on emotion expression.

❊ **Progressive Muscle Relaxation (PMR):** PMR is a technique where you intentionally tense up and then relax different muscle groups in your body to help you feel calmer and reduce stress. It works because when you tense your muscles, it creates physical tension, but when you let go and relax them, it helps release that built-up stress.

❊ **Tense and Release Your Jaw:** When you're stressed, you might not even realize you're clenching your jaw. Take a moment to squeeze your jaw tightly (like you're holding in a yawn) for 5 to 10 seconds, then release. This can help with tension headaches or general stress. It's a subtle but effective way to reset.

❊ **Shoulder Shrug and Drop:** Tense your shoulders up to your ears as if you're shrugging, hold it for a few seconds, then drop them down like you're letting go of all the weight you're carrying. This one is perfect if you've been hunched over a desk or on your phone for too long.

* **Hand Squeeze and Release:** If you find your hands are tense, try making fists, hold them as tightly as you can, then slowly release them. Doing this gives your body a chance to reset and stop holding all that stress in your hands.
* **Leg Tensing:** Sit comfortably and stretch your legs out in front of you. Tighten your leg muscles like you're pushing your feet into the floor, hold for a few seconds, then relax. This can help you physically "loosen up" when you're feeling restless or anxious.
* **Foot Flex:** Sit back and stretch your legs out again. Flex your feet—point your toes up toward your face as much as you can, hold it for a few seconds, then relax. This is a great way to release tension in your lower body and calm yourself down after a long day of sitting or standing.

SELF-CARE AND USING A RELAXATION ROUTINE

Engaging in activities that support your physical, emotional, and mental well-being is essential for replenishing your energy and reducing stress. Prioritizing self-care through exercise, hobbies, and creative outlets helps you invest in your long-term health and resilience. When stress starts to build up, having a go-to routine is key—this way, you don't have to come up with something new when you're already feeling overwhelmed and unfocused. For example, doesn't this routine sound like an ideal way to wind down, say, on a Sunday night, as a maintenance strategy?

* **Create a Relaxing Space:** Start by dimming the lights or lighting a scented candle with a calming fragrance (like

lavender or eucalyptus). You could also add some fairy lights or set up some soft lighting if that helps create a peaceful vibe.

* **Calming Music:** Put on some chill music. It could be instrumental, nature sounds, or even a favorite calming playlist you've put together. Music is a powerful way to shift your mood. You might try apps like Calm or YouTube channels that specialize in relaxing sounds.

* **Deep Breathing:** While you're soaking in the calm, start taking slow, deep breaths. Breathe in for four seconds, hold for four, and exhale for four. Do this for a few minutes. It'll help you shift out of fight-or-flight mode and bring your focus back to your body.

* **A Warm Shower or Bath:** If you're able to, hop into a warm shower or bath. Let the water be a kind of reset for your mind. You don't need to do anything special—just focus on how the warm water feels, breathing deeply as you let the tension of the day wash away.

* **A Moment of Stillness:** Once you're done with the shower, sit or lie down in a quiet spot for a few minutes. This is your time to just *be*. No distractions, no social media, no work or school pressure. Just breathe, reflect, and focus on being present.

* **Affirmations (a Must):** End the routine with some affirmations, like, "I am safe, I am calm, I can handle this." It's a simple way to leave the routine feeling grounded and more in control.

KNOW YOUR VALUES

Your values are the things that really matter to you. They're the beliefs, rules, and standards you live by, whether you realize it or not. Figuring out what's most important to you helps you navigate life in a way that feels authentic and true to yourself. It's like having a personal guidebook for hard decisions, goals, and even friendships.

You're at a time when you're figuring out who you are and what you stand for. It can be easy to feel swayed by peer pressure, social media trends, or what everyone else expects of you. Knowing your values gives you that extra confidence to stay true to yourself and make choices that match your own beliefs.

Here's how some common values can look in action:

- ☼ **Respect:** You treat people the way you want to be treated, and you stick to your boundaries, understanding that others have different opinions, backgrounds, and needs, and you treat them with kindness and dignity. This doesn't just mean respecting people in real life, but also online. If respect is important to you, you're more likely to stay away from drama, gossip, or anything that undermines others.

- ☼ **Honesty:** Being true to yourself is huge when you're a teen. You don't have to pretend to be someone you're not. If honesty matters to you, you'll choose not to lie about who you are, even if it's tempting to go along with what's popular or what people expect. Honesty involves saying what's real, even when it's hard to be vulnerable.

- ☼ **Creativity:** If you're into music, drawing, writing, or any other creative outlets, living according to your values might mean you make space for these things in your life. Creativity is about expressing your unique perspective. You might find that prioritizing creativity in your life helps you feel more fulfilled.

* **Equality:** Maybe you believe everyone should have a fair shot in life. If equality is one of your values, you're likely to stand up against injustice and support causes that promote fairness, whether it's gender, race, or opportunities. This could mean speaking out when you see something wrong, or simply being inclusive in your friend groups.

* **Empathy:** If you can put yourself in someone else's shoes and genuinely care about their feelings, you're likely to show up when someone's having a hard time. Empathy is about listening and being there for others. In high school or college, this could mean supporting a friend who's going through deep stuff, or speaking up against bullying.

* **Growth:** Life is all about learning and evolving, whether that's improving your skills, expanding your mindset, or working on yourself. If growth is something you value, you'll probably make time for things that push you forward—whether it's reading a book, learning a new hobby, or even getting out of your comfort zone (thank you for reading this book) to try something different.

SAFETY PLANNING

Creating personalized safety plans provides a sense of security during or in the aftermath of potentially threatening situations when you feel overwhelmed or emotionally unsafe. You can navigate difficult circumstances with greater confidence and resilience with these specific steps:

* **Recognize When You Feel Unsafe:** Identify what sets off your distressing feelings—whether it's specific people, situations, conversations, or environments—and have a

plan in place for how to handle them (e.g., taking a break, stepping outside for a few minutes).

* **Set Boundaries:** If a relationship or situation feels unsafe or emotionally draining, practice setting clear boundaries. You can say, *"I need some time to myself right now"* or *"I'm not comfortable with that topic,"* and walk away if needed.

* **Emergency Contacts:** Have a list of trusted people you can contact during difficult moments, like a friend or family member, and know how to reach them quickly for support.

COGNITIVE COPING STRATEGIES

Challenging and reframing negative thoughts and beliefs is key to breaking free from self-blame and hopelessness. Our minds often get caught in patterns of thinking that make things feel worse than they are. These patterns, known as cognitive distortions, are negative thought habits that make us see situations in extreme or unbalanced ways. These distorted thoughts can amplify stress, anxiety, and low self-esteem, and they often fuel feelings of helplessness. Cognitive distortions are an important part of CBT (cognitive behavioral therapy), a widely used therapy approach designed to help people identify and challenge these unhelpful thought patterns. While cognitive distortions are a normal part of the human experience, learning to recognize and address them is key to breaking free from their grip. By shifting these patterns, you can develop a more compassionate inner dialogue that celebrates your strengths rather than putting you down. This can ultimately improve your emotional well-being and how you handle challenges. Here are a few common cognitive distortions and examples of how they might show up in your thinking:

- ✦ **All-or-Nothing Thinking:** Viewing situations in black-and-white terms, with no middle ground. *Example:* "If I don't get 100% on this test, I'm a complete failure."
- ✦ **Overgeneralization:** Taking one negative event and assuming it will happen every time. *Example:* "I didn't get the job I interviewed for; I'll never get hired anywhere."
- ✦ **Mental Filtering:** Only focusing on the negative aspects of a situation while ignoring the positive. *Example:* "I made a small mistake in the group project, so the whole thing is a disaster."
- ✦ **Disqualifying the Positive:** Rejecting positive experiences or accomplishments as being unimportant. *Example:* "People say I did well on my presentation, but they're just being nice. It wasn't that great."
- ✦ **Jumping to Conclusions:** Making negative assumptions without solid evidence. *Example:* "I didn't get a reply to my text, so they must be mad at me."
- ✦ **Personalization:** Blaming yourself for things outside your control. *Example*: "My friend is upset, so it must be my fault."
- ✦ **Should Statements:** Putting unnecessary pressure on yourself with "should" or "must" statements, leading to guilt or frustration. *Example:* "I should be able to handle everything on my own, and I shouldn't feel stressed."
- ✦ **Labeling and Mislabeling:** Attaching a negative label to yourself or others based on a single event. *Example:* "I didn't do well on that assignment, so I'm just dumb."

✸ **Fortune-Telling:** Predicting a negative outcome without any evidence. *Example:* "I'm going to fail my exam; I just know it."

✸ **Magnification (or Minimization):** Making a big deal out of a small issue, or minimizing something important. *Example:* "If I make a mistake in this presentation, it's going to ruin everything."

More importantly, here are a few strategies to help you manage these faulty ways of thinking:

✸ **Reframe Negative Thoughts:** If you catch yourself thinking, *"I always mess up,"* counter it with, *"I made a mistake, but that doesn't define me. I can learn and improve next time."* This is a way to fight *all-or-nothing thinking*, where you believe that one mistake makes everything bad. Instead, remember that everyone makes mistakes, and it's an opportunity to grow.

✸ **Challenge Your Inner Critic:** When you catch yourself thinking, *"I'm not good enough,"* ask yourself, *"Would I say this to a friend?"* If not, then treat yourself with the same kindness and understanding. This helps fight *catastrophizing*, where you imagine the worst-case scenario. Instead, practice showing yourself the same compassion you would show someone else who's struggling.

✸ **Use Positive Affirmations:** Start your day by repeating a few affirmations, like *"I am capable,"* or *"I can handle whatever comes my way."* This sets a positive tone for the day and helps rewire your thinking to focus on your strengths and abilities rather than the negative. This practice can be especially helpful if you tend to overgeneralize or see things in a negative light.

RELATIONSHIP BUILDING

Building supportive relationships is crucial for providing a sense of belonging and validation during your healing process. Trusted individuals can offer empathy and encouragement, helping you feel less isolated and more resilient in the face of adversity.

* **Reach Out to Friends:** Make an effort to stay in touch with people who support and understand you. Even a quick text or call can strengthen bonds and remind you that you're not alone.

* **Seek Mentorship:** Find a mentor or role model who can guide you through hard times. This could be a teacher, coach, or someone you look up to who has been through similar challenges.

* **Join a Community or Club:** If you're feeling isolated or disconnected, joining a group or community can help you find like-minded people who get where you're coming from. Whether it's a school club, sports team, volunteer group, or an online community around a hobby or interest, being part of something bigger than yourself can give you a sense of belonging and purpose. Plus, it's a great way to make friends who can offer support and empathy when you need it most.

* **Set Up Regular Check-Ins:** Sometimes we get so caught up in our own stuff that we forget to reach out. Setting up regular check-ins with a friend or family member can help keep you grounded. Whether it's a weekly coffee or a text chain, having a consistent space to share thoughts, vent, or just connect can make a huge difference. It's all about creating a routine of care and communication that doesn't feel forced but feels supportive.

✿ **Volunteer or Offer Support to Others:** It might sound counterintuitive, but helping others can strengthen your own support network. Volunteering or offering a helping hand to friends or family can build relationships while also giving you a sense of fulfillment. When you show kindness to others, you'll likely find that it circles back to you when you need it most. Helping others can make you feel more connected to your community and remind you that we all need each other.

SEEKING HELP

Reaching out for help is one of the most important steps in taking care of your mental and emotional well-being. It can be hard to ask for support, but doing so helps lighten the load and gives you access to resources and perspectives you might not have on your own. Seeking help doesn't mean you're weak—it's a sign of strength and a proactive way to cope with life's challenges.

✿ **Talk to a Professional:** If you're feeling overwhelmed, reaching out to a therapist or counselor can provide a safe, non-judgmental space to explore and process your emotions.

✿ **School Support:** Don't hesitate to connect with a teacher or school administrator if you're struggling. They're there to listen and can help you find the resources you need.

✿ **Talk to Parents or Guardians:** Your parents or guardians can often provide emotional support and guidance, helping you figure out next steps or simply being there when you need someone to talk to.

✿ **Peer Support:** Sometimes, talking to someone who understands what you're going through can be incredibly helpful. Joining a support group—whether in person or online —can connect you with others facing similar challenges.

TELLING YOUR STORY

Sharing your story can be a powerful step toward healing. While this book won't dive deeply into processing trauma, it will help you explore ways to express what you've been through and guide you in integrating your experiences in a way that empowers you. Telling your story, when you're ready, can move you from feeling isolated to feeling more connected, both to yourself and others.

- ✿ **Journaling:** Writing regularly about your thoughts and emotions can help you process and make sense of your feelings. It's a safe space where you can be completely honest with yourself. You might start with just a few lines each day, or write more extensively when something's weighing on you. Over time, this can give you clarity on your own experiences.

- ✿ **Speak to a Trusted Person:** When you feel ready, consider opening up to someone you trust—whether it's a friend, family member, or mentor. Sharing parts of your story with someone who listens without judgment can help reduce feelings of isolation and help you feel seen and supported.

- ✿ **Join a Support Group:** Whether online or in person, connecting with others who've gone through similar experiences can be incredibly powerful. Hearing other people's stories can make you feel less alone, and sharing your own can be a step toward healing. It also helps you build a sense of community with others who understand.

✵ **Write a Letter:** If talking feels too hard or you're not sure how to start, consider writing a letter to someone you trust, or even to your past self. This can be a way to express your feelings without the pressure of an immediate conversation, and it can serve as a powerful tool for reflecting on your journey.

By practicing these basic self-regulation skills, you'll start to build a toolkit for managing your emotions, staying calm under pressure, and handling life's challenges with more flexibility and confidence. Remember: Practice leads to progress, and progress opens new possibilities.

Now, let's dive into even more evidence-based strategies for tackling different challenges you might face along the way. For example, if you're feeling stressed about politics, turn to Chapter 18; if you're feeling down about your family relationships, head to Chapter 13. And if you ever need a refresher on the basics of self-regulation, feel free to revisit here in Chapter 1 anytime you need.

CHAPTER 2

EMOTIONAL DISCONNECTION

~~~

COMMONLY VOICED

* "I guess I'm... okay? I mean, I don't feel sad exactly, but I don't feel happy either. There are a lot of emotions and nothing going on at the same time. What do you want me to say?"
* "My feelings overwhelm and exhaust me. All I want to do is just stay in my room and draw all the curtains down. Wake me up when I'm 30."
* "I hate when people ask me how I'm feeling. I don't like being put on the spot."
* "I don't understand why I feel the way I do; I just do?"

UNDERSTANDING EMOTIONAL DISCONNECTION

In my work with first-time therapy clients, I'm consistently impressed by their emotional intelligence—the ability to recognize, understand, and manage both their own emotions and those of others. My excitement when I encounter these emotionally aware young people stems from the anticipation that our work together will be deep, fascinating, and ultimately, effective. I believe emotions are to our experiences what the alphabet is to language.

Barbara Fredrickson's broaden-and-build theory sheds light on the crucial role emotions play in building relationships, making decisions, and enriching our lives. According to her theory, positive emotions expand our thinking and behaviors, enabling us to forge lasting connections and develop resilience.[13] By sharing our feelings, we foster trust and strengthen our relationships, allowing our instincts to guide our decisions. In essence, understanding and articulating our emotions are key to effective emotional regulation and overall mental health.

The advanced emotional literacy I've seen in my clients seems influenced by the decreasing stigma around mental health (yay!) and the impact of social media, which has exposed us to a rich emotional vocabulary and new ways to express ourselves.[14] For instance, I once overheard two teens at a café chatting about a mutual friend. One said, "Yo, did you see her Instagram story? Big mood, she's lowkey slaying in that outfit, but I'm salty I missed her party last night." While this exchange might seem casual, I was struck by their sophisticated emotional awareness. As a language enthusiast, I found their conversation layered and eloquent, conveying feelings, thoughts, and values all at once (and don't worry—I respected their privacy and didn't eavesdrop beyond this snippet).

In therapy, one of my primary goals is to understand how my clients connect with their emotions. I often start with a simple question like, *"Tell me about your most recent birthday."*

The variety of responses can be surprising—some clients dive deep into their emotional experiences, while others might simply say, *"It was fun"* or *"I'm not sure."* This exercise reveals how well they can articulate their feelings, so feel free to give it a try yourself!

My guideline is that if I need more than a couple of follow-up questions to help someone open up about their emotions, it may be time to provide some basic education on emotional connection and disconnection. This approach recognizes that emotional connectedness is fundamental to who we are and how we navigate life. So, what happens when we find ourselves emotionally disconnected? Emotional disconnection can stem from various sources, including past experiences, current stressors, or mental health challenges like depression and anxiety.[15] Here are some common issues someone experiencing emotional disconnection might face:

Difficulty Identifying Feelings: When you're emotionally disconnected, pinpointing your feelings can be challenging. For instance, while scrolling through social media and seeing friends having a great time, you might find yourself feeling nothing at all or caught in a confusing mix of emotions you can't quite name. You might be someone who might respond to a simple "How are you?" with a vague "I'm okay," even if you're overflowing with a myriad of other feelings, like a soda bottle that's been shaken and ready to burst.

Avoidance of Emotional Discomfort: Emotional disconnection often results in avoiding situations that could evoke strong feelings.[16] For example, after a breakup, you might steer clear of mutual friends or avoid places that remind you of your ex. Although this may seem like a protective move, it can leave you feeling even more isolated and hinder your ability to form new connections. Ironically, engaging with others—the very thing you're avoiding—might be what helps you heal.

Physical Symptoms: Numbing or ignoring your emotions can show up in physical ways. You might experience constant fatigue, trouble sleeping, or changes in appetite—like binging on snacks during late-night gaming sessions or feeling too drained to cook. These physical signs are your body's way of signaling that something isn't right emotionally, reminding you that caring for your mental health can have a profound impact on your physical well-being.[17]

Impact on Relationships: Emotional disconnection can create significant barriers in all types of relationships, especially romantic ones. If you find it hard to express your needs or feelings, misunderstandings and frustration can easily arise. Imagine wanting to share your thoughts with a partner but struggling to find the words—it can feel like you're building a wall instead of a bridge. This lack of communication may leave your partner feeling confused or distant, deepening the disconnection.

Burden of Expectations: If you're under significant pressure to succeed and be accepted—whether academically, socially, or professionally—but don't feel internally motivated to pursue these goals for yourself, it can lead to a sense of living for others. Over time, this constant drive to meet societal expectations can result in emotional detachment. You might find yourself going through the motions—attending classes, hanging out with friends, or working—yet feel like you're not truly engaged in your life. This detachment can make it difficult to enjoy your successes or figure out what you genuinely care about.

Struggles with Vulnerability: Being vulnerable or emotionally open can feel risky, especially in a world where everyone seems to showcase their "best selves" constantly. If you exist in an environment that discourages emotional expression, you may struggle to open up to others. This reluctance can result in shallow connections, making it harder to find support when you need it most.

Consider Alex's struggles with emotional awareness and intimacy with others—you might find parts of yourself reflected in their experience.

Alex's Story

Alex, a 17-year-old high school student, is navigating a complex predicament. Their struggles with emotional disconnection began early, shaped significantly by their family dynamics. Growing up in an environment where emotional expression was not encouraged, Alex learned to suppress their feelings to maintain peace. When emotions did surface, they often went unacknowledged, minimized, or invalidated, leading Alex to believe that hiding their emotions was the better option.

At school, Alex faced difficulties connecting with peers who were more expressive. During class presentations, Alex would feel a surge of emotions but struggled to pinpoint or articulate them. Instead of expressing nervousness or excitement, they masked these feelings behind a calm facade, unable to communicate their true state. This tendency to conceal their emotions left Alex underprepared, feeling misunderstood and isolated, even in moments of praise or encouragement from classmates.

In social situations, Alex often resorted to avoidance as a coping mechanism. During group hangouts, when conversations turned personal, they would retreat into their phone or make excuses to step away, claiming they needed to study. Friends noticed this emotional distance and expressed concern, but Alex deflected their inquiries, sidestepping deeper discussions about their feelings. This pattern of avoidance further alienated them from their friends, leaving Alex feeling disconnected and unsure of how to make the most out of their friendships.

When it came to decision-making, Alex frequently allowed others to choose for them, avoiding the sharing of their own preferences. Friends and family often made assumptions about Alex's likes and dislikes based on this perceived indifference, leading to decisions being made without their input. This lack of assertiveness reinforced Alex's feelings of being overlooked and disregarded, deepening their emotional disconnection.

Physically, Alex often dealt with headaches and stomachaches, especially during stressful periods like exams or social events. Despite seeking medical evaluations, doctors couldn't pinpoint the cause of these physical ailments. This disconnect between their emotional and physical health compounded Alex's frustration and fatigue, emphasizing the toll that unaddressed emotions were taking on their well-being.

In summary, Alex's emotional disconnection—rooted in family upbringing, social pressures, and ineffective coping strategies—underscores a pressing need to bridge the gap between their internal feelings and external interactions.

🔍 SELF-REFLECTION

If any part of Alex's story resonates with you, further self-exploration is highly recommended. Here are some questions to help you reflect on your own levels of comfort with emotion identification, exploration, expression, and regulation. Remember, have your pen and notebook available to answer these questions and take some notes, since you will likely want to return to your thoughts in the future.

* **Identifying Emotions:** What emotions do I frequently experience in my daily life? Can I list them?

* **Recognizing Emotions:** When I feel a strong emotion, how do I identify it? What physical sensations, thoughts, or behaviors help me recognize that emotion?

* **Recent Emotional Experiences:** During a recent situation where I felt strong emotions, what specific emotion did I experience, and what set it off specifically?

* **Ease of Expression:** Which emotions do I find easy to express? Are there any emotions that I struggle to share? Why might that be?

* **Emotional Responses:** How do I typically respond to different emotions? Do I tend to avoid, suppress, or express them openly? Can I identify patterns in my responses?

* **Aftermath of Emotional Expression:** After I express or cope with my emotions, how do I feel? Do I notice any changes in my mood or overall well-being?

* **Cultural Influences:** Are there cultural, societal, or family factors that shape how I perceive or express my emotions? How do these influences affect me?

⟨♀⟩ SELF-REGULATION STRATEGIES

Feeling emotionally disconnected, like Alex, is something many of us go through, and it doesn't have to be something you accept as permanent. We all experience moments when our feelings seem distant, or our relationships don't feel as deep as we'd like them to be. You *can* reconnect with your emotions and discover healthier ways to express and manage them. It might feel a little scary at first, but exploring your emotions and building deeper connections is a brave and personal decision.

The good news is emotions themselves aren't dangerous. They're just signals from your brain—they are neutral, and helpful in guiding your decisions. In fact, acceptance and commitment therapy (ACT) sees emotions as natural responses that can teach us valuable things about ourselves, like what we need or how we might best respond to situations.[18] Rather than viewing emotions as something to avoid or fear, it's more helpful to embrace them as part of being human.

ACT encourages us to notice and accept our feelings without judgment, giving us the space to sit with them instead of trying to push them away. This kind of acceptance can help us become more emotionally flexible, allowing us to respond more effectively to whatever comes our way. When we approach our emotions with curiosity and compassion, we can learn what they're trying to tell us and use that insight to guide our actions. For example, if you're feeling disconnected like Alex, reaching out to a friend who's empathetic, understanding, and able to offer a new helpful perspective might be a good first step. You could say, *"I've been feeling a bit off lately and could really use someone to talk to."*

Emotions can also be reminders of what truly matters to you—your values. These values, like connection or authenticity, guide your choices and shape what's important in your life. When you're in touch with your feelings, you're better able to make decisions that align with your true self. For instance, if you value connection, recognizing feelings of loneliness can motivate you to reach out to friends, helping you nurture deeper relationships that resonate with who you are at your core.

Below, you'll find trauma-informed self-regulation strategies that can help you connect with your emotions, express yourself more openly, and find the support you need when life gets overwhelming. It's all about trying different approaches to see what works best for you and knowing that it's okay to ask for help when you need it. After all, even the strongest ships need a crew to navigate through a storm.

Permission to Feel: Giving yourself permission means allowing yourself to experience your emotions without judgment or pressure to immediately "fix" them. Give yourself room to be kind and patient with yourself, recognizing that it's okay to feel whatever you're feeling, even if those feelings are uncomfortable. When you're overwhelmed, instead of pushing yourself to "get over it" or pretending you're fine, take a moment to sit with the emotions. Imagine if you were comforting a friend—they'd need time and space to process their feelings, and you'd give that without rushing them. Do the same for yourself. For example, if you're upset after an argument, instead of pushing through the emotions, you could say, *"I'm really upset, and that's okay. I don't need to have* *all the answers right now. I just need a little time to process this.*" You might go for a walk, listen to music, or journal. By giving yourself this space, you let the emotions settle before reacting, which helps prevent them from building up and becoming overwhelming. In essence, giving yourself permission to feel is a compassionate approach that helps you process your experiences clearly and move forward at your own pace.

Identify Physical Reactions: Your body often sends signals when your emotions are out of balance, like stomachaches, headaches, or restlessness. If you notice tension building up, it's a good sign that it's time to pause and reset. You might try stepping outside for a walk, dancing to your favorite song, or doing a few stretches. If you're into fitness, a quick workout or even some yoga can help release tension and clear your mind. These small actions can make a big difference in easing stress and helping you feel more grounded.

Radical Acceptance: Radical acceptance is the practice of fully embracing your reality, no matter how difficult or uncomfortable it might be. Being radical considers things as they are, without fighting against them or wishing they were different. When you're upset after an argument, for example, it's easy to start replaying the conversation over and over in your mind, thinking about how you "should" have acted differently or how unfair the situation was. But radical acceptance asks you to stop fighting with your emotions or the situation itself, and encourages you to acknowledge, *"This is how I feel right now, and that's okay."* It doesn't mean you approve of the situation, but it allows you to process your feelings without piling on guilt or shame. Radical acceptance doesn't mean you have to like everything that happens or that you're giving up on improving situations. It's simply about accepting that, in this moment, things are as they are, and you don't have to add more suffering by denying your emotions. It creates the mental space to move forward, rather than staying stuck in resistance.

Emotion Charts: Sometimes it's hard to name what we're feeling. That's where emotion charts come in handy. There are tons of charts and graphics online that show different emotions with colors and faces to help you identify your mood. For example, after a frustrating interaction with a parent, you might feel a mix of frustration and anxiety. Having a chart on your phone or in your journal can help you break it down. It might help you realize that you're not just mad, but also hurt or confused. Once you label the emotions, it can be easier to talk about it with someone—like saying, *"I was really hurt by what was said, and I didn't know how to handle it."*

Be Inquisitive: Being inquisitive about your emotions means asking yourself why you're feeling a certain way instead of just reacting to those feelings. It's like being a detective in your own life. By understanding the *why* behind your emotions, you can deal with them more effectively. For example, if you're anxious about a test, ask yourself, *"What am I afraid of if I fail?"* You might realize you're worried about disappointing others or feeling behind. Once you identify the fear, you can make a plan to study more or ask for help, instead of just stressing out. Similarly, if you're feeling sad about a situation, ask, *"Why does this make me feel sad?"* It might help you uncover deeper feelings, like feeling neglected or misunderstood. Understanding your emotions helps you process them calmly and makes it easier to take action. Consider writing, as it gives you the freedom to express yourself without judgment, helping you untangle your thoughts. You might notice patterns or uncover things you hadn't realized, like feeling frustrated in a friendship. This can help you decide if you need to talk to someone or set boundaries.

Creative Expression and Emotional Release: Expressing emotions through creativity is a form of acceptance. For example, if you're feeling sadness about a breakup, creating a poem or song about it helps you face that sadness rather than suppress it. Instead of trying to push the emotions away, you allow yourself to experience them, which can reduce their power over time. Writing a song about a hard day at school or a falling out with a friend could help you process those emotions and turn them into something personal and creative. If you're angry or frustrated, put on some music and move your body however feels right. You can jump, spin, or even just do a few deep stretches to release that energy. If you're feeling isolated, you might photograph nature, like a single leaf on the ground, to reflect your feelings of loneliness or solitude. You could create a digital artwork that uses colors or symbols to represent the conflict you're feeling, or design a digital journal page that tracks your emotional ups and downs. If you're upset about something, you might film a "day in my life" type of vlog where you narrate what happened and how you're processing it, or you could create a short film about the challenges you're facing. After a tiring week, you might dress in cozy, comfortable clothes to give yourself a sense of security, or wear bold, vibrant outfits when you're feeling confident. The possibilities are endless. Do what comes naturally to you and don't be too concerned about getting it just right.

Read More Books: Reading fiction nurtures many of the core skills of emotional intelligence—empathy, self-awareness, emotional regulation, and social understanding. By engaging with characters and their emotional journeys, you not only expand your emotional vocabulary but also build the skills to manage your own emotions and connect more deeply with others. So yes, diving into a good novel is not just entertaining—it's an effective tool for developing your emotional intelligence.

Seek Connection: When things get overwhelming, finding spaces where you can connect with people who truly get what you're going through is incredibly important. You can find support and understanding on platforms like TikTok or Instagram, where young people openly share their struggles and coping strategies. Joining mental health-focused groups on Discord or Reddit can also provide a sense of community. These groups often offer peer support and advice on everything from school stress to relationship struggles.

It's also helpful to be selective about who you're connecting with online. Not all advice is good advice, and some people may not be well-equipped to help with serious issues. Make sure you're engaging with communities that promote healthy, positive conversations about mental health. If you're going through something more serious or need professional support, it's always a good idea to reach out to a trusted adult or therapist for guidance.

Deep Conversations/Active Listening: Having those "real" conversations with close friends or family can make a huge difference. Talk about what's on your mind—maybe how anxious you're feeling about a big decision or how drained you are after a tough week. Share your thoughts, but also ask about theirs. For example, *"I've been feeling really over-whelmed lately, how do you handle moments like that?"* These kinds of chats create deeper bonds, letting you feel support and to be supported.

Sometimes, being a good listener is just as important as talking about your own feelings. If a friend is sharing something tough, try to really listen without interrupting. Show them you care by saying things like, *"That sounds rough,"* or *"I hear you, that must have been so frustrating."* It's these small gestures that help strengthen your friendships and let them know you are emotionally available.

Interpersonal Effectiveness/Assert Preferences: Interpersonal effectiveness is about asking for your own needs while respecting others. When setting boundaries, it's important to use a calm and respectful tone to avoid conflict. For example, instead of shutting down someone's feelings, you might say, *"I understand you're upset, but I need to focus on my own feelings right now. Can we talk later when I'm in a better headspace?"* This way, you're both acknowledging the other person's emotions and taking care of your own. Or if you feel overwhelmed when a friend constantly brings up drama or negative situations, you could say, *"Hey, I need to focus on something positive right now. Can we talk about something that lifts both of us up, like our favorite new shows or something fun we're looking forward to?"* It's okay to gently steer conversations away from topics that drain you emotionally.

☾ POSITIVE-CHANGE KICKSTARTER

Healthy Expression Strategies: When you're feeling overwhelmed, what healthy strategies can you use to express your emotions?

_____

_____

_____

Creative Outlets: What creative outlets, like writing or drawing, could help you process your emotions?

_____

_____

_____

Support System: Who do you feel comfortable talking to about your emotions? How do they typically respond to you? Can you reach out to them today?

_____

_____

_____

Consideration of Professional Support: Have you thought about seeking support from a counselor or therapist? Your school likely has counselors available who may be able to support you directly or refer you to a professional who might. What are your thoughts or concerns regarding this option? What can you do to remove the barriers to establishing professional care for yourself?

_____

_____

_____

 # RESOURCES

WEBSITES

ReachOut (au.reachout.com): Provides online resources, articles, and forums specifically designed to support young people's mental health and well-being.

UCLA Mindful app (www.uclahealth.org/ulcamindful/ucla-mindful-app): Offers mindfulness exercises, guided meditations, and articles on mindfulness tailored for teens and young adults.

Headspace (www.headspace.com): Offers guided meditations, mindfulness exercises, and sleep stories to help manage stress and improve overall well-being.

Calm (www.calm.com): Provides meditation sessions, breathing exercises, and relaxation techniques to reduce anxiety and promote relaxation.

MoodTools (moodtools.org): Offers tools and resources for tracking mood, managing stress, and practicing self-care strategies.

MOBILE APPS

Use **mood-tracking apps** to record emotions and share insights regularly such as:

Daylio (daylio.net)

Moodfit (www.getmoodfit.com)

BOOKS

Becoming Safely Embodied: A Guide to Organize Your Mind, Body and Heart to Feel Secure in the World, by Deirdre Fay (Morgan James Publishing, 2021).

The Emotionally Intelligent Teen: Skills to Help You Deal with What You Feel, Build Stronger Relationships, and Boost Self-Confidence, by Melanie McNally (New Harbinger Publications, 2023).

The Language of Emotions: What Your Feelings Are Trying to Tell You, 2nd Edition, by Karla McLaren (Sounds True, 2023).

CHAPTER 3

ANXIETY

~~~~~

COMMONLY VOICED

✵ "I'm always second-guessing myself and worrying about messing up the simplest things."

✵ "I wish I could just chill out and enjoy things like other people do, but my worries and fears always get in the way."

✵ "I'm always on edge, like something bad's about to happen. My mind's constantly racing with what-ifs and worst-case scenarios."

✵ "Going to school, talking to people, and even just leaving the house sometimes can be really hard for me."

UNDERSTANDING ANXIETY

Anxiety is something many of us face, often stemming from various sources—like the pressure to ace the SATs, the trials and tribulations of relationships, or simply our tendency to overthink everything. The term "anxiety" has an intriguing origin, derived from the Latin *anxietas*, meaning "uneasiness" or "distress." This, in turn, comes from the verb *angere*, which means "to choke" or "to strangle," perfectly capturing the physical tightness and discomfort often associated with anxiety.

I vividly recall my first post-college interview for a copy-writer job on Wall Street. After successfully navigating several rounds with different team members, I felt confident—until I walked into the twenty-seventh floor, corner office of the VP of marketing, greeted by breathtaking views of the city's skyscrapers, framed perfectly by the East River and clear skies. The sheer magnitude of this view took my breath away, and in that moment of awe, I felt so small and out of place. I completely blanked. When they asked, "Kathy, tell me about yourself," I felt like I was born yesterday, my throat dried up, and I stumbled through an answer that was far from coherent. All the preparation I had done evaporated, leaving me with a long, awkward ride home on the subway, replaying that moment over and over.

You might experience a similar rush of anxiety before something significant, like a driver's test, or find yourself carrying around a persistent, heavy bag of worry. Understanding anxiety means recognizing how it shows up in your life—whether as a temporary spike in response to a specific event or a more chronic feeling that lingers. By exploring these experiences, you can better discern when anxiety moves beyond fleeting concerns and becomes something that deserves our compassionate attention.

NOT ALL STRESS IS BAD

Daily stress and situational anxiety are part of life, but surprisingly, these pressures can also offer chances for personal growth. I can't tell you how many times I've been grateful for the pause that comes from feeling the weight of potential embarrassment before speaking in public. That natural pressure to come across as thoughtful has helped me avoid saying something I might regret later.

Think about your own experiences: juggling academic deadlines—like a research paper, a case interview, or a senior thesis—might keep you up at night, but it's also a chance to sharpen your time-management skills. The stress of performing well in a sports game or an extracurricular activity can push you to practice harder and improve your abilities.

Family and school expectations, like maintaining good grades or being involved in various activities, might feel overwhelming, but they can also help you develop a strong work ethic. Plus, navigating friendships and resolving conflicts within your social circle not only challenges your emotional well-being but also teaches you valuable communication skills.

WHEN ANXIETY BECOMES OVERWHELMING

Anxiety often emerges when your brain perceives a threat—real or imagined. It's like your body's alarm system going off, preparing you to fight, flee, or freeze. This happens because of a rush of stress hormones that heighten your senses and make your heart race.

Over time, if you keep avoiding the things that make you feel anxiety, your brain learns that those situations are dangerous, which can make the anxiety feel even stronger. It's like building a habit of fear; the more you avoid, the more your brain believes it should be afraid. Understanding this can help you challenge those thoughts and gradually reduce anxiety by facing your fears step by step.

When anxiety becomes overwhelming, it often crosses a critical threshold from being a manageable part of life to a debilitating condition. This threshold is marked by the intensity, duration, and impact of anxiety on your daily functioning. While anxiety is a normal emotional response, it becomes problematic when it *interferes* with your ability to carry out everyday activities, maintain your relationships, or pursue your personal goals.

Take generalized anxiety disorder (GAD), for example. It's when you find yourself worrying way too much about everything—school, relationships, the future. This constant worry can make it hard to focus on anything, leaving you feeling restless and fatigued. It's like being stuck on a treadmill that just won't stop, and that can wear you down fast.

Then there's panic disorder. This is when you suddenly feel a wave of intense fear, like your heart is racing and you can't catch your breath. These panic attacks can hit out of nowhere, making you want to avoid places, people, or situations where they've happened before. Over time, that can really limit your life and keep you from doing things you enjoy.

Social anxiety disorder is another common one. It's that paralyzing fear of being judged in social situations, which can turn even simple hangouts into major stress-fests. You might start sweating or shaking, making it super hard to even chat with people. When the fear of judgment holds you back, it can feel really isolating.

Let's talk about specific phobias and agoraphobia. If you have a specific phobia, like a fear of spiders, you might go to great lengths to avoid them, even if it means skipping a fun outing. Agoraphobia takes it a step further, making you fear situations where you can't easily escape, leading to avoiding crowds or even leaving home altogether. This can create a bubble that feels safe but also incredibly limiting.

Conditions like PTSD, obsessive-compulsive disorder (OCD), and separation anxiety disorder can also complicate things. PTSD might show up as flashbacks or nightmares after a traumatic event, making you feel unsafe and anxious. OCD involves getting stuck in a loop of repetitive thoughts and behaviors—like washing your hands over and over because you're worried about germs—which can be exhausting. And separation anxiety isn't just for kids; it can affect teens and young adults too, causing major stress about being apart from loved ones.

Isn't it wild to learn that there are so many ways that anxiety manifests? Let's look at Ace's story—it really dives into how anxiety impacts lives and what keeps it going. If any of their story resonates with you, I hope you see that you're not alone in your struggles.

Ace's Story

Ace, a 20-year-old college student majoring in computer science, began their college experience with excitement about greater independence and academic exploration. However, by the second semester of their first year, overwhelming anxiety started to take hold.

As coursework became more demanding and competitive, Ace felt immense pressure to achieve perfect scores. They set impossibly high standards for themselves, leading to perfectionism that made every assignment feel like a high-stakes challenge. This pressure was exacerbated by feelings of homesickness, making it difficult to focus.

During their sophomore year, a particularly challenging programming project required long hours of debugging. Despite their efforts, Ace received a lower grade than expected. This setback initiated a loop of negative self-talk, where Ace thought, "I'm terrible at everything," reinforcing feelings of inadequacy through overgeneralization, which in CBT means when you take one bad thing that happened and make it feel like it's going to happen all the time or to every situation. (Reference the list of cognitive distortions in Chapter 1.)

Simultaneously, Ace heard about their peers enjoying social events and securing prestigious internships at top tech companies. They began to catastrophize, imagining the worst-case scenarios, such as "If I don't land an internship, I'll never succeed in this field." These thoughts led to increased anxiety about measuring up to their classmates.

To cope, Ace started isolating themself, spending more time studying and revising, often sacrificing sleep to ensure their work was flawless. This avoidance of social activities felt easier in the moment but only intensified their feelings of loneliness and anxiety.

As academic pressures mounted, Ace's sleep patterns became erratic, leading to fatigue and difficulty concentrating during lectures. Physical symptoms, such as frequent headaches and muscle tension, emerged because of chronic stress. Ace found themself in a state of hypervigilance, obsessively monitoring their classmates' reactions in social situations, which kept their anxiety at a peak.

Socially, Ace became increasingly self-conscious, engaging in mind reading, which, again, is when you assume you know what other people are thinking, without any real proof. Ace worried that their peers thought they were awkward just because they didn't seem as engaged in a couple of conversations during class, further fueling their anxiety. This led to withdrawal from group activities, creating a habit of isolation that compounded their feelings of inadequacy.

Over time, the cumulative stressors led to panic attacks, creating an overwhelming sense of uncertainty. The interplay of academic pressure, fear of failure, and social anxiety combined with ruminative thoughts about past failures made Ace's daily life increasingly challenging.

🔍 SELF-REFLECTION

Are you someone who finds it unbearably hard to sit with uncertainty, needing to account for everything about your future? Like Ace, who felt overwhelmed by the pressure to achieve status and worried about what their peers thought, do you find yourself fixating on others' perceptions? Ace's path through anxiety, marked by negative self-talk and the fear of falling behind, highlights how easily we can become trapped in our minds. Here are some ways to reflect on your personal relationship with anxiety:

* **Daily Stress Experience:** How do I notice stress manifesting in my daily life? What physical sensations, thoughts, or behaviors accompany my stress?
* **Vulnerabilities and Patterns:** What specific things or situations tend to worsen my anxiety? Can I identify any recurring patterns in what sets me off?

* **Coping Strategies:** How do I usually cope with feelings of worry? What strategies or activities help me regain a sense of control?
* **Impact on Relationships:** In what ways does anxiety affect my relationships and social interactions? Are there particular challenges I face when connecting with others or participating in social activities?
* **Concerns and Fears:** What are my primary concerns or fears related to my anxiety? Are there specific outcomes or scenarios that I find myself dreading?
* **Self-Talk During Stress:** What thoughts do I tend to have during stressful moments? Are there recurring beliefs or messages I tell myself that may contribute to my anxiety?
* **Physical Changes:** Have I noticed any changes in my sleep patterns, appetite, or energy levels that seem related to my anxiety?

SELF-REGULATION STRATEGIES

So, how can you manage anxiety in an effective way? It's important to find strategies that work best for you and your specific form of anxiety, and to seek support when you need it. At the most basic level, we know that mindfulness-based stress reduction is a powerful tool for reducing anxiety symptoms and improving overall quality of life. Cognitive-behavioral techniques are also beneficial; they help you identify and challenge negative thought patterns, which are key to overcoming the psychological mechanisms that underlie anxiety. Research supports the effectiveness of these techniques for improving mental health outcomes.[19]

Since my embarrassing Wall Street interview, I have developed specific coping strategies to manage my anxiety in similar situations. Before interviews, I practice mindful breathing to center myself; I take a few deep breaths to calm my racing heart. I also visualize my favorite safe corner of my closet (not a corner office) and my responses ahead of time, which helps create familiarity and reduces the shock of the unexpected. Additionally, I remind myself that interviews are conversations, that it's okay to talk favorably about myself to strangers, and that the stakes aren't as high as I make them out to be. This shift in mindset allows me to approach them with more confidence.

Understanding anxiety's role in your life can empower you to manage it more effectively. As Maya Angelou once said, "I can be changed by what happens to me. But I refuse to be reduced by it." This quote reminds us that while challenging experiences may shape us, anxiety can also motivate growth and resilience. By employing effective coping strategies and seeking support, you can mitigate anxiety's impact and focus on your personal development and well-being.

Understand Your Past Experiences: Understanding how your past might influence your current anxiety is key to developing compassion and insight. Experiences, especially in childhood, can shape how you react to stress today. We learn that past challenges can ignite anxiety in the present, but this knowledge allows us to separate past experiences from current emotions. Books like *The Body Keeps the Score* by Bessel van der Kolk or watching videos on anxiety can help you understand why your body reacts the way it does, and working with a therapist can help you integrate this knowledge into your life.

Anxiety as a Natural Response to Stress: Anxiety is a natural response to stress, and recognizing it as such helps normalize your feelings. Learn to accept anxiety rather than try to be rid of it forever. Viewing anxiety as your body's way of preparing for action can reduce the fear around it. For example, when you're nervous about an upcoming test, remind yourself, *"This anxiety is helping me focus and prepare."* Affirmations like *"It's normal to feel anxious"* help you reduce resistance and allow anxiety to be part of your experience without letting it control you. The more you practice acceptance, the less anxiety will interfere with your life.

Practice Cognitive Defusion: Cognitive defusion, an ACT technique, helps you see anxious thoughts as passing events, not permanent truths. Visualizing anxious thoughts as clouds drifting by or thinking, *"I'm having the thought that I'm going to fail"* instead of *"I'm going to fail"* helps you detach, or defuse, from those thoughts. Another way to think about it is like a text message thread. When an anxious thought pops up, like *"I'm going to make a fool of myself,"* imagine it as just another text in a group chat. You can choose to notice it without reacting to it or let it control the conversation. Just like you'd swipe away a text you don't need to respond to, you can let that thought pass by without it defining your entire experience. By observing these thoughts without judgment, they lose their power and become easier to manage.

Reduce Avoidance: Avoiding emotions or situations that make you uncomfortable (like anxiety) may provide temporary relief, but it often makes the fear grow stronger over time. During exposure, you may feel anxiety, but learning to sit with that feeling without judgment helps you manage it. Remind yourself, *"It's okay to feel anxious. I don't need to avoid* *it, and I can handle it.*" Over time, this acceptance reduces the power of anxiety.

Start Small and Build Up: Imagine you're anxious about public speaking. Start with the least threatening situation, like reading a short speech in front of a mirror. Once you're comfortable with that, film yourself speaking and watch the video. The next step might be presenting to a close friend, then to a small group of people, and finally to a larger audience. Each step helps desensitize you to the anxiety until you're able to handle the full situation.

Remember to Breathe: Simple mindful breathing techniques like box breathing is an easy and effective technique that can help ground you and calm anxiety. This rhythmic pattern interrupts the racing thoughts caused by anxiety and refocuses your mind on your breath. Box breathing is especially helpful when you feel overwhelmed and need to take a pause to regain control of your emotions. Imagine a box in front of you. Inhale for four counts, hold for four counts, exhale for four counts, and hold again for four counts. Repeat for five minutes.

Visualize a Calming Place: Visualization involves imagining a peaceful, calming place to help reduce anxiety and shift your focus from stressors. It helps reduce stress by creating a mental "escape" that calms your mind and body. It can be especially helpful if you need a quick mental reset, such as before a test or when you're about to face a stressful situation. Do it by closing your eyes and imagining a place where you feel safe and at peace—a beach, a quiet forest, or your favorite spot. Use all your senses: Imagine the sounds, smells, and sights around you. Picture yourself in this peaceful place, feeling calm and at ease.

Emotional Freedom Technique (EFT) or Tapping: This is a form of acupressure combined with mindfulness, where you tap on specific points of your body (mainly the head and upper body) while focusing on a specific issue or anxiety. Tapping has been shown to reduce anxiety by combining physical touch with verbal affirmation. It can help release trapped emotions and calm the nervous system in moments of distress. This is how it works: Tap with your fingers on certain points of your body (such as the side of your hand, between your eyebrows, and on your collarbone) while repeating phrases like, *"Even though I feel anxious, I deeply and completely accept myself."*

Other Self-Soothing Techniques: Self-soothing activates your parasympathetic nervous system, helping your body move from a state of fight-or-flight into a calm, restful state. It's a great way to manage moments of heightened anxiety. Try appealing to all your senses to help calm your nervous system by holding a warm cup of tea, listening to the sound of water coming from a faucet, or wrapping yourself in a cozy blanket. Engage your sense of smell with calming scents like lavender or vanilla, or use textured objects like a soft pillow or a stress ball to ground yourself.

⊘ POSITIVE-CHANGE KICKSTARTER

Strengths and Resources: What strengths or resources can you draw on to cope with anxiety? Reflect on past experiences or strategies that have been effective for you and try one today.

_____

_____

_____

Balanced Approach to Anxiety Management: What steps can you take to create a more balanced approach to managing your anxiety? What does your ideal future look like in terms of stress management, and what is one action you can take today or this week to get there?

_____

_____

_____

Feelings About Seeking Help: How do you feel about the idea of seeking help or support for managing your anxiety? What barriers or concerns prevent you from reaching out for assistance?

_____

_____

_____

 RESOURCES

WEBSITES

American Psychological Association (APA; www.apa.org): Provides resources on anxiety disorders, treatment options, and stress-management techniques.

Nemours Teens Health (https://mentalhealthliteracy.org): Offers articles, guides, and tools for understanding and managing anxiety.

BOOKS

Anxiety Relief for Teens: Essential CBT Skills & Mindfulness Practices to Overcome Anxiety & Stress, by Regine Galanti (Zeitgeist Young Adult, 2020).

DBT Skills for Teens with Anxiety: Practical Strategies to Manage Stress and Strengthen Emotional Resilience, by Atara Hiller (Zeitgeist Young Adult, 2023).

First, We Make the Beast Beautiful: A New Story About Anxiety, by Sarah Wilson (Dey Street Books, 2018).

CHAPTER 4

DEPRESSION

~~~~

COMMONLY VOICED

❋ "It's like there's this black hole inside me that sucks away all my energy and joy. It's hard to even get out of bed in the morning."

❋ "It all just feels pointless. I don't have the motivation to do anything anymore."

❋ "No matter how hard I try, I can't shake this blah feeling."

❋ "I want to be grateful for what I have, but I doubt if I'm deserving of joy or happiness."

UNDERSTANDING DEPRESSION

Your age group often faces unfair scrutiny for how you express yourselves. Society tends to misinterpret your emotional variability as signs of instability or immaturity. I witness this firsthand when I mention that I work with teens and young adults; people often react with a mix of pity and bemusement, as if to say, *"You're brave—good luck!"* In response, I emphasize that your emotional sensitivity reflects the normal ups and downs that come with navigating a complex stage of life filled with significant changes. In fact, it's you who are the brave ones!

Things get more complicated when feelings of sadness, hopelessness, or emotional numbness persist, potentially leading to depression. These feelings can creep in gradually or strike suddenly. While the *Diagnostic and Statistical Manual of Mental Disorders* (DSM-5) states that symptoms of depression must last at least two weeks to qualify as a major depressive episode, depression can manifest in unique ways for teens and young adults that may go unnoticed.[20]

Many young people may not show classic signs of sadness; instead, you might experience increased irritability, withdrawal from social interactions, or changes in appetite and sleep patterns. This can lead to your struggles being misinterpreted as "typical teenage behavior," obscuring the seriousness of your emotional pain. Additionally, the pressure to maintain a certain external image can heighten feelings of inadequacy and loneliness, creating a situation where your internal struggles remain hidden.

When you're depressed, it can feel like walking through thick mud—every step requires immense effort, and the harder you try to move forward, the more you feel pulled back. Just getting out of bed can be a struggle, even when you should feel well-rested. Everyday responsibilities—like going to work or school, managing chores, or socializing—can seem monumental. This constant fatigue and lack of motivation can lead to procrastination, creating a backlog of responsibilities that heightens feelings of inadequacy and guilt.

Take Billie Eilish's song "Bellyache," for example. In this track, Eilish captures the essence of being overwhelmed by her thoughts, wrestling with sadness, guilt, and confusion.

Her lyrics about wondering where her mind went, or thinking she'd feel better, perfectly convey the sense of being trapped in your emotions.[21] If her music resonates with you, it may be because she articulates those hidden feelings of sadness and frustration that can be hard to express.

Recent studies indicate that hormonal changes, such as fluctuations in estrogen and testosterone, can lead to mood swings and increase the risk of depression.[22] These hormonal shifts can disrupt emotional regulation, resulting in deep sadness or irritability. Family dynamics also play a crucial role; conflicts at home or a lack of support can intensify feelings of depression and anxiety, making daily stressors harder to manage. Major life events—like academic pressure or a challenging breakup—can cause moods to shift downward. Additionally, social media can add another layer of stress, with research showing that excessive use can diminish self-esteem and amplify feelings of inadequacy, especially when comparing yourself to the seemingly perfect lives portrayed online.[23]

Living with depression can feel isolating, even when surrounded by loved ones. This disconnection can be worsened by a reluctance to share your feelings, often stemming from fears of being judged or misunderstood. The stigma surrounding mental health can make seeking help even more challenging, leaving you to struggle in silence.

Reflecting on your experiences with depression can provide valuable insights into your emotional state and coping strategies. To illustrate this further, consider Rowan's story—a vivid example of how depression can impact an individual, and how support and self-care can foster healing and recovery.

Rowan's Story

At 19, Rowan was a college student who had once found immense joy and solace in photography. With a special talent for capturing breathtaking cityscapes and their inhabitants, they would often spend hours perfecting their images. Photography wasn't just a hobby for Rowan; it was a sanctuary that allowed them to escape the pressures of college life. It boosted their self-worth, as it was one of the few things that felt completely natural to them, and it helped foster some of their most meaningful relationships.

However, during one particularly challenging semester, everything changed. Rowan had developed deep feelings for their close friend Parker, with whom they spent countless hours bonding over photography and dreaming of traveling the world together as photographers. After much internal struggle, Rowan finally decided to confess their feelings, only to find that Parker didn't share the same romantic interest. This rejection felt like a heavy cloud descending over Rowan's once-bright life. They lost the hope of a romantic relationship, and it dimmed their vision for the future. Their friendship with Parker became strained and awkward, leaving Rowan feeling isolated and misunderstood.

In the aftermath of this heartbreak, signs of depression began to creep in. Sleepless nights became the norm, as Rowan lay awake with their mind racing over the rejection. Their grades began to slip, and focusing on assignments felt impossible. Physical symptoms emerged too—frequent headaches and stomachaches that stemmed from the emotional turmoil they were experiencing.

The rejection shattered Rowan's sense of emotional safety and stability. They found themselves caught in a rotation of negative thoughts, convinced that this experience reflected their own shortcomings. Pervasive thoughts like *"I'm unlovable"* and *"I'll never find someone who cares about me"* sank deeper into their mind, further entrenching their feelings of worthlessness.

Rowan's fears of being alone echoed larger patterns of emotional vulnerability and interpersonal struggles. Cognitive distortions, which are again patterns of irrational or biased thinking, contribute to Rowan's emotional distress and unhealthy behaviors. Rowan engaged in all-or-nothing thinking, which is the tendency to view situations in black-and-white terms, with no middle ground. Rowan saw rejection as complete failure rather than understanding it as a normal part of life and relationships. They also engaged in catastrophizing, which involves expecting the worst possible outcome or viewing a situation as far worse than it is. Rowan thought, *"If I get rejected, it means I'll always be alone,"* blowing a single event out of proportion. Instead of recognizing that rejection is a common experience, Rowan internalized it as proof of their inadequacy. This deepened their emotional distress and made it increasingly difficult to reach out for support or engage in the activities that once brought them joy.

SELF-REFLECTION

Have you experienced depressive feelings or symptoms, such as the ones demonstrated by Rowan? Here are questions to explore how depression may be touching your life:

- **Recent Feelings and Experiences:** How have I been feeling lately, particularly regarding my experience with depression? What specific emotions have I been struggling with?
- **Current Coping Mechanisms:** How do I typically cope with heavy emotions, and what strategies have I found helpful in the past? Are there new coping methods I'd like to explore?
- **Patterns and Triggers:** Have I noticed any specific moments or situations that worsen my feelings of depression? What situations, people, or activities tend to improve or worsen my mood?
- **Impact of External Factors:** How do external factors, like stress or changes in routine, affect my mood? What are my predominant thoughts during depressive episodes, and do I notice any negative thinking patterns, such as catastrophizing?
- **Self-Perception and Future Outlook:** How do my thoughts about myself, the world, and the future influence my depressive moments?
- **Concerns About Seeking Help:** What are my concerns or barriers regarding seeking help for my feelings?

⟨?⟩ SELF-REGULATION STRATEGIES

Here are some important words of caution: Recognizing your depressive symptoms and reaching out for support is extremely important. If you're engaging in self-injurious behaviors—like cutting, head-banging, or acting recklessly—or having thoughts about ending your life, please reach out to a professional or talk to a trusted adult right now. Don't wait. There's no time to hesitate when it comes to your safety. You can find contact numbers in the resources section at the end of this chapter.

It's also essential to understand that sadness, along with its variations, serves important functions for us. It helps us process experiences, motivates us to seek change, and fosters empathy for ourselves and others. Being open and curious about these feelings, rather than pushing them away, can lead to valuable insights into your experiences.

To reduce depression and regain a sense of functionality, start by leaning on a supportive network of friends, family, or support groups. Asking for help isn't a sign of weakness; it's an acknowledgment that you need assistance, something we all need from time to time. After all, if you could overcome your feelings of depression on your own, you likely would have done so already, right? There's something truly restorative about sharing your story with others. I can't tell you how often my clients have realized that once they decided to share their burdens with a loved one (by the way, you call them loved ones because their job is to love you), they shifted from feeling like they would be depressed forever to understanding that they were experiencing a challenging but temporary or manageable emotional state.

A trustworthy friend or family member might offer valuable insights on how they navigated their own challenges, or at the very least, they could take you out to help distract you from what's bothering you. If you're feeling disappointed about a rejection or lacking confidence, chances are someone else has faced similar feelings, and recognizing this shared experience can be uplifting. Additionally, when you're feeling down, it's easy to lose sight of your own worth, so having someone remind you of your positive qualities can help break the habit of negative self-talk.

If you don't have an empathic person to turn to during emotional times, consider reaching out to a professional, like a guidance counselor or therapist. By "empathic," I mean someone who won't simply tell you to "just get over it" or insist that "you have nothing to be sad about." Instead, look for someone who can truly listen and understand what you're going through.

Below are more specific steps that can help you move toward recovery and build resilience. You're not alone in this, and it's okay to feel sad sometimes—it's a part of being human.

Be Kind to Yourself: When you're going through a melancholic time, it's all too easy to fall into that pattern of self-criticism. You might think, *"I'm not good enough. I should be doing better."* Being harsh on yourself, though, only makes everything feel harder. Instead, try practicing kindness and compassion toward yourself.

For example, after a bad day or a moment when things didn't go the way you hoped, rather than beating yourself up, try saying something like: *"This is really hard, and I'm doing the best I can. It's okay to struggle sometimes. I'll get through this in time."*

By talking to yourself like you would talk to a friend or innocent child—kindly and without judgment—you help soften the emotional load. It's a reminder that it's okay to feel how you're feeling, and you don't have to be perfect to be worthy. You're putting in the effort, and that's plenty!

Your Thoughts Aren't Facts: When you're feeling down, it can be easy to believe that your thoughts are the absolute truth. However, recognizing that thoughts are *just opinions*—not facts—can help you create some space between you and the negative things your mind might tell you.

For example, imagine you're scrolling through Instagram and see someone posting about getting into a top college, or having the perfect day with their group of friends. Immediately, your brain might jump to thoughts like, *"I'm such a mess. I'll never be enough. I'm low-key failing at life."* It's natural to feel bad in that moment, but instead of immediately believing those thoughts, try to pause and observe them.

You might say something like: *"I'm having the thought 'I'm a loser.' Okay, that's just a thought. It doesn't mean it's true. I'm know I'm not loser, and this thought doesn't define who I am."*

The key is recognizing that your thoughts are not facts. You don't have to believe everything your mind tells you, especially when they're not helpful. It's like when someone tries to invade your space—just because they're there doesn't mean you have to let them stay. You can choose to not let that negative thought rent space in your brain anymore.

The more you practice this, the easier it gets to notice when your thoughts aren't helping you, and let them go before they can take over your emotions. You have the power to decide which thoughts you give attention to.

Self-Validation and Willingness to Feel Uncomfortable: Imagine you just got your test results back, and you didn't do as well as you hoped. You might be feeling a mix of sadness, frustration, and maybe even anger toward yourself. It's tempting to push those feelings away or tell yourself you shouldn't be upset, but instead, try validating your emotions.

Say something like, *"It makes sense that I'm upset. I worked hard, and things didn't go the way I wanted. It's okay to feel frustrated."*

By saying this, you're acknowledging that your feelings are valid and normal. Instead of judging yourself or trying to ignore what you're feeling, accept it. Let yourself feel the disappointment without piling on guilt.

Then, say to yourself: *"I'm willing to feel sad right now. It's okay to be disappointed. I'll keep going."* This doesn't mean you like the sadness, but you're giving yourself permission to experience it without letting it control you. You're allowing the emotion to pass naturally, rather than holding on to it and letting it take over.

This approach can help you move through difficult emotions more quickly, so they don't stay stuck and impact everything else. There is a lot of power in accepting your feelings as part of being human, and then taking the next step forward, even if it's small.

Check the Facts Before Spiraling: If you didn't get invited to a party or hangout and start believing that nobody likes you or that you're always left out, it can feel really discouraging. But before you spiral into those negative thoughts, it's important to take a step back and check the facts with these steps:

✧ **Pause and ask yourself, "Is it true that generally nobody likes me?"** Sometimes our brains can jump to conclusions, but just because something didn't go the way we expected doesn't mean it's the whole story. Think about the times when you have connected with your friends or felt included. Have there been moments when they reached out to you before? Have they supported you in the past?

✧ **Consider other reasons why you might not have been invited.** It's possible that the invite list was really small, or maybe the hangout was more of a last-minute thing, and they didn't think to invite everyone. There could be a lot of different reasons, and most of them have nothing to do with your worth as a person.

✧ **Challenge the thought, "I'm always left out."** One instance doesn't define you. Just because this one time you weren't invited doesn't mean it will always happen. Ask yourself: *"Have I had fun with my friends before? Have I been included in the past?"* The fact that you've had positive experiences with them shows that they value you.

✧ **Remind yourself that this is temporary.** This one moment doesn't define your friendships or your worth. It's just a small setback, not proof that you're not liked or important.

By checking the facts and separating those negative thoughts from reality, you can start to see that your friendships and your value aren't determined by one situation. Setbacks don't mean you're not good enough. It's just a moment, and you can move forward from it.

Behavioral Activation: When you're feeling low, it can be hard to get moving, but taking even small actions can help shift your mood. DBT's **TIPP** skills are quick ways to change your emotional state, especially when you're stuck in a cycle of negative feelings.

✷ **Temperature:** Splash cold water on your face or hold something cold against your skin. The cold helps reset your emotions and makes you feel more awake and alert, breaking through the emotional fog.

✷ **Intense Exercise:** Even if you're stuck in bed, a few minutes of intense exercise can help lift your mood by releasing endorphins. Try doing five minutes of jumping jacks or running in place. It's a quick way to get your body moving and release built-up tension.

✷ **Paced Breathing:** If you're feeling anxious, especially before something like a social event or presentation, slow down your breathing. Inhale for four counts, hold for four, and exhale for six. Repeat a few times. This helps calm your nervous system and brings you back to the present moment.

✷ **Progressive Relaxation:** If you're feeling overwhelmed, especially at the end of the day, try tensing and relaxing each muscle group, starting from your toes and working your way up to your head. This helps release the physical tension that builds up with emotional stress and calms your body before sleep.

By using these simple techniques, you can quickly shift your emotional state and feel a little more in control, even when you're struggling.

☺ POSITIVE-CHANGE KICKSTARTER

Enjoyable Activities and Well-Being: What activities or hobbies do you still enjoy despite feeling sadness or depression? What small steps can you take to prioritize your well-being?

_____

_____

_____

Support and Self-Care: How do you feel about seeking support from others? How can you care for yourself physically, emotionally, and mentally during this time?

_____

_____

_____

Values and Goals: What is important to you in life, even during rough times? What short-term or long-term goals would you like to pursue despite feeling down, and how can you stay connected to your values and interests?

_____

_____

_____

 RESOURCES

HOTLINES AND HELPLINES

988 Suicide & Crisis Lifeline (988lifeline.org): This national hotline is available 24/7. Dial 988.

Crisis Text Line (www.crisistextline.org): Text HOME to 741741 at any time of day to speak with a crisis counselor.

WEBSITES

Anxiety and Depression Association of America (adaa.org): Offers information and resources on depression, including self-help tips and links to support groups.

Mental Health Literacy (mentalhealthliteracy.org): Provides comprehensive information, resources, and tools specifically for teens dealing with mental health issues, including depression.

BOOKS

The Depression Workbook for Teens: Tools to Improve Your Mood, Build Self-Esteem, and Stay Motivated, by Katie Hurley (Instant Help Books, 2016).

Mindfulness for Teen Depression: A Workbook for Improving Your Mood, by Mitch R. Abblett and Christopher Willard (Instant Help Books, 2016).

Radical Acceptance: Embracing Your Life with the Heart of a Buddha, by Tara Brach (Bantam Books, 2003).

CHAPTER 5

ANGER

~~~~~

COMMONLY VOICED

✸ "There's always a fire burning inside me, and it keeps me on edge nonstop."

✸ "I blow up easily over the smallest things—my fuse is super short, and I explode at the tiniest stuff."

✸ "I'm constantly arguing with people, and it's wrecking my relationships. I hate feeling like this angry, aggressive person."

✸ "When I get mad, I just see red—I can't think straight and end up lashing out without realizing it. It's scary how out of control I feel."

UNDERSTANDING ANGER

I may not have seen every movie in the Marvel-verse, but I've watched enough to discern that anger is a reliable and recurring theme in the arc of most of its protagonists. Anger seems to act as a catalyst for character development and conflict, both internal and external. Take *Black Panther*, for example. T'Challa, the hero, wrestles with intense feelings of anger and betrayal after uncovering the truth about his family's past and the death of his father. This emotional turmoil highlights how anger can be a powerful force that drives us to change. As T'Challa processes his emotions, he realizes that while anger might push him to seek vengeance against Killmonger, the villain, it also risks leading him down a destructive path that could harm his relationships and hinder his ability to effectively lead Wakanda.[24]

This example underscores the importance of managing anger carefully to prevent negative outcomes. Unlike other primary emotions such as fear or sadness, which often lead to withdrawal or avoidance, anger is inherently action-oriented. It acts as a signal that something is unfair or threatening, pushing us to confront the situation. This active nature of anger is supported by its role in activating the body's fight-or-flight response, preparing us to address perceived challenges. This response is governed by the amygdala, which detects threats, and the prefrontal cortex, which helps regulate our emotions. Together, these brain regions enable us to confront problems, defend ourselves, or initiate change.[25]

EFFECTS OF UNCHECKED ANGER

How well do you manage anger? Has it, like T'Challa, served as a powerful motivator for your personal growth? When managed well, it can be epic—a sight to behold. However, if left unchecked, anger can lead to destructive behaviors such as cursing, shouting, slamming doors, property damage, or physical confrontations. These actions might offer temporary relief but can cause long-term damage to your relationships and well-being. Chronic anger is also linked to deeper mental health issues, including depression and anxiety, and can increase risks for serious health problems.

Specifically, individuals who struggle with chronic anger may use it as a coping mechanism to mask feelings of sadness or anxiety, leading to an outcome where unresolved emotions fuel further anger. Additionally, chronic anger can set off the body's stress response, resulting in elevated levels of cortisol and adrenaline. Over time, this prolonged activation can contribute to various health problems, including increased blood pressure, heart rate, and inflammation, which heighten the risk for cardiovascular issues like heart disease.[26]

Frequent anger and aggression can strain relationships, leading to conflicts and misunderstandings. A 2023 study reveals that persistent anger and aggression contribute to dissatisfaction in relationships and increased conflicts.[27] Anger also impairs cognitive processes and communication skills, making it challenging to engage in constructive dialogue. After an angry outburst, you might experience feelings of guilt or regret as you reflect on your actions. This internal struggle represents the conflict between your desired reactions and the impulses driven by your anger.

See how chronic anger has made Taylor's life more challenging and see if you can relate to their experiences.

Taylor's Story

Taylor, a 16-year-old, struggled with chronic anger that hindered their growth. As a transracial adoptee, Taylor has had to deal with a very complex mix of identity struggles, attachment issues, and feelings of belonging. From a young age, they struggled with the implications of being raised in a family that did not share their racial or cultural background, which often left them feeling isolated and different. This disconnect heightened their sensitivity to perceived slights or rejections.

A key factor in Taylor's anger was the experience of not fully belonging anywhere. They frequently encountered microaggressions (i.e., subtle, often unintentional or unconscious comments or behaviors that convey a negative or dismissive message toward marginalized or disadvantaged groups) from peers and even family members who, despite their love and support, struggled to understand Taylor's experiences. This lack of understanding sometimes manifested in well-meaning but misguided comments about race or identity, leading Taylor to feel invalidated or even targeted. For instance, when friends made jokes about Taylor's cultural background using exaggerated accents, they felt a mix of anger and confusion, believing these comments undermined their sense of self. In those moments, they often withdrew or lashed out, struggling to articulate why the remarks were hurtful.

Attachment issues also played a crucial role in shaping Taylor's emotional responses. Their early years spent in a different environment before adoption left them with lingering feelings of abandonment. This background led Taylor to develop a heightened vigilance regarding relationships, often interpreting neutral or ambiguous actions as betrayals. When friends or family canceled plans or didn't respond to messages right away, Taylor instinctively assumed they were being rejected. This black-and-white thinking intensified their anger, prompting defensive or aggressive reactions instead of seeking clarification.

Taylor's experiences in school further compounded their emotional challenges. They felt immense pressure to excel academically, driven by a desire to prove themself to their adoptive family and society at large. This pressure created an interplay of frustration and anger when things didn't go as planned. For example, when a teacher offered feedback that Taylor perceived as critical, it brought about deep-seated feelings of inadequacy. Their defensiveness often led to arguments with teachers, further isolating them and reinforcing the belief that they were not fully accepted.

In social situations, Taylor's heightened emotional responses were often exacerbated by their expectations of fairness. They believed that everyone should understand their struggles and treat them accordingly. When this didn't happen, it felt like a personal attack, leading to confrontations and strained relationships. This pattern was evident in group projects, where Taylor felt overwhelmed and resentful if they sensed others weren't contributing equally. Their anger would boil over, resulting in accusations and withdrawal, perpetuating feelings of loneliness and frustration.

🔍 SELF-REFLECTION

Taylor's personal experiences of feeling othered in their social circles understandably fueled their expressions of anger, but this unresolved anger ultimately deepened their sense of alienation. Have you ever felt similarly? Reflecting on the following questions can help you explore the roots, expressions, and impacts of your anger:

❋ **Triggers and Reactions:** What situations or people typically activate my anger, and how do I usually react when I feel anger rising?

- ✿ **Accompanying Emotions:** What other emotions, such as frustration or sadness, often accompany my anger?
- ✿ **Expression and Physical Response:** Do I tend to suppress my anger or express it outwardly? How does my body physically respond to anger? Do my muscles tense? Does my heart race?
- ✿ **Patterns and Influences:** Are there recurring patterns in the situations that make me angry? How did my family or caregivers influence my approach to handling anger?
- ✿ **Impact of Past Experiences:** Have past experiences or traumas affected my current anger management, and how does my anger impact my relationships?
- ✿ **Relationship Strain and Repair:** Has my anger damaged or strained any relationships? If so, how have I tried to repair these relationships?
- ✿ **Management Strategies:** What strategies do I use to manage my anger, and are they effective? What motivates me to use healthier coping methods for anger?

⦿ SELF-REGULATION STRATEGIES

As you can see from Taylor's situation, anger is a complex emotion that can cause a lot of harm if left unchecked. It's important to recognize that chronic anger often stems from deeper, underlying issues—such as stress, trauma, or unmet needs—that need to be addressed for your overall well-being. If you're prone to intense anger or outbursts, it's likely that you feel unheard or undervalued, which can lead to a build-up of frustration. Over time, this frustration can escalate into anger or rage—not just in response to a specific situation, but as a reaction to a broader sense of inadequacy, neglect, or powerlessness. Understanding the root causes of your anger is the first step toward managing it in a healthier way.

By understanding that anger can be a signal pointing to these unmet needs, you can shift your perspective. Instead of simply viewing anger as a negative emotion, you can see it as a message, urging you to pay attention to what is truly lacking in your life. Therefore, honoring your underlying needs can allow you to approach anger with empathy rather than shame or blame. This understanding opens the door to constructive dialogue and self-reflection. For example, if Taylor realized that their anger was rooted in feeling unseen, they could have taken proactive steps—like having a candid conversation with the people around them who might be able to provide affirmations of their value.

Applying effective management strategies allows you to harness anger's energy for positive outcomes. Techniques like reframing negative thoughts and practicing mindfulness, supported by recent research, can help you manage anger in a way that fosters better relationships and enhances personal well-being. Mindfulness can help in recognizing these unmet needs as they arise, providing tools to address them before they escalate into anger.

Ultimately, this compassionate understanding of how your anger presents itself can create a space for healing and growth, both for yourself and for those around you. When we acknowledge and address our unmet needs, we can transform our anger into a catalyst for change, leading to deeper connections and a more fulfilling life.

Here are several specific strategies that are trauma-informed:

Take Two: When you feel anger escalating, take a two-minute pause. Use this time to engage in deep breathing, or simply to sit quietly without speaking or reacting. The two-minute pause allows you to separate yourself from the intensity of your emotions, giving you enough time to regain control. It's a quick but effective way to cool down before making any decisions or engaging in a conversation. Pausing also allows you to gain emotional distance from the situation and prevent saying or doing things you'll regret. It gives you time to think about your feelings and respond thoughtfully rather than impulsively.

Reframe Your Thoughts Behind Your Anger: Practice changing your perspective on anger-provoking situations. For example, if you're upset because a friend is late, try, *"I'm disappointed they're late, but this doesn't define our friendship."* Instead of focusing on your anger, focus on how you want to react. Remind yourself, *"I can express my frustration calmly and respectfully."*

Be Assertive, Not Aggressive: Express your feelings directly and respectfully. Instead of blaming others when you're upset, use "I" statements to express how you feel. For example, instead of saying, *"You never listen to me,"* say, *"I feel ignored when I'm not heard."* This keeps the conversation focused on your feelings and needs, rather than attacking the other person. Being assertive means standing up for yourself while maintaining respect for the other person.

Keep an Anger Log: When you feel angry, write down what happened, how you felt, and the thoughts that went through your mind. This helps you become more aware of your vulnerabilities and emotional patterns. Over time, you may notice specific situations that consistently activate your anger.

Reflecting on these patterns can help you prepare for similar situations in the future. Review your experiences regularly. Take time once a week to look back at your journal and see if any patterns emerge. Are certain people, situations, or thoughts contributing to your anger? Ask yourself, *"How can I respond differently next time?"* This three-part reflection will help you make better choices when faced with anger-inducing situations:

1. Identify the Problem: Instead of simply reacting to anger, take a step back and identify what the real problem is. Is it the situation, someone's behavior, or your expectations? Be specific: *"I'm angry because I wasn't included in the group decision,"* versus a vague *"I'm angry because people don't respect me."*

2. Generate Solutions: Once you've identified the problem, brainstorm possible solutions. For example, if you're angry because someone is late, think about how you could address it. Could you set clearer expectations or address it calmly when the person arrives? Make sure the solutions you consider are realistic and manageable. It's important to act in a way that helps resolve the situation, not escalate it.

3. Implement and Review: Choose the solution you think will work best and implement it. For example, if you choose to speak up calmly about feeling disrespected, make sure you do so without aggression. Afterward, reflect on how the solution worked. Did it resolve the issue? Did it make you feel better? If not, think about alternative solutions for next time.

Use Humor to Disperse Anger: Humor can be a powerful way to shift your perspective and de-escalate anger. By finding something funny in an annoying situation, you take away some of its power. Try finding something absurd about the situation or imagine a humorous alternative version of events. Imagine your frustration as a grumpy cat—he's just making things difficult for you. Instead of letting him win, laugh at how silly he looks and tell him, *"Not today, Grumpy Cat!"*

Take a Different Perspective: Compassionate reframing is about trying to see the other person's actions from a compassionate lens rather than assuming negative intent. This technique involves using empathy to shift your emotional response. For instance, if someone cancels plans with you last minute, instead of getting angry, try thinking, *"Maybe they are dealing with something personal or stressful."* Reframing the situation helps you develop more compassion and lessens the anger.

Create Anger-Free Zones: Create certain places, activities, or times in your life where anger is not allowed, such as during meals or in your car. By setting boundaries for when you will and won't allow yourself to get angry, you can prevent unnecessary outbursts. It also helps you train yourself to respond differently by setting limits on how long you'll let your anger linger.

Use the "SOS" Technique (Stop, Observe, Shift): When you begin to feel anger rising, immediately *stop* what you're doing, *observe* how your body feels (tight muscles, clenched fists), and *shift* your focus to something calming, like your breath or a positive thought. This simple technique from DBT can disrupt your automatic reaction of anger and allow you to choose a more measured response. The SOS steps are like stopping a video game when a boss fight gets too intense—taking a moment to breathe and think will help you level up your calmness!

Develop a Cooling-Off Routine: Designate a specific activity to do every time you feel anger bubbling up, such as taking a walk, having a cold nonalcoholic drink, or listening to a calming song. Having a go-to routine for when anger arises can help you cool down before reacting impulsively. Over time, you'll associate the routine with calming yourself down, making it easier to deescalate in the moment.

Create a "Letting Go" Ritual: When you feel anger building up, engage in a ritual that helps you release it—like writing a letter (you don't need to send it), drawing a picture of your anger, or smashing something safe like a stuffed animal or a pillow. This allows you to physically express and release pent-up frustration in a controlled way, reducing the need to hold onto or act out on anger. Afterward, you can reflect on the release and feel lighter.

Engage in Forgiveness: Holding onto grudges often fuels ongoing anger. Try practicing forgiveness, even if you don't feel like the person deserves it. The process doesn't mean excusing their behavior, but it helps you unburden the emotion. By forgiving, you create emotional freedom for yourself. Imagine the person you are angry at as a flawed human being, like everyone else. You might say, *"I forgive you for this, not because you deserve it, but because I deserve peace."*

ⓛ POSITIVE-CHANGE KICKSTARTER

Management Strategies: What strategies do you use to manage your anger, and are they effective? Are there healthier coping methods, such as mindfulness or exercise, that you could explore today?

_____

_____

_____

Impulse Control and Self-Improvement: How well do you control your impulses when angry, and what can you do to improve your self-control during these moments?

_____

_____

_____

Responsibility and Learning: Are you ready to take responsibility for your anger and its effects? What can you learn from your experiences with anger, and how can these insights help you become more self-aware and resilient?

_____

_____

_____

Areas for Personal Growth: What specific areas for personal growth could improve your anger management?

_____

_____

_____

 RESOURCES

BOOKS

The Anger Workbook for Teens, by Raychelle Cassada Lohmann (New Harbinger Publications, 2019).

Nonviolent Communication, A Language of Life: Life-Changing Tools for Healthy Relationships, by Marshall B. Rosenberg (PuddleDancer Press, 2015).

Why We Get Mad: How to Use Your Anger for Positive Change, by Ryan Martin (Watkins Publishing, 2021).

MOBILE APPS

Mindfulness Coach (mobile.va.gov/app/mindfulness-coach): This is an app developed by the US Department of Veterans Affairs (VA), to help individuals improve their mental health through a variety of guided mindfulness exercises aimed at reducing anger, stress, anxiety, depression, and promoting overall well-being.

CHAPTER 6

PERFECTIONISM

~~~~~

COMMONLY VOICED

- ☼ "I feel like I must achieve flawlessness all the time, and it's draining. No matter how hard I try, it's never enough."
- ☼ "I'm so afraid of making mistakes that I avoid trying new things altogether. I'm paralyzed by the idea of failure."
- ☼ "I beat myself up over every small mistake. I'm constantly striving for more, but it always seems just out of reach."
- ☼ "I know nobody's perfect, but I still must be. The feeling of satisfaction is short-lived since my brain always goes to the next thing I should be doing."

UNDERSTANDING PERFECTIONISM

Have you ever come across the story of the quest for the perfect pearl? It's a tale that pops up in many cultures, and I love sharing my version with clients because it serves as such a poignant metaphor for chasing unattainable ideals. In this story, a traveler sets out on an epic journey to find a legendary pearl, rumored to be the most flawless and beautiful of them all. While we may not know exactly why this seeker is on this quest—perhaps it's fame, fortune, beauty, or a longing for completeness—the quest itself is packed with challenges.

Our traveler faces raging seas, fierce storms, and encounters with all kinds of characters. But when they finally discover the pearl, a profound realization hits: the trip's toll has overshadowed the joy of finding the pearl. The story teaches us that while the pursuit of perfection can be enticing, the true treasures lie in the adventure itself and the relationships we build along the way.

As you navigate this pivotal stage of your life—full of personal growth, academic exploration, and career ambitions—it's easy to feel like you're running on a treadmill in search of that perfect pearl. Whether you're aiming for top grades, excelling in sports or extracurriculars, juggling a busy social life, or curating an ideal social media presence, the pressure can feel overwhelming. Perfectionism isn't just about setting high standards; it can take a serious toll on your mental and physical well-being.

In academia, striving for perfect grades and accolades can provide a temporary boost, but it often leads to burnout and dissatisfaction. Research indicates that an excessive focus on external validation can diminish our intrinsic motivation—the drive to engage in activities for their own sake—resulting in feelings of emptiness and decreased well-being.[28] For instance, concentrating solely on achieving straight A's may increase anxiety about failure rather than fostering a genuine enjoyment of the learning process.

Social media doesn't help either. Platforms like Instagram and TikTok create an environment of "Insta-perfection," where the idealized versions of life can fuel social comparison. This can really chip away at your self-esteem, especially when you're comparing your real life to someone else's high-light reel. Studies show that constant exposure to curated images can heighten feelings of anxiety and inadequacy.[29]

Cultural expectations also add to this pressure. In high-achievement cultures, the focus on success can lead to increased psychological distress. For young people, the emphasis on excelling in academics, sports, or career aspirations can be daunting. In the US and other Western countries, the idea of the "American Dream" encourages competition, but it can leave you feeling stressed and unfulfilled if you don't measure up.

For those in minority and immigrant communities in the US, this struggle can be even more complex. Balancing cultural heritage with the demands of a new society often leads to intensified perfectionism. High parental expectations, driven by hopes for a better future, can further fuel this pressure. And the challenge of finding acceptance in a new cultural context can lead to perfectionism to prove one's worth.[30]

All these factors create an environment where you believe you need to meet impossibly high standards, increasing your stress and anxiety. The effects of perfectionism can be immediate and intense. You might find yourself feeling overwhelmed by the constant pressure to achieve flawlessness. This often leads to frustration and self-criticism when things don't go perfectly. You may even procrastinate because the fear of not achieving perfection makes it hard to get started or finish tasks.

Over time, this stress and self-criticism can erode your mental well-being. You might struggle to enjoy your accomplishments or feel satisfied with your efforts, leading to burnout. The incessant pursuit of perfection can undermine your self-esteem and sense of fulfillment.

Let's look at Casey's story to see the effects of perfectionism and its impact on their overall mental health. Please pay attention to where you might relate to Casey.

Casey's Story

Casey is an 18-year-old senior in high school and a dedicated fencing athlete with dreams of competing in the Olympics. While known for their impressive fencing skills and academic achievements, they live with intense perfectionism that significantly impacts their daily life and aspirations.

In fencing, Casey trains laboriously for hours each day, aiming for flawless performances in every match and practice session. They meticulously analyze every move, seeking perfection in their footwork and strategy. They report failing if they don't achieve a perfect score, overshadowing their successes in local and regional competitions. For example, if they lose a single bout, Casey might think, "I can't do anything right," disregarding their overall performance.

Academically, Casey maintains top grades while juggling rigorous training schedules. They obsess over every assignment and exam, feeling immense anxiety over even minor mistakes. If they receive a B, they catastrophize the situation, thinking, "This will ruin my chances of getting into a good college," ignoring their strong academic record. Despite praise from teachers and classmates, Casey's fear of failure drives them to spend countless hours studying, often sacrificing sleep and social activities. They engage in mental filtering by fixating on critical feedback, concluding, "I'm always bad at this subject," which reinforces a sense of hopelessness.

Socially, Casey finds it challenging to relax and connect with peers both outside and inside of fencing. They worry about being perceived as anything less than successful, leading to overgeneralization; if they feel excluded from a gathering, they might think, "They must not like me anymore," or "They must hate me because I'm their competition," exacerbating feelings of isolation. Their reliance on should statements, like "I should always be the best," sets unrealistic expectations, causing frustration when they inevitably fall short.

In pursuit of their Olympic aspirations, Casey's perfectionism extends to physical conditioning and self-care routines. They adhere strictly to training diets and exercise plans, believing that any deviation could compromise their performance. If they indulge in a treat or skip a workout, they might think, "I've ruined my chances," reinforcing the belief that their worth as an athlete hinges on maintaining peak physical and mental condition.

🔍 SELF-REFLECTION

Does any part of Casey's story ring true for you? To better understand how your pursuit of high standards and perfectionism influences various aspects of your life, consider these self-reflection questions. Reflect on your personal expectations, emotional responses, and relationships to gain deeper insights into your drive for achievement:

- ✤ **Setting High Standards:** Do I set excessively high standards for myself in academics, sports, or personal goals? How does this impact my mental health and well-being?
- ✤ **Feelings Around Expectations:** How do I feel when I don't meet my own expectations or when I make mistakes? What physical symptoms of stress do I notice related to my drive for achievement?
- ✤ **Striving for Excellence:** How does striving for excellence affect my emotions, behaviors, and relationships with friends, family, and teammates?
- ✤ **Triggers for Perfectionism:** What situations or tasks initiate my need for perfection the most? Are there specific times when the pressure to succeed feels particularly intense?
- ✤ **Thought Patterns:** Do I have recurring thoughts about success and failure that drive my perfectionism? How do I usually respond to setbacks or failures?

⟨🧠⟩ SELF-REGULATION STRATEGIES

Fortunately, there are some effective ways to cope with perfectionism and boost your mental health. Alongside the story of the perfect pearl, there's another beautiful tale that I learned from a mentor that offers a different perspective on perfectionism. In this story, a water bearer has two pots: one is perfect, and the other is cracked. Each day, he fills both pots with water at the well and carries them home. While the perfect pot is proud of its flawless performance, the cracked pot feels ashamed for leaking water. But over time, the cracked pot realizes that its imperfections have nourished the flowers growing along the path, adding to their beauty. This lovely story reminds us that our flaws can lead to unique contributions and growth, and they don't take away from our worth.

When it comes to dealing with perfectionism, therapeutic approaches like CBT and mindfulness-based interventions have been shown to help individuals challenge those perfectionistic thoughts and develop healthier coping strategies. Learning to set realistic goals, practicing self-compassion, and reaching out for support from trusted adults, mentors, friends, and counselors are all crucial steps toward building resilience and reducing the pressure of perfectionism.

Your worth isn't defined by flawless achievements or how you stack up against others. Just like the cracked pot, embrace those imperfections as part of your growth, and recognize the value you bring to the world, even in your most vulnerable moments. Prioritizing your mental and emotional well-being is key. By understanding and addressing perfectionistic tendencies early on, you can pave the way for a healthier, more fulfilling future.

Here are some strategies specifically tailored for managing perfectionism:

Set Achievable Goals: Use the SMART goal framework (developed by George T. Doran, a management consultant and teacher, in 1981) to set *Specific, Measurable, Achievable, Relevant,* and *Time-bound* goals. This framework will help you break down often unrealistic and overwhelming expectations into more manageable and realistic steps. Instead of a general goal of getting an A on a paper, a SMART goal would look something like this: "I will complete a five-page report summarizing the project results by next Friday at 5 p.m. I will write one page each day for the next five days, spending one hour revising at the end of each day. I will review and make minor revisions on the last two days, ensuring the report is clear, coherent, and meets the necessary requirements. I will submit the report by the deadline, focusing on completing it rather than making it perfect."

Redefine Personal Success: Reflect on what success means to you, rather than adhering to societal or parental standards. For example, if you value creativity, consider success as engaging in artistic projects or finding innovative solutions, rather than simply achieving top grades. If you prioritize health and well-being, set a goal to practice mindfulness or exercise regularly, rather than focusing solely on academic performance. This shift can lead to more meaningful achievements that resonate with your true self.

Redefine Personal Failure: Redefine failure by challenging your beliefs around it. Do you have a fearful relationship with failure, where you'd rather avoid challenging tasks to prevent being seen as having failed? Do you feel that not achieving something at the highest level would bring dishonor or shame to you or your family? Instead, embrace the idea that failure doesn't define you—it simply means you're taking risks, learning, and pushing your boundaries. Shift your focus to the lessons you gain from failure, recognizing it as a necessary step toward success.

Experiment with Minor Risk: Set aside time each week to do something you think you're terrible at—whether it's asking someone out, singing in the shower, or ordering food in a new language. Keep a journal to reflect on what you learned and how you felt. This helps foster a healthier relationship with mistakes over time. Instead of viewing mistakes as failures, treat them like science experiments. Ask yourself, *"What happens if I try this new method?"* or *"What if I take a different route home?"* By adopting a mindset of curiosity, you reduce the pressure to be perfect.

Social Media Detox: Take a break from social media or follow accounts that showcase "real" lives, embracing flaws and failures. This can help lessen the pressure to compare yourself to unrealistic standards. Even a few hours or a day away from perfection-driven platforms can remind you that not everything needs to be "picture-perfect."

Follow Inspiration, Not Comparison: Be selective with your social media feeds by following content that promotes authenticity and vulnerability. This could include body positivity advocates or mental health influencers who openly discuss their struggles with perfectionism. Let their honesty serve as a counterbalance to the curated, flawless images that might bring about perfectionist thoughts.

Growth Mindset Playlist: Curate a playlist of songs that inspire a growth mindset, where mistakes are part of the journey. Play it while working or studying to remind yourself that learning is about trying, failing, and trying again. On my list are songs like *"Let It Be"* by The Beatles, *"Unpretty"* by TLC, and *"Perfectly Imperfect"* by India.Arie.

Go on Side Quests for Learning: Engage in activities that challenge you to learn new things, like taking on a random DIY project or picking up a new skill. Focus on the process, not the outcome. Being a beginner is a great reminder that no one starts perfect, and learning is a beautiful part of the journey. Break large goals into smaller steps and celebrate your progress along the way. Also, set an occasional "wild card" goal where the process matters more than the result—

like writing a short story without editing or worrying about grammar, or spending an afternoon doing something spontaneous and creative, even if it gets messy.

Show Your Kindness: Shift your focus to making a positive impact on others in an imperfect way. For example, give a genuine compliment, volunteer, or do something kind for a stranger without expecting anything in return. These small acts can help break the cycle of self-judgment and redirect your energy toward positive, meaningful contributions.

Create "Fail Moments": Record yourself doing something silly or imperfect, like attempting a funny dance or tackling a challenging activity. When you're feeling stressed about perfection, play the recording and laugh at how much joy can come from embracing imperfection. For example, I've had plenty of funny #MommyFail moments that, looking back, I'm so grateful for—they turned out to be some of my best growth moments and helped me become a better parent.

Don't Take Yourself Too Seriously: Embrace humor by watching comedy shows like *Ted Lasso* or *The Office*, or listening to podcasts like *The Perfectionism Project* by Sam Laura Brown, which highlight the ridiculousness of perfectionism. Laughing at our perfectionist tendencies can lighten the load and remind us that life doesn't always have to be so serious. Similarly, create routines that promote play and relaxation without the pressure to be perfect. For instance, try a "no pressure" workout where you move however feels good, or cook a meal without stressing over measurements or timing.

POSITIVE-CHANGE KICKSTARTER

Management Strategies: What strategies do you use to manage stress and anxiety related to high standards? What are healthier coping mechanisms that you can use to alleviate self-imposed pressure today?

Goals Setting: Are the goals you have set for yourself your own, or do they belong to someone else? What ways can you take fuller ownership of your goals?

Taking Pride: Taking pride in our achievements can be incredibly fulfilling. Think about a recent success—big or small—that brought you joy. Reflect on what you did to reach that goal. Give yourself that well-deserved pat on the back!

 RESOURCES

BOOKS

The Anxious Perfectionist: How to Manage Perfectionism-Driven Anxiety Using Acceptance and Commitment Therapy, by Clarissa W. Ong and Michael P. Twohig (New Harbinger Publications, 2022).

How to Be Enough: Self Acceptance for Self-Critics and Perfectionists, by Ellen Hendriksen (St. Martin's Essentials, 2025).

The Perfectionism Workbook for Teens: Activities to Help You Reduce Anxiety and Get Things Done, by Ann Marie Dobosz (Instant Help, 2016).

The Perfectionist's Dilemma: Learn the Art of Self-Compassion and Become a Happy Achiever, by Tara Cousineau (Alcove Press, 2025).

When Perfect Isn't Good Enough: Strategies for Coping with Perfectionism, by Martin M. Antony and Richard P. Swinson (New Harbinger Publications, 2009).

CHAPTER 7

BURNOUT

~~~~~

COMMONLY VOICED

✧ "I'm always tired, no matter how much I chill. Feels like I'm running around 24/7."
✧ "I used to be so into my hobbies, but now everything seems like a drag. I'm too busy to enjoy any of it."
✧ "Balancing school, activities, and everything else is killing me. I'm stretched so thin; I barely have time for myself."
✧ "I'm stuck in this never-ending cycle of stress and responsibilities. The thought of having to adult scares me."

UNDERSTANDING BURNOUT

It's concerning to see how the demands placed on you and your peers can sometimes overshadow the joys of learning and discovery. The pressure to excel academically, juggle extracurricular activities, and navigate social complexities can feel overwhelming, especially along with the other unique challenges we each face.

Experiencing burnout is like watching your phone's battery slowly drain despite your best efforts to recharge it. At first, things seem manageable, and you juggle responsibilities with relative ease. But as stress, demands, and complexity of tasks pile up, the battery depletes faster and faster. No matter how many quick fixes you try, the charge never fully recovers, leaving you with low battery alerts, struggling to stay productive, and feeling drained despite your best efforts.

About 30% to 40% of high school students report feeling overwhelmed by academic and extracurricular pressures, while 40% to 60% of college students face burnout during their studies.[31] Why are so many young people reporting burnout?

You might be feeling more pressure now than your parents and grandparents did at your age due to intensified academic and career demands and economic challenges. Today's higher standards for college admissions and increased competition have created a high-pressure environment, leading to long nights of studying and weekends filled with advanced placement courses, standardized tests, and a broad curriculum. Moreover, facing a volatile job market and economic uncertainty adds to the stress. To stand out, you and many of your peers likely feel compelled to excel academically and gain extensive experience through internships and extracurricular activities.

Burnout shares similarities with perfectionism, depression, and anxiety. While both burnout and perfectionism stem from pushing yourself too hard, burnout specifically results from prolonged stress and overcommitment. Perfectionism revolves around unrealistic standards and self-criticism, while depression and anxiety can have various causes and affect your emotional state and daily life more profoundly.

The roots of burnout often lie in academic pressures, demanding schedules, and high expectations—whether they come from within or outside sources. A significant factor of burnout is how it changes your perception of time. With academic deadlines, extracurricular commitments, and social obligations all converging, time can feel both rushed and endless. The constant pressure to "do more" and "achieve more" can create a sense of time scarcity, where every moment is filled with tasks and responsibilities. This relentless rush can make it hard to take breaks, leading to burnout that's difficult to escape.

As burnout sets in, you might feel increasingly cynical and disconnected. Tasks that once had meaning now seem like an endless list of obligations. This detachment can even extend to relationships, making it hard to connect with others amidst the exhaustion.

Compounding this challenge, you may face judgments from adults who might not fully understand your experiences. Adults often perceive complaints of burnout as signs of weakness or lack of resilience. They may dismiss these feelings as having too much free time or failing to manage responsibilities properly. Such judgments can include comments like, *"You're just not used to hard work yet,"* or *"You should learn to handle stress better."* These attitudes can exacerbate feelings of isolation and frustration, making it even harder for you to seek help or feel validated in your struggles.

Physically, burnout manifests as headaches, stomachaches, and muscle tension, with disrupted sleep only making things worse. In the short term, it leads to trouble concentrating, irritability, and a sense of emotional depletion. These issues impact academic performance and affect your overall mood and social interactions.

Looking ahead, burnout can significantly alter future perceptions and life choices. For instance, if burnout leads to chronic stress and emotional exhaustion, you might develop a heightened sense of anxiety and depression that colors your outlook on future opportunities. This could manifest as a reluctance to pursue ambitious career goals or a hesitancy to take on new challenges, driven by fear of repeated failure or stress. You might think to yourself, *"If I'm already feeling overwhelmed and unhappy, why should I or how can I push myself even harder for the future?"* It can be difficult to see the point of putting in more effort or striving for success if it only leads to more stress and unhappiness. This mindset can make it hard to find purpose in your work or in life itself if it's only about enduring constant pressure and hardship.

Over time, this shift in perspective can limit your potential, affecting both personal and professional growth. Additionally, the internalized pressures and judgments experienced during burnout might make you more cautious or skeptical about taking risks, impacting your overall well-being and life satisfaction.

To see how these questions might manifest in real life, consider Riley's story as an example of how balancing responsibilities and managing stress can impact well-being.

Riley's Story

Riley, a 15-year-old teenager known for their vibrant energy and dedication to academics and extracurricular activities, found themselves increasingly overwhelmed. Balancing schoolwork, sports, and community service had always been demanding, but recent challenges exacerbated their stress. Riley's younger sibling was diagnosed with leukemia, requiring frequent hospital visits and adding emotional strain to Riley's already hectic schedule. Meanwhile, their parents' divorce proceedings became a constant source of tension at home, with Riley feeling torn between supporting both parents amidst their emotional turmoil.

Academically, Riley had always excelled, but the pressure to maintain top grades became burdensome. Long hours spent studying and completing assignments left them feeling mentally drained and struggling to concentrate in class. Despite their efforts, Riley started missing practices for their beloved soccer team and volunteer shifts at the animal shelter, feeling guilty for not being able to meet their commitments.

At home, Riley tried to navigate the emotional strain caused by their parents' divorce. They attempted to be supportive to both parents while coping with their own feelings of sadness and confusion. The constant tension and emotional upheaval further drained Riley's energy, leaving them emotionally exhausted and withdrawn. They began declining invitations from friends and avoiding social gatherings they once enjoyed, feeling disconnected and unable to muster the energy to engage.

Physically, Riley's lack of restful sleep became apparent. Despite feeling exhausted, they struggled to fall asleep at night, their mind racing with worries about school, their sibling's health, and their parents' relationship. The resulting fatigue compounded their difficulties, affecting their mood and ability to function during the day.

Navigating social media, once a source of connection and enjoyment, became a prompt for Riley's insecurities. Scrolling through posts of peers achieving milestones or presenting idealized lives led Riley to compare themselves unfavorably, questioning their own achievements and worth.

🔍 SELF-REFLECTION

As you juggle the demands of life, it's important to periodically look at how well you're managing your responsibilities and maintaining your well-being. Use the following questions to reflect on your current balance, stress levels, and emotional health:

✿ **Assessing Responsibilities and Balance:** Am I currently taking on too many responsibilities? How do I evaluate my balance between school, work, extracurricular activities, and personal time?

✿ **Evaluating Goal Realism:** Are my goals realistic, or do I feel a pressure to achieve perfection? What criteria can I use to assess the feasibility of my goals?

✿ **Analyzing Sleep Quality:** How would I rate my sleep quality? Do I feel rested upon waking, and what factors might be affecting my sleep patterns?

✿ **Identifying Physical Symptoms:** Have I noticed any physical symptoms like headaches, fatigue, or changes in my appetite? How do these symptoms relate to my overall stress levels?

✿ **Exploring Emotional Well-Being:** Emotionally, how do I feel daily? Am I experiencing mood swings, irritability, or a sense of emptiness? What might be causing these feelings?

* **Understanding Stress Responses:** How do I typically respond to stress? Do I ignore it, push through it, or take breaks? Are my current coping strategies effective, or should I consider trying new approaches?
* **Evaluating Motivation and Accomplishment:** Have I noticed a decline in my motivation or sense of accomplishment in school, hobbies, or social life? What factors might be contributing to this change?
* **Assessing Relationships and Support:** How would I describe my relationships with friends and family? Do I feel supported, and am I comfortable discussing my challenges with them?

SELF-REGULATION STRATEGIES

In today's hustle culture, there's this pervasive belief that constant productivity is the only path to success. Many of my clients express regrets about noticing early signs of stress but feeling compelled to push through anyway. That inner voice—often fueled by societal expectations—tells you that if you're not grinding every moment, you're falling behind. But it's crucial to challenge that narrative.

As Tricia Hersey writes in *Rest Is Resistance,* "Rest is a form of liberation. It is a way to reclaim our time, our bodies, and our minds."[32] While ambition and hard work are admirable, they shouldn't come at the expense of your well-being. When you're caught up in the hustle, it's easy to overlook your own needs. You might find yourself trapped in a habit of overcommitting, neglecting essential self-care practices like exercise, mindfulness, and reaching out for support. Ignoring the distress signals from your body and mind is like refusing a life vest when you're drowning.

Taking time for self-care isn't a sign of weakness; it's a strategic move. Think of it as filling your tank so you can keep moving forward. When you prioritize your well-being, you'll find that you have more energy and clarity to tackle the challenges ahead. Set small, achievable goals for self-care every day. This might mean carving out just 10 minutes a day for mindfulness or taking a break to enjoy something you love. Celebrate these small wins! They're crucial for maintaining balance and reminding yourself that your worth isn't solely tied to how much you accomplish.

Here are some other strategies for dealing with burnout:

Adapt an "I Can Handle It" Attitude: Burnout often comes with negative self-talk, such as *"I can't handle this"* or *"I'm not good enough."* Cognitive reframing helps to change these thoughts into more realistic or positive ones, improving mental clarity and focus. If you're thinking, *"I have so much work and I'll never finish,"* reframe it as, *"I have a lot to do, but I can break it down into manageable steps. I'm making progress and I can do hard things."*

Time Management and Prioritization: One of the biggest cognitive challenges during burnout is feeling overwhelmed by tasks. Learning to prioritize and break tasks down can improve cognitive efficiency and reduce mental exhaustion. Create a to-do list and prioritize items using color codes or a numbering system. Start with the most important task and break it down into smaller actions, like "write outline" or "review notes" instead of "complete essay." Google "Eisenhower Matrix" to learn more about this effective prioritization tool.

The Pomodoro Technique (Time Blocking with Breaks): The Pomodoro Technique (developed by Francesco Cirillo in the late 1980s) helps with cognitive fatigue by providing intervals of focused work followed by short breaks. This can improve focus, productivity, and reduce mental exhaustion. Set a timer for 25 minutes of focused work on one task. When the timer goes off, take a five-minute break to stretch, walk around, or do something else. After four "Pomodoros," take a longer break (15 to 30 minutes).

Nutritional Support for Brain Function: A healthy diet rich in omega-3 fatty acids, antioxidants, and other nutrients supports brain function, reduces inflammation, and improves mood, all of which can help cognitive performance during burnout. Eat brain-boosting foods such as salmon, blueberries, spinach, walnuts, and dark chocolate. Stay hydrated with water or herbal teas, as dehydration can impact cognition.

Visualize Self at Finish Line: Visualization can help improve concentration, reduce anxiety, and enhance cognitive performance by "training" the brain in a relaxed state. Take a few minutes to close your eyes and visualize completing a task successfully or overcoming a challenge. Imagine the steps and the positive emotions you'll feel after accomplishing it.

Gratitude Wall or "Feel Good" File: Create a gratitude wall in your room or dorm, and every day, write down one thing you're grateful for on a sticky note and add it to the wall. Over time, this builds a visual reminder of all the positive things in your life, which can really shift your mindset. If you're more into digital stuff, you can create a "Feel Good" file on your phone or computer where you save positive messages, compliments, or memories that lift your spirits when you need them most.

Join a Self-Care Squad: When burnout hits, having a solid support system makes the experience less lonely. Try organizing a weekly virtual hangout with friends where you can all talk about how you're feeling and do something self-care related together—watch a movie, do face masks, or play a relaxing game. You can also create a *"Burnout Buddy Challenge"* with a friend, where you hold each other accountable for fitting in daily self-care, like taking short breaks and checking in throughout the week. If you're into journaling, swap prompts with a friend or share what you've written with someone you trust to process emotions together. These activities help you stay connected and remind you that self-care doesn't have to be a solo mission.

Keep Moving: When you're deep in the grip of burnout, the last thing you might feel like doing is moving your body, because curling up like a human burrito feels way more soothing. But the truth is, moving your body can help release built-up stress and lift your mood almost immediately. So, throw yourself a little dance party in your room! Create a playlist of your favorite upbeat songs and dance it out for 10 minutes, whether solo or with friends. If dancing isn't your thing, try putting together a simple stretching routine to do every morning or before bed. You can follow a YouTube video or just make your own. Stretching is especially helpful if you're feeling stiff after a long day of studying or sitting at a desk. And for something a bit more calming, consider trying a virtual yoga class. Search for short tutorials on YouTube or yoga apps that focus on relaxation. It's a great way to clear your mind and reduce burnout—all without needing any fancy gear.

◉ POSITIVE-CHANGE KICKSTARTER

Prioritizing Self-Care: Do you make regular time for relaxation and self-care? What activities help you recharge, and are you incorporating them into your daily routine?

Recognizing Social Isolation and Joy: Do you feel isolated from social activities? Have you lost interest in hobbies or activities that once brought you joy? What can you do to reconnect with those interests today?

Managing Life Changes: How have recent life changes, such as family dynamics or academic pressures, affected your well-being? What strategies can you use to manage these changes?

Aligning Goals and Commitments: Are your long-term goals aligned with your current commitments and priorities? What boundaries can you set to protect your mental and physical health?

 # RESOURCES

BOOKS

The Book of Burnout: What It Is, Why It Happens, Who Gets It, and How to Stop It Before It Stops You!, by Bev Aisbett (HarperCollins, 2024).

Burnout: The Secret to Unlocking the Stress Cycle, by Emily Nagoski and Amelia Nagoski (Ballantine Books, 2020).

The Teenager's Guide to Burnout: Finding the Road to Recovery, by Naomi Fisher and Eliza Fricker (Robinson, 2025).

CHAPTER 8

BEHAVIORAL ADDICTION

~~~~

COMMONLY VOICED

- ✣ "I'm totally addicted to my phone."
- ✣ "I'm trying to break my online shopping addiction, but it's so hard."
- ✣ "Can't stop scrolling. My "For You Page" is basically my life."
- ✣ "My family is always on my case about my gaming, but it's hard to stop."

UNDERSTANDING BEHAVIORAL ADDICTION

One of my neighbors sets up an elaborate Halloween display each year that always makes me think. They have a lineup of over a dozen life-sized human skeletons elevated on stilts, each adorned with old electronics like headphones and cellphones. I've never had the chance to ask what message my neighbor intends to convey, but with public art, the interpretation is often left to the observer, right?

To me, this scene seems like a commentary on the insidious effects of behavioral addiction to social media and smartphones—suggesting that even in death, we can't pry our phones from our hands. It also hints at how we might be withering away because we neglect our basic needs, becoming so absorbed in our screens that we overlook the world around us. Yes, I may be reading too much into what might just be spooky lawn decorations, but when you learn more about behavioral addictions, you might see my point.

Behavioral addiction occurs when you get so wrapped up in activities like gaming, social media, or online shopping that they start interfering with your daily life. Unlike substance addiction, which involves physical dependence on drugs or alcohol and can lead to cravings and serious health problems, behavioral addiction revolves around being hooked on repetitive actions. These behaviors create a psychological dependence, leading to intense cravings and a loss of control, but without the physical withdrawal symptoms typical of substance addiction. While behavioral addiction primarily impacts mental well-being—causing issues like social isolation, slipping grades, or financial troubles—the experience of addiction isn't so different from that of substance addiction.[33]

Look at the behavioral addiction cycle:

1. The Beginning—Excitement and Reward: Behavioral addiction starts with seemingly harmless activities like gaming for hours, scrolling through social media, or binge-watching shows. These activities are often seen as normal and even encouraged in daily life. Whether it's leveling up in a video game, getting likes on your latest post, or joining the latest binge-worthy TV show, these activities can initially give you a rush and offer an escape from stress, providing instant pleasure and a sense of belonging.

2. Getting More Engaged—The Thrill of the Chase: As time goes on, the initial excitement can start to wear off, making you dive deeper into these activities to get that same rush. This means you might spend even more time gaming, scrolling endlessly through social media, or watching series after series. The need to chase that initial high can take over your daily routine, making it harder to keep up with other important parts of your life.

3. Facing the Consequences—When Things Start to Go Wrong: When these behaviors start taking over, they can really mess with other areas of your life. For example, spending too much time on social media can hurt your school performance, while compulsive gaming or streaming can lead to social isolation or financial strain.

4. Struggling to Break Free—The Challenge of Control: Trying to cut back or stop these activities can be incredibly difficult. You might feel irritable, have trouble focusing, or experience strong cravings, similar to withdrawal symptoms seen in substance addiction. It can be overwhelming to manage these urges and reduce your involvement in these activities, even if you know they're causing problems.

5. Relapsing and Starting Over: Relapse is a common part of dealing with behavioral addiction. It's normal to fall back into old habits, which can be disheartening.

In the short term, behavioral addictions can lead to increased stress and anxiety, especially if you're constantly checking notifications or trying to achieve high scores in games. This constant engagement can disrupt your concentration, making it hard to focus on other important tasks such as schoolwork or job responsibilities. Sleep patterns can also be significantly affected; activities like late-night gaming or excessive social media use can lead to insomnia or poor sleep quality. Additionally, excessive involvement in these behaviors can result in social withdrawal, as you might find yourself spending less time interacting with family and friends.

Over the long term, behavioral addictions can have more severe impacts on your mental health, potentially leading to chronic conditions such as depression and anxiety. The incessant pursuit of satisfaction from these behaviors can exacerbate these issues, creating a combination of dissatisfaction and emotional distress. Social relationships can also suffer, with long-term isolation from family and friends becoming a common issue. The negative effects on social interactions can further isolate you and impair your ability to form new relationships. Academic or work performance may decline due to the persistent distraction and loss of focus caused by these addictions. Financial problems can escalate over time as well, with ongoing compulsive spending leading to significant debt and instability. Overall, these long-term effects can severely diminish your quality of life, causing a lack of fulfillment and missed opportunities for personal and professional growth.[34]

Read about Quinn's struggle with addiction to online gaming and gambling, and the toll it took on their social, physical, and financial well-being. Notice how their behaviors may compare or contrast with your own experiences.

Quinn's Story

Quinn, a 20-year-old figuring out life after high school in a quiet rural town, chose to stay close to home rather than heading off to college. They took on various jobs to support themself and explore different interests. While Quinn enjoyed the tight-knit community and the slower pace of rural life, they also struggled with boredom and a feeling of isolation. Without the structured environment of school, Quinn found themself searching for ways to stay engaged and connected.

During this time, Quinn started using their smartphone more, diving into social media and online gaming for entertainment and social interaction. What began to pass the time soon turned into a major part of their daily routine.

As Quinn became more absorbed in online gaming and social media, the impacts on their life became increasingly evident. Their job at the local hardware store began to suffer as they missed shifts and showed up late, leading to tensions with their boss and a reduced work schedule. Their performance in online courses also declined, with missed deadlines and poor grades, as their focus shifted away from academics.

Socially, Quinn withdrew from friends and family, declining invitations to hangouts and family gatherings. This withdrawal led to strained relationships and a growing sense of isolation. At home, Quinn neglected household chores and personal errands, resulting in a disorganized living space and mounting unpaid bills.

Quinn's impulsive spending on in-game purchases and gambling led to significant financial stress and instability. They began spending most of their earnings each week, yet had very little to show for it. While Quinn understood the importance of "saving for a rainy day," they didn't fully grasp the long-term consequences of their actions, leaving them feeling behind compared to their peers, who seemed much better off on social media. This insecurity hit a breaking point when they couldn't afford new tires after a flat on the way to the hardware store. Forced to borrow money from their parents, Quinn felt infantilized, which only heightened their anxiety and deepened the cycle of financial struggle and inadequacy.

Physically, the sedentary lifestyle from extended gaming sessions caused issues such as poor posture, eye strain, and sleep disturbances. Relationships with family and friends became strained as they expressed concern over Quinn's excessive online habits. Additionally, Quinn's addiction limited their opportunities for personal growth and exploration of new interests, affecting their overall potential for development.

🔍 SELF-REFLECTION

Reflecting on your behavioral addictions and their impact can be a crucial first step in understanding and addressing addiction. Use these questions to evaluate how addictive behaviors might be affecting your life and consider steps toward healthier coping mechanisms and recovery:

✻ **Frequency and Patterns:** How often do I engage in these specific behaviors, and can I identify any patterns in my frequency?

* **Concerns from Others:** Have others expressed concerns about my behavior? What feedback have I received from friends or family regarding this?
* **Sense of Control and Attempts to Change:** Do I feel out of control with these behaviors? Have I tried to cut back or stop in the past, and what were the outcomes of those attempts?
* **Coping Mechanisms and Triggers:** Am I using these behaviors to cope with stress or emotions? What specific situations lead me to engage in these behaviors?
* **Context and Influences:** Are there particular times, places, or people that influence my likelihood of engaging in these behaviors? How do these contexts affect my decisions?
* **Emotional Experience:** How do I feel before, during, and after engaging in these behaviors? What emotional changes do I notice throughout this process?
* **Impact on Relationships and Performance:** How has this behavior affected my relationships with others, and has it impacted my performance at work or school?
* **Financial Consequences:** Have I experienced any financial issues due to this behavior? How has it affected my budgeting or spending habits?

⟨👤⟩ SELF-REGULATION STRATEGIES

It's common for people to turn to activities like online gaming or social media to cope with boredom, stress, or feelings of isolation, especially during major life changes or when life feels unstructured or daunting. With devices always within reach, breaking free from these behavioral habits can be harder than it seems. The activities we get caught up in are easily accessible and woven into the fabric of our daily lives. For instance, I can't even count how many times I found myself sucked into addictive pimple-popping or furniture restoration videos on YouTube when I should've been studying for my board exam. At the time, I always felt guilty for what I considered a complete waste of study time. However, I now find some comfort in recent research that highlights the therapeutic potential of these study-break, ASMR (autonomous sensory meridian response) videos, particularly for managing stress and improving sleep.[35] These videos bring about a soothing, tingling sensation, often described as a relaxing chill or shiver, typically felt on the scalp, neck, or spine. This calming effect is sparked by specific auditory or visual stimuli, such as soft-spoken voices, tapping, crinkling sounds, or gentle movements. While I understand what makes these videos so appealing and how they can offer a temporary escape, they also have the potential to create challenges and interfere with other areas of our lives. For me, the loss of time and the guilt that came with it weren't worth the brief moments of stress relief during my studying.

To manage behavioral addictions and regain balance, it's crucial to set clear limits on the time spent on these activities. This can help create more structure in your day. For instance, using a timer can remind you when it's time to stop gaming or scrolling. Additionally, scheduling specific times for essential activities—like work, socializing, or exercise—can help you maintain balance and prevent online habits from taking over. Regularly checking in with yourself to assess how you feel before and after engaging in these activities can also be beneficial. For instance, when guilt set in for me when watching my stress-reducing YouTube videos, I knew I had met my threshold of diminishing return. This practice can help you identify any maladaptive patterns and adjust your behavior as needed, ensuring you don't end up "withering away to skin and bones," much like my neighbor's skeletons display.

Here are some specific self-regulation strategies to help reduce the hardships that come with behavioral addiction:

Learn More About Your Addiction: Keep a behavioral addiction reflection journal where you track your urges to engage in addictive behaviors, what sets them off, and how they make you feel. By tracking patterns, you can gain insight into why certain activities pull you in, and you can create a healthier relationship with them. Make it interactive by adding stickers, emojis, or drawings to keep it creative and fun.

Digital Declutter Party: Every few weeks, host a gathering with friends (via Zoom or in person) to clean up your devices, deleting unnecessary apps, games, or accounts that contribute to addictive behavior. You can swap tips on how to set app usage limits, customize your screen time settings, and discuss how to set healthier boundaries online. Make it fun with music, snacks, and virtual hangouts while you all work through your screens.

"Unfollow and Reconnect": Start the practice of mindful social media use by regularly unfollowing accounts that contribute to your behavioral addictions (like endless scrolling or unrealistic expectations). Focus on following accounts that promote positivity, inspiration, or your personal interests. This mindful approach ensures that social media becomes a tool for growth rather than an outlet for unhealthy distractions.

The Five-Minute "Toxic Break" Timer: Set a five-minute timer whenever you catch yourself feeling the urge to indulge in a behavioral addiction. Instead of immediately giving in, commit to doing something else for just five minutes— whether it's stretching, drawing, or even taking a quick break to scroll in a mindful way (like checking in with friends or watching something educational). The goal is to interrupt the cycle and reset your mind in small increments.

Small Wins Matter: Create a reward system to help break any behavioral addiction. Every time you make a positive choice or break a pattern, give yourself a small reward—like a favorite treat, a fun activity, or even a break with a favorite hobby. Gradually increase the rewards for breaking larger, more persistent habits and track your progress to stay motivated.

Invest in Yourself: Every time you feel the urge to make an impulsive purchase, deposit the amount you would have spent into a physical jar or a savings account for a future goal (like a vacation or new gear you actually want). Track the progress and, when you hit milestones, reward yourself with something you can truly enjoy—without breaking your financial health.

Pre-Decided List of Alternative Behaviors: Make a list of activities that can distract and engage your mind, like a five-minute dance, journaling, stretching, or even playing a board game. Keep this list where you can access it easily, and reward yourself when you successfully choose a healthier action instead.

Accountability Buddy System: Buddy up with a friend, sibling, or family member. Share your goals, track progress together, and regularly check in with each other. Make it fun by celebrating small wins; hype each other up and show compassion toward each other.

◎ POSITIVE-CHANGE KICKSTARTER

Self-Esteem and Coping Strategies: How does your addictive behavior affect your self-esteem? What healthier ways can you cope with stress and negative emotions?

_____

_____

_____

Rediscovering Joy: Are there activities you used to enjoy before this behavioral addiction took over? How can you reintroduce them into your life?

_____

_____

_____

Avoiding Exposure and Commitment to Change: What steps can you take to avoid temptations for these addictive behaviors? Why do you want to change, and how would your life improve if you overcame this behavior?

_____

_____

_____

Challenges and Fears: What challenges or fears do you have about addressing this addictive behavior? Are you ready to commit to a recovery process, and what steps can you take to affirm that commitment today?

_____

_____

_____

 # RESOURCES

MOBILE APPS

SMART Recovery (smartrecovery.org): Provides support for all types of behavioral addictions using a self-empowering approach.

Forest App (www.forestapp.cc): A unique app that helps you stay focused by planting virtual trees. The longer you stay off your phone and focus on your tasks, the more your tree grows. If you exit the app to check social media or get distracted, your tree dies. It's a fun and rewarding way to track your focus time and reduce phone distractions. Plus, for every tree you grow, the app contributes to planting real trees in the world, combining productivity with environmental impact.

Habitica (habitica.com/static/home): An app that turns habit-building into a role-playing game (RPG), where you create a character and earn rewards for completing real-life tasks and breaking bad habits. You can invite friends to join, adding a social and supportive element that makes the process feel more like a fun game than a mundane task.

Focus@Will (www.focusatwill.com): An app designed to improve focus and productivity by providing music specifically curated to enhance concentration. It offers a variety of music channels tailored to different work styles and cognitive needs, helping to reduce distractions and improve focus. The music is scientifically engineered to boost attention and sustain mental energy, making it a great tool for studying, working, or staying on task.

BOOKS

Digital Minimalism: Choosing a Focused Life in a Noisy World, by Cal Newport (Penguin Random House, 2019).

Dopamine Nation: Finding Balance in the Age of Indulgence, by Anna Lembke (Dutton, 2021).

CHAPTER 9

NEURODIVERGENCE

~~~~~

COMMONLY VOICED

✿ "I feel like I'm always trying to catch up with everyone else, but it's like I'm running in a different race altogether. It's hard to keep up when my brain works differently than everyone else's."

✿ "I have trouble with things that seem easy for my friends, like organizing my thoughts or remembering things."

✿ "I struggle with social situations, like knowing what to say or how to act around other people. It's like I'm speaking a different language, and I'm constantly worried about saying or doing the wrong thing."

✿ "I feel like I'm always misunderstood by others, like they don't see the 'real' me. It's like I'm wearing a mask to hide my struggles, and I'm afraid to let people see the 'messy' parts of myself."

UNDERSTANDING NEURODIVERGENCE

I sometimes joke that the reason we haven't been taken over by an alien species isn't that they don't know we exist, but because they're still trying to make sense of our fascinating and perplexing brains. With around 86 billion neurons forming intricate networks, the complexity of our brains presents a daunting challenge to comprehend. I imagine how an alien observer might be flummoxed by how our brains process sensory information, learn, and adapt, all while showcasing incredible creativity and problem-solving skills. Yet, despite these remarkable abilities, we remain vulnerable to mental health issues, trauma, and cognitive harms.[36]

This hypothetical alien would likely marvel at the diversity within human cognition, noticing how you and others perceive and interact with the world in unique ways. The spectrum of neurodiversity highlights both strengths and challenges. They might ponder how your brain, for instance, can experience profound emotional depth, given that feelings like love, empathy, and anxiety likely significantly influence your behavior and relationships. To them, your brain might appear not just as a center of logic and reasoning, but as a hub of complex social dynamics, cultural expressions, and an innate drive for connection. This complexity could be a bit daunting for them to fully comprehend, as we humans are a mix of mystery and predictability.

Our neurodiversity could be seen as one of the most fascinating aspects of humanity, possibly even a key to our species' ongoing survival. The term "neurodivergence" encompasses individuals whose neurological development and functioning differ from what is considered typical, including conditions such as autism, ADHD, dyslexia, dyscalculia, and dyspraxia. Should you be an individual who has received a diagnosis or suspects that you are neurodivergent, you likely experience variations in cognition, behavior, learning styles, and social interactions that set you apart from the neurotypical population. For instance, you may process information differently, leading to unique ways of thinking and problem-solving. If you have ADHD, you might excel in creative brainstorming but struggle with sustained attention on tasks you find uninteresting. In contrast, neurotypical individuals typically exhibit more uniform cognitive processing, following conventional learning and thinking patterns that align with societal expectations.[37]

Social interactions can also pose challenges for you. You might find it difficult to interpret social cues, leading to misunderstandings or feelings of isolation. For example, if you're on the autism spectrum, you may struggle to read body language or engage in small talk, making social connections more challenging. Neurotypical individuals, on the other hand, usually navigate social situations with greater ease, understanding and responding to social cues in ways that are generally accepted by society. Emotional regulation further differentiates you from neurotypical individuals, as you may experience heightened or distinct emotional responses, leading to challenges in managing your emotions. You might feel overwhelmed in busy environments due to sensory processing issues, whereas neurotypical individuals go on unbothered and may respond to emotional situations in ways that align with social norms.

Your learning style likely varies significantly from that of neurotypical individuals. You may have unique learning preferences, such as strong visual thinking skills if you have dyslexia or hyperfocus abilities if you have ADHD. These preferences can lead to alternative approaches to education and problem-solving. Neurotypical individuals, by contrast, typically benefit from standard educational methods that emphasize sequential and linear processing of information. Daily functioning can present additional challenges for you; you might face specific difficulties with tasks that neurotypicals find straightforward, such as organization, time management, and planning—often due to executive functioning difficulties. Ultimately, neurotypical individuals usually manage daily tasks and responsibilities without significant barriers, adhering to conventional approaches to organization and planning.

Sadly, many individuals who are neurodivergent experience higher rates of anxiety, depression, and burnout, a trend supported by recent research.[38] The reasons behind this increased vulnerability are complex and multifaceted. One significant factor is social stigma, which can manifest in various forms, such as misunderstanding, discrimination, and lack of acceptance. You might face negative stereotypes and misconceptions about your condition, leading to feelings of shame and self-doubt. For instance, someone with ADHD might be unfairly labeled as lazy or undisciplined, while an autistic individual may be seen as aloof or unempathetic. These misconceptions can contribute to a sense of isolation and exacerbate mental health issues as you grapple with the pressure to conform to neurotypical norms.

If you're on the autism spectrum, you might find it difficult to initiate conversations, making it hard to form meaningful connections. This lack of social support can create distress, further impacting your mental health. Studies have shown that the absence of a supportive social network can intensify feelings of anxiety and depression, highlighting the importance of community and understanding.[39]

The pressure to conform to societal expectations also adds to your mental health burden. You might feel compelled to mask your true self to fit in, which can be psychologically exhausting. This need for conformity can lead to chronic stress, anxiety, and feelings of inadequacy. Research indicates that the act of constantly suppressing your natural behaviors and traits can result in significant psychological distress, as you struggle to reconcile your authentic self with the expectations imposed by society.[40]

Finally, sensory overload is another critical factor affecting your mental health. Many report heightened sensitivity to sensory stimuli, which can lead to exhaustion and burnout, particularly in crowded or noisy environments. For example, a busy classroom or a loud public space may become overwhelming, causing anxiety and fatigue. This sensory overload can hinder your daily functioning and exacerbate feelings of stress, further impacting your overall mental well-being.[41]

Consider someone like Cameron, who suspects themself to be neurodivergent. Their experience can shed light on how social structures may not always be inclusive of neurological differences. By exploring Cameron's story, we can better understand the challenges and strengths that come with being neurodivergent in a world that often overlooks these unique perspectives.

Cameron's Story

Cameron, a 20-year-old community college student, had been deeply passionate about climate advocacy, but this commitment came with significant personal challenges. Despite a strong interest in environmental issues, Cameron struggled with managing their academic workload and maintaining their well-being. Their enthusiasm for climate activism, which had once been a source of joy, became overshadowed by feelings of burnout and stress.

Academically, Cameron found themself overwhelmed by the demands of their courses. They often procrastinated on assignments and felt anxious about their performance. This anxiety led them to avoid tasks, which only increased their stress and frustration. Cameron's difficulties with organization and time management made it hard for them to keep up with their studies, contributing to a growing sense of inadequacy.

Outside the classroom, Cameron experienced persistent fatigue and a noticeable decline in their enjoyment of activities they had once loved, such as participating in environmental clubs and volunteering for climate initiatives. Their sleep was frequently disrupted, leading to physical symptoms like headaches and stomachaches, which added to their emotional distress. Cameron's once-vibrant interest in climate advocacy was now marred by a sense of exhaustion and disinterest.

Socially, Cameron felt isolated. They had trouble connecting with others and began withdrawing from social activities due to feelings of being overwhelmed and misunderstood. This sense of isolation exacerbated their emotional struggles and made it difficult for them to maintain friendships and support networks.

Cameron's symptoms suggested the presence of neurodivergent traits such as executive functioning difficulties, sensory sensitivities, and challenges with social communication. These traits manifested as problems with organization, sensory overload, and

difficulties in maintaining relationships, which all contributed to Cameron's current and lifelong difficulties.

Q SELF-REFLECTION

Here are some questions to help you reflect on your unique
neurodivergent experiences, which can help you understand
your strengths and challenges, and find strategies for personal
growth and well-being.

* **Understanding Neurodiversity:** How do I define my
  neurodiversity, and how does it shape my daily life,
  including my interactions with family, friends, and
  colleagues?
* **Challenges and Rewards:** What specific aspects of my
  neurodivergence do I find most challenging or rewarding,
  and how do these traits impact my emotional responses?
* **Coping Strategies and Self-Care:** What coping mechanisms have I developed to manage my neurodivergent
  traits, and what self-care practices do I engage in to
  support my well-being?
* **Acceptance and Understanding:** Do I feel that those
  around me understand and accept my neurodivergent
  traits, and how does this affect my relationships?
* **Routines and Organization:** What routines or structures
  help me stay organized and manage my daily tasks, and
  how do I handle sensory sensitivities in my environment?
* **Sources of Stress:** What are the main stressors I experience
  related to my neurodivergence, and how do I address
  them while celebrating my successes and acknowledging
  my achievements?

⟨💡⟩ SELF-REGULATION STRATEGIES

Neurodiversity is the concept that neurological differences, such as those seen in conditions like ADHD, autism, dyslexia, and others, are a natural part of human variation. Rather than viewing these differences as disorders that need to be cured, neurodiversity emphasizes the idea that they should be recognized and valued as part of the spectrum of human experience.[42]

The term promotes the understanding that neurodivergent individuals like yourself can possess unique strengths and perspectives, and it advocates for inclusion, acceptance, and accommodation in society. In essence, neurodiversity challenges traditional views of normalcy and encourages a broader appreciation for the diverse ways that people think, learn, and interact with the world.

Until only recently, our society has unfortunately not been structured to embrace neurodiversity or support those who are neurodivergent. Even my own field of psychology has predominantly adopted a medicalized model, focusing on disorders and illnesses rather than taking a more comprehensive approach that considers the social and systemic origins of individual distress. Often, when someone struggles to function optimally, we assume there's something wrong with their brain, neglecting to examine how our classrooms, workplaces, and even families may be set up in ways that hinder those who think differently from the so-called "normal" person.

This perspective is simplistic and perpetuates misunderstanding and stigma. Instead of labeling individuals who are neurodivergent as "deficient" or "disordered," we should be asking essential questions about our environments. How can we make our schools better for different ways people learn? How can workplaces foster inclusivity and harness the unique strengths that neurodivergent individuals bring?

Seeing things from a more open perspective means also appreciating what neurodivergent people bring to the table. Their unique ways of thinking can spark new ideas and creativity that traditional systems might hold back. If we move away from just focusing on what's 'wrong' and instead try to understand each other, we can create spaces where everyone's differences are celebrated and everyone can succeed.

Fighting for changes in things like how we learn, the tech we use, and the rules at work can totally change how people experience the world and how society sees things. A society that truly includes everyone would recognize neurodiversity as a natural and valuable part of who we are, making us all smarter and pushing us forward together.

Ultimately, we are concerned about fostering a culture where all minds are valued and where diversity of thought is recognized as a strength rather than a barrier. By reframing the conversation around neurodiversity, we can work toward a more equitable society that appreciates the unique challenges and extraordinary potential of all its members.

While our world is still figuring out how to be more human and inclusive (and maybe even welcoming some aliens one day!), there are things you can do right now to make life easier—like easing the weight of masking and helping yourself fit in more comfortably.

Seek a Comprehensive Neuropsychological Evaluation: Talk to a psychologist or counselor who specializes in neurodivergence to get a deeper understanding of how your brain works. This will help you know what strengths you can focus on and how to handle challenges more effectively. Before your appointment, jot down personal struggles, experiences, and any past evaluations. This can guide the conversation and make sure all your needs are addressed.

Connect with Your School's Support Services: Make the most of tutoring and academic resources offered by your school. Don't forget about community programs or online resources that offer support for learning challenges. Joining study groups with friends can also be a helpful way to share ideas and learn together in a more social setting. Reach out to your school counselor or special education services for accommodations, like extended test times or access to additional support during classes. These can make a big difference in reducing stress and helping you stay organized. Keep checking in to ensure everything is in place.

Set Realistic Goals and Stay Organized: Create clear, small goals to work on each week. This could be something like organizing your room, completing homework by a certain time, or making time for self-care. Use a planner, either physical or digital, to track these tasks. Keeping a to-do list can help you stay on top of things and avoid feeling overwhelmed.

Create a Sensory-Friendly Environment: At home, make sure you have a designated quiet space where you can relax or focus without distractions. You can add things like noise-canceling headphones, weighted blankets, or dim lighting to make your environment feel calmer. If noise or lights overwhelm you, try using earplugs or switching to softer lighting throughout the day.

Practice Social Skills in Real Life: Practice social interactions in your everyday life—whether it's chatting with a family member, joining a community activity, or participating in group events. It's okay to start small, like having short conversations with friends or meeting new people in low-pressure situations, like at the park or a local event.

Develop a Healthy Daily Routine: A good routine can be your anchor outside of school or work. Try to wake up and go to bed around the same time each day to keep your body's rhythm in sync. Balance your day with scheduled time for tasks like chores, study, rest, and hobbies. This will help manage stress and create predictability, reducing anxiety.

Take Breaks When Overwhelmed: If you start feeling overwhelmed, it's important to take breaks. Go for a walk, listen to calming music, or do something quiet to reset. Breaking up your day into smaller, manageable chunks helps prevent burnout.

Find Your Tribe: Connect with people who understand your neurodivergence—whether it's friends, family, or online support groups. They can offer a listening ear or even help you navigate challenging situations. Don't hesitate to talk to someone when you need emotional support or guidance.

Reframe "Different" as "Me": Instead of focusing on what feels different, try shifting your perspective to celebrate what makes you stand out. Whether it's your creativity, attention to detail, or problem-solving skills, these qualities can be assets. Keep reminders of your strengths and successes, no matter how small, so you can remind yourself of your value. Shift the way you think about being different. Instead of seeing it as something negative, view it as an advantage. You bring perspectives and ideas that others might not have, and that's incredibly valuable. Consider writing about your feelings of difference and how they might actually help you stand out in positive ways. Make it a habit to tell yourself things that reinforce your self-worth and uniqueness. Positive affirmations like *"I am enough," "My differences are valuable,"* or *"I contribute something important"* can help shift your mindset and build confidence over time.

Focus on Personal Growth: Instead of trying to be "normal" or fit into a box, focus on growing as your authentic self. Set goals that align with your interests and values. Celebrate your progress and accept that growth comes with challenges. The key is to be proud of how far you've come, not how you compare to others.

Set Boundaries with Toxic Comparisons: Social media and peer pressure can sometimes make you feel like you need to "fit in" or be like everyone else. But remember, what you see online is often a highlight reel, not the whole story. Try to limit comparisons and focus on your personal growth. If you're feeling overwhelmed by others' posts, take a break from social media and give yourself space to just be.

⚙ POSITIVE-CHANGE KICKSTARTER

Goal-Setting and Personal Growth: How do you approach goal-setting and planning, and what adjustments could better align these processes with your neurodivergent traits and strengths?

_____

_____

_____

Communication Preferences: What are your preferred methods of communication—whether they're written, verbal, or auditory? And how can you handle situations where those preferences aren't met? For example, if you prefer written instructions but your teacher wants to meet in person, you could ask if it's possible to follow up with a note or email afterward to give yourself time to process and respond thoughtfully. What are some other ways you could ask for your communication needs to be better supported?

_____

_____

_____

Self-Advocacy and Resources: How can you effectively advocate for yourself in various settings, and what resources or support systems can you seek out to enhance your understanding of neurodivergence?

_____

_____

_____

Joy and Fulfillment: What activities bring you joy and fulfillment, and how can you prioritize them in your life while balancing acceptance of neurodivergence with personal growth?

RESOURCES

BOOKS

Different, Not Less: A Neurodivergent's Guide to Embracing Your True Self And Finding Your Happily Ever After, by Chloé Hayden (Murdoch Books, 2023).

The Dyslexia, ADHD, and DCD-Friendly Study Skills Guide: Tips and Strategies for Exam Success, by Ann-Marie McNicholas (Jessica Kingsley Publishers, 2020).

Neurodiversity Playbook: How Neurodivergent People Can Crack the Code of Living in a Neurotypical World, by Matthew Zakreski (Gifted Unlimited, 2024).

Smart but Scattered—and Stalled: 10 Steps to Help Young Adults Use Their Executive Skills to Set Goals, Make a Plan, and Successfully Leave the Nest, by Richard Guare, Colin Guare, and Peg Dawson (The Guilford Press, 2019).

Unmasking Autism: Discovering the New Faces of Neuro- diversity, by Devon Price (Harmony, 2022).

PART II
ENHANCING INTERPERSONAL SKILLS

"People and relationships never stop being a work in progress."

—Nora Roberts

CHAPTER 10

LONELINESS & SOCIAL ISOLATION

~~~~

COMMONLY VOICED

✻ "I'm always on the sidelines, while everyone else is out there living their best lives."
✻ "My social life is just a series of missed connections and awkward moments where I'm not really part of the group."
✻ "I keep seeing everyone's group pics and adventures, and I'm just here, trying to figure out where I fit in."
✻ "Sometimes it feels like I'm invisible. I'm right here, but it's like nobody even looks my way or acknowledges I'm around."

UNDERSTANDING LONELINESS AND SOCIAL ISOLATION

John Green, author of *The Fault in Our Stars*, encapsulates the challenges of loneliness perfectly: "The world is full of people who are just waiting to be noticed, even though they're standing right in front of you."[43] This sentiment resonates deeply with those who, despite being surrounded by crowds and social opportunities, still experience a profound sense of disconnection and isolation.

Psychologically, loneliness occurs when there is a disparity between our current social interactions and our ideal social life. John T. Cacioppo describes it as the emotional state that emerges when our social reality falls short of our social aspirations.[44] It's akin to watching others effortlessly connect while feeling perpetually on the outside. For instance, social media platforms often amplify this feeling by showcasing curated images of vibrant social lives, leading individuals to compare their own less glamorous realities and feel increasingly isolated.

Existentially, loneliness reflects a fundamental separation inherent in the human experience. Philosophers such as Jean-Paul Sartre and Martin Heidegger have explored this separation, emphasizing that loneliness involves not just physical isolation but a profound disconnection at a deeper level.

Sartre's idea of *"being-for-itself"* talks about how we, as individuals, are constantly defining ourselves through our actions and choices.[45] It means that we're aware of who we are, what we do, and how we impact the world, but at the same time, we're always aware that we're separate from everyone else. It's like realizing that, no matter how much you connect with others, you're still an individual—thinking, feeling, and experiencing life on your own terms. This awareness can make you feel lonely because, in a way, you're always "by yourself" in your experience, even if you're surrounded by people.

Heidegger's idea of *"being-toward-death"* is about how we all know that we'll eventually die, and that knowledge shapes the way we live. It's like the ultimate reminder that, no matter what, we're all going to face our own death one day, and this can make you feel isolated because no one can truly experience death for or with you. You're the only one who can face it, and that reality makes you more aware of your individuality and how separate you are from others. So, even if you have close relationships, you can't share the exact same experience of life's end with anyone else—it's something you face alone.[46]

Together, these ideas show that the awareness of our individuality (how we're separate from others) and the reality of death (the ultimate solitude) can create feelings of existential loneliness. You're aware that no matter how connected you might feel to others, there's always a part of you that stands apart.

Ultimately, several factors influence loneliness, including socioeconomic status, the depth of digital interactions versus real connections, mental health challenges, social skills, family dynamics, cultural background, and life transitions. For example, individuals from lower socioeconomic backgrounds may face additional barriers to forming and maintaining social connections due to financial constraints or lack of resources.[47] Similarly, those who rely heavily on digital interactions might experience a sense of loneliness due to the superficial nature of online relationships compared to face-to-face connections.

LONELINESS AS A MODERN EPIDEMIC

In our era of instant and constant connectivity, loneliness has emerged as a significant concern, often described as an "epidemic." Despite unprecedented ways to connect digitally, many people still feel profoundly isolated. A recent comprehensive study of many studies on the loneliness epidemic revealed this paradox: While we are digitally connected, many of us experience emotional loneliness because these interactions often lack the depth and fulfillment of face-to-face connections.[48]

The COVID-19 pandemic magnified this issue, transitioning many from daily in-person interactions to primarily virtual connections. Lockdowns, social distancing, and remote learning highlighted the importance of face-to-face interactions for emotional and psychological well-being. Studies found that these changes significantly increased feelings of loneliness among young people, with the effects of isolation, limited social interactions, and reliance on virtual connections extending into young adulthood.[49]

The pandemic's impact was particularly severe for young adults, with a significant number of individuals aged 18 to 29 reporting symptoms of depression and anxiety related to loneliness during this time.[50] This period of isolation underscored the crucial role of in-person interactions in maintaining emotional health.

Loneliness is not just a fleeting emotion; it can profoundly impact various aspects of your life. One significant area affected is emotional and psychological health. Loneliness often acts as a major predictor of mental health issues like depression and anxiety. Imagine being trapped in a dark room where every negative thought feels amplified—this vividly illustrates the intense emotional toll that loneliness can exact on you.

Moreover, loneliness can hinder your academic and occupational success. This issue was particularly noticeable during the pandemic, when remote learning became widespread. Remember trying to focus on an assignment while feeling disconnected from your peers and instructors? Loneliness can make educational and professional challenges feel even steeper. The effects of social disconnection can disrupt your ability to engage fully in learning and work environments.

Additionally, loneliness impedes the development of essential social skills that are crucial for future success and happiness. Missing out on interactions that foster communication, empathy, and connection can hold you back from forming meaningful relationships. It's like being sidelined from a game you want to play—every missed opportunity to interact can significantly impact your future successes and connections with others.

Finally, chronic loneliness is linked to higher risks of illness and chronic health conditions. The pandemic exacerbated these health impacts, leading to changes in physical activity and sleep patterns. Over time, neglecting exercise, proper meals, and adequate rest can result in serious physical health problems, demonstrating that loneliness affects more than just your emotional well-being; it can have far-reaching consequences for your overall health.

Loneliness that extends into adulthood may influence your ability to form relationships and achieve personal goals. Ongoing loneliness can establish patterns of social isolation and emotional distress. The pandemic highlighted how severe loneliness can have enduring effects, underscoring the importance of support systems for mental health and personal growth.

Ellis's story offers a glimpse into the emotional and psychological challenges faced by many international students who leave the comfort of home for a new life abroad. Their journey reflects the gap between expectations and reality when navigating a new environment, and how loneliness can quietly affect every aspect of life, from academics to mental health. Even if you are not an international student, how can you relate or not relate to Ellis's experience of loneliness?

Ellis's Story

Ellis, an 18-year-old international student, arrived at a dynamic urban university in a new country with high hopes for a successful academic life. Hailing from a small town with a close-knit circle of friends and a supportive family, Ellis was excited about the opportunities for personal and professional growth that studying abroad promised. They had also grown up with two beloved pets—an energetic dog and a calm, affectionate cat—that had provided stability and comfort throughout their life. Ellis envisioned thriving in the lively campus environment, eager to embrace new experiences and forge lasting connections.

However, their initial excitement quickly gave way to deep, persistent loneliness. Despite being surrounded by people and immersed in the vibrant campus life, Ellis felt isolated and disconnected. For example, while walking through the crowded campus quad, they saw groups of friends laughing and chatting but felt invisible and unable to break into these social circles. It was as if they were living in a parallel world, watching others form friendships and enjoy their university experience from a distance.

This loneliness began to impact Ellis's academic performance. They struggled to focus during lectures and found it increasingly difficult to engage in group projects. In study sessions, Ellis often sat quietly on the periphery, unable to contribute meaningfully. The pressure to maintain high grades, combined with their disconnection from classmates and professors, only added to their stress. Ellis described a lack of motivation and a sense that every academic challenge was magnified by their feelings of isolation. They frequently spent late nights in their dorm room trying to catch up on work, but felt unproductive and drained.

Socially, Ellis struggled to initiate and sustain meaningful relationships. Despite attending social events like campus mixers and club meetings, and joining student groups such as the international students' association and a local hiking club, they felt out of place. For instance, at a welcome party for new students, Ellis tried to join conversations but found it difficult to connect, leaving them feeling awkward and disconnected. Their attempts at making friends often seemed futile, with conversations fizzling out quickly or never moving beyond superficial small talk. This left Ellis feeling even more isolated and frustrated.

The emotional weight of leaving behind their pets further intensified Ellis's sense of displacement. Their pets had provided a source of comfort and routine, and their absence created a profound void. Ellis missed the everyday moments with their pets, who had been a constant source of joy and grounding.

Emotionally, Ellis battled anxiety and occasional depressive episodes. They often felt overwhelmed by their loneliness, which fueled worries about their future. Ellis described a persistent sense of emptiness and pervasive sadness that clung to them throughout the day. Their mental health issues were compounded by physical symptoms, including irregular eating habits—such as skipping meals or overeating due to stress—inconsistent sleep patterns, and a lack of physical exercise, which they had previously enjoyed. These issues created a vicious pattern of feeling down and being unable to engage in activities that might improve their mood.

🔍 SELF-REFLECTION

Reflecting on your feelings and experiences can help you identify the sources of your loneliness and explore ways to address it. Here are some self-reflection questions to guide you on this expedition:

- ✵ **Understanding Loneliness:** When did I first notice feeling lonely? What situations contribute to this feeling? How do I distinguish between being alone and feeling lonely?
- ✵ **Thoughts and Feelings:** What thoughts arise when I reflect on my loneliness, and is it difficult for me to talk about it? If so, why?
- ✵ **Impact on Well-Being:** How does loneliness affect my mood, overall well-being, and self-esteem? In what ways does it impact my relationships with friends and family, as well as my schoolwork or career goals?

* **Health and Self-Care:** How does loneliness impact my health and self-care practices?
* **Coping Mechanisms:** What are my main ways of coping with loneliness, and what have I learned from these experiences?
* **Personal Growth and Self-Perception:** How has dealing with loneliness changed my view of myself and my future? Do I feel embarrassed or guilty about being lonely?

⟨ၐ⟩ SELF-REGULATION STRATEGIES

Chronic loneliness is grueling, and if you're feeling it, know that you're not alone. It's something nearly everyone experiences at some point in their lives, even if it feels incredibly isolating at the time. In fact, the late Dr. Ruth Westheimer, a renowned sex therapist, was appointed as New York City's Ambassador to Loneliness, which underscores how widespread and impactful this issue really is. In the introduction to her book *The Joy of Connections*, Dr. Ruth draws attention to the common stigma and shame that both people struggling with their sex lives and those dealing with chronic loneliness often face. I can relate to this, especially with my younger clients, many of whom feel a deep sense of embarrassment when they admit to me that they feel lonely.

I believe there should be ambassadors for loneliness at every major life milestone—one for kids, teens, emerging adults, midlife, and older age. Loneliness shows up in different ways at each stage. For children, it may manifest as a feeling of disconnection from peers or being misunderstood at home. During the teenage years, the struggle to belong often takes center stage. This is a time when we're still figuring out who we are, and the pressure to fit in can leave us feeling isolated, even in a crowd. In young adulthood, loneliness becomes more complex—it could stem from unmet expectations, the weight of career pressures, or the loneliness that comes with breakups and the challenges of building long-term relationships. For those of us in midlife or later, loneliness may arise from a sense of lost purpose, the empty nest, or just the absence of deep social connections as life becomes busier and more focused on responsibilities. But at every stage, loneliness points to a need for connection, belonging, or closeness that hasn't been fulfilled.

No matter where you are in life, it's important to show yourself some grace. It's easy to fall into negative self-talk, comparing yourself to others or even to a version of yourself you think you've lost. But loneliness isn't a reflection of who you are or your worth—it's simply a signal that something is missing, and it's temporary. Start with small, intentional steps to nurture yourself. This could mean sticking to a comforting routine, finding activities that bring you joy, or even taking up a new hobby to shift your focus and rediscover a part of yourself.

It may feel overwhelming now, but with time, patience, and a bit of bravery, things will change. The more you engage with your environment and give yourself permission to connect with others, the more you'll find opportunities to fill the gaps that loneliness creates. As you move through this process, you'll also learn more about yourself and how to take better care of your emotional health.

Here are a few self-regulation strategies that can help you navigate loneliness and support your emotional well-being.

Learn More About Loneliness: Understanding loneliness can be a powerful tool in managing it. Explore articles, videos, or podcasts that talk about loneliness, its effects, and how others cope. Knowing you're not alone in feeling lonely can be a huge relief. Try looking into resources like the book *Lonely: Learning to Live with Solitude* by Emily White or podcasts like *The Lonely Hour.*

Create Your Own Comfort Kit: When loneliness strikes, have a "go-to" kit. This could include favorite hobbies, comfort snacks, or even a playlist of songs that lift your mood. If you know the loneliness usually hits in the evenings, keep a fun puzzle or your favorite journal nearby to distract you and connect with yourself.

Feel Connected Through Volunteering: Volunteering is not only a way to help others but also a powerful way to combat loneliness. You might volunteer at a shelter, help tutor younger students, do a park clean-up, or organize community events. Giving to others fosters a sense of belonging and purpose, which can alleviate feelings of isolation.

Practice Conversations in Low-Pressure Situations: Try practicing small talk with strangers, like asking someone about their day or complimenting them on something they're wearing. Over time, these small moments can help build your confidence in social situations. Start small! Set a goal to speak up during one class discussion or say "hi" to someone new at lunch. Gradually, these small social wins will build your comfort and social confidence.

Explore Art or Music Therapy: Use drawing, painting, or even digital art to explore how you're feeling. Art can be a cathartic way to express emotions you might not have words for and helps you process your feelings creatively. Create music to express your emotions, or learn an instrument. Music has been shown to improve mood and can be a great way to bond with others when shared in groups or online communities.

Exercise to Boost Your Mood: Physical activity isn't just good for your body—it's also great for your mind. Whether it's going for a run, doing yoga, or dancing to your favorite tunes, exercise releases endorphins that help reduce feelings of loneliness and anxiety.

Join or Form a Stammtisch: In Germany, regular social hangouts that occur at the same time each week are often referred to as *"stammtisch."* The term originally referred to a regular's table at a pub or restaurant, where people would gather to chat and enjoy drinks. Today, it can also refer to any recurring social gathering that happens regularly, such as a weekly meet-up for a certain sport, a board game night, a language exchange, or just a casual social gathering. It's also common for student groups or clubs to organize these kinds of weekly meetups at cafes, parks, or community spaces.

Find Community in Spiritual Practices: If you're spiritually inclined, getting involved in a community group like a youth group, a religious gathering, or a spiritual practice (like meditation or yoga) can help create a sense of belonging.

Changing Up Your Thinking: Addressing the mindsets that contribute to feelings of isolation or loneliness is key to managing these emotions more effectively. Sometimes, the way we think about ourselves, others, or situations can keep us stuck in feelings of loneliness. Here are some common mindsets and ways to shift them:

✴ **"I'm the only one who feels this way"**: This mindset makes you feel isolated in your emotions, as if no one else can relate. But the reality is, everyone experiences loneliness at some point. When you realize that others have felt or are feeling the same way, it can help you feel more connected to others, even if you're not physically close to them. Think instead, *"Many people feel lonely at times, and I'm not alone in this."*

✴ **"I don't fit in, and I never will"**: Feeling that you don't belong can be incredibly isolating. This mindset often stems from comparing yourself to others or believing you're different. Shifting to a more open mindset allows you to see that while it might take time, there are always opportunities to connect with people who appreciate you for who you are. The right people are out there, even if it takes time to find them. Doesn't saying this instead work better: *"I may not fit in right now, but I have the ability to connect with others who share my interests"*?

✴ **"No one understands me"**: It's easy to feel like no one gets you, especially when you're feeling disconnected. But by shifting this mindset, you open yourself up to finding those who do understand, whether through friends, groups, or online communities. You're more likely to find meaningful connections if you believe they exist. Instead, shift to this: *"I can find people who understand my experiences, even if it takes some effort."*

✴ **"I have to do everything on my own"**: This mindset can create a barrier to reaching out for support when you need it. Loneliness often comes with the pressure of believing that you have to handle everything by yourself. Learning that it's okay to ask for help or lean on others can create opportunities for deeper connections and remind you that you're not alone in facing challenges.

* **"People don't want to spend time with me"**: When you feel lonely, it's easy to assume that people aren't interested in you or don't care. But often, this mindset is shaped by our own insecurities or assumptions. Shifting it allows you to recognize that people might be busy, have their own struggles, or not know how to reach out. It's not a reflection of your worth or likability. Go with something like this instead: *"Some people might not reach out, but that doesn't mean others don't want to connect."*

* **"I'll always be alone"**: Loneliness can feel permanent, but it's important to remember that it's a temporary feeling, not a permanent state. By taking steps to reach out and engage with others, you can create opportunities for connection. Try reframing this to: *"Loneliness is temporary, and I have the power to change my situation."*

* **"I'm not interesting or valuable enough for others to want to spend time with me"**: Low self-esteem can fuel loneliness, but everyone has qualities that make them worthy of connection. Embrace your uniqueness and recognize that people value you for who you are. Instead, tell yourself: *"I am worthy of connection, and I have unique qualities to share."*

* **"I'm too different from others to fit in"**: It's easy to feel like you're too different from everyone else, but your differences are what make you special. Embrace them, as they can help you find others who appreciate your individuality. Think of it this way: *"My differences make me unique and interesting, and they can attract the right kind of people."*

✼ **"I have to be perfect to be loved or accepted"**: Needing to be perfect can stop you from making connections with others. Remember, authenticity is what truly matters. Try reminding yourself: *"I don't need to be perfect to connect with others. Authenticity is more important."*

⊘ POSITIVE-CHANGE KICKSTARTER

Building Connections: What can you do to feel less lonely, and how can you build deeper connections with others? What activities might help you feel more connected?

_____

_____

_____

Support and Resources: What support or resources are available to help you address your loneliness?

_____

_____

_____

Future Changes: How might your life change as you actively work to address your loneliness and enhance your connections with others?

_____

_____

_____

RESOURCES

BOOKS

It's Kind of a Funny Story, by Ned Vizzini (HarperCollins, 2006).

The Joy of Connections: 100 Ways to Beat Loneliness and Live a Happier and More Meaningful Life, by Ruth K. Westheimer, Allison Gilbert, and Pierre Lehu (Rodale Books, 2024).

Platonic: How the Science of Attachment Can Help You Make and Keep Friends, by Marisa G. Franco (G. P. Putnam's Sons, 2022).

Tribe: On Homecoming and Belonging, by Sebastian Junger (Twelve, 2016).

CHAPTER 11

IDENTITY DISCRIMINATION

COMMONLY VOICED

- It's like everyone's just focused on how I look instead of what I'm actually like, and it's just so unfair."
- "I know I should speak up about sexism, ableism, racism, and all that, but I'm scared of making things worse. It's tiring to stand up for myself when I already feel so vulnerable and alone."
- "I feel like I'm walking around with a target on my back, and I never know when someone's going to take a shot at me."
- "I try to shake off the hurtful comments and jokes, but they keep chipping away at my self-worth. It's hard to feel confident when it seems like everyone's either judging me or has already decided what I'm worth."

UNDERSTANDING IDENTITY DISCRIMINATION

If you could choose anyone, living or deceased, to be your friend, who would it be? It's likely that the person you pick embodies traits of a strong sense of self and a well-formed identity. For instance, I would say celebrated poet and writer Maya Angelou fits this bill for me. Her powerful voice as a writer and poet, along with her unwavering commitment to justice and equality, showcases a remarkable sense of self. Angelou's life and work, from her acclaimed autobiography *I Know Why the Caged Bird Sings* to her activism in the Civil Rights Movement, reflect deep resilience and a clear sense of purpose. Her ability to use her experiences and talents to inspire and uplift others exemplifies the traits of a well-defined identity.[51]

Identity encompasses more than just your name, social security card, or background; it includes your cultural heritage, languages, beliefs, and how you perceive your role in society. This self-discovery can be challenging, especially when faced with identity discrimination. This type of discrimination happens when others unfairly judge or mistreat you based on factors like race, ethnicity, gender, age, ability, or sexual orientation. For example, you might encounter discrimination at school because of your race, face gender bias in sports or clubs, or deal with prejudice based on your sexual orientation. Such experiences can deeply affect how you view yourself and interact with others.

Your identity development is shaped by personal experiences, social interactions, and societal expectations. Discrimination can complicate this process by introducing negative stereotypes and pressures that hinder self-exploration and acceptance. For instance, if you face racial or gender discrimination, it can make it harder to explore and embrace your identity fully, impacting your self-esteem and sense of belonging.

Understanding how discrimination impacts identity development can be eye-opening. Think of it this way: Just like you're figuring out who you are and where you fit in, there are also psychological theories that try to explain how this process works. But remember that everyone's experience is different, and these theories just give a general picture.

Erik Erikson's Psychosocial Development Theory: Erikson thought that our sense of identity grows through different stages as we age. Teen years and young adulthood are especially important for this. During these times, you're trying out different roles and figuring out who you are in the eyes of society. [52]

James Marcia's Identity Status Model: Marcia's model breaks identity development into four main stages. Here's a quick rundown:

- **Identity Diffusion:** You're not sure about your beliefs or goals and haven't really explored them yet.
- **Identity Foreclosure:** You've made commitments to certain values or roles without exploring other options. This is often based on what others expect of you.
- **Identity Moratorium:** You're actively exploring different options and beliefs but haven't committed to any yet.
- **Identity Achievement:** You've explored various options and have made clear commitments to specific roles and beliefs.

Discrimination can mess with this process of growth. For instance, a transgender person facing discrimination might settle on an identity too quickly or feel pressured to fit into societal norms, which can limit their exploration and affect their self-view.[53]

Social Identity Theory: This theory says that part of who we are comes from the groups we belong to, like race or gender. If you're discriminated against based on these groups, it can hurt your pride and sense of belonging. For example, racial discrimination might make someone feel disconnected from their cultural heritage, affecting their overall sense of identity.[54]

Intersectionality Theory: Intersectionality looks at how different aspects of your identity—like race, gender, ability, and sexuality—overlap and shape your experiences. Discrimination isn't just about one part of who you are; it can affect you in multiple ways at once. For example, a young Black woman might face challenges related to both her race and gender, making it even more complicated to develop a strong and empowered sense of self.[55]

These theories offer useful insights into identity development, but your own experiences are unique and may not fit perfectly into these models. The key takeaway is that understanding these concepts can help you make sense of how discrimination impacts your task of self-discovery.

Identity discrimination can significantly impact your psychological well-being in both short-term and long-term ways. In the short term, psychological distress often manifests as increased anxiety and fear. For instance, a young Asian American student who faces racial slurs at school might develop heightened anxiety, leading them to avoid social situations to escape potential future encounters. Emotional numbness can also occur. A transgender teenager repeatedly misgendered by peers may emotionally withdraw, becoming detached from both positive experiences and their peers. Social isolation is another common response; an immigrant student teased for their accent might withdraw from friends and family to avoid the discomfort of judgment, exacerbating feelings of loneliness. Additionally, self-doubt and internal conflict might arise in a 2SLGBTQ+ individual facing bullying, causing them to question their worth and identity, which can lead to a sense of not belonging.[56]

Over the long term, the effects of discrimination can be even more profound. Academic and career hesitation might develop; for example, a Black student experiencing systemic racism may begin to doubt their academic capabilities, potentially leading to reluctance in pursuing higher education or career opportunities. Chronic stress from ongoing discrimination can also result in serious health issues, such as headaches, gastrointestinal problems, or high blood pressure. Identity confusion and fragmentation may arise in a young Latina who faces stereotypes about her cultural background, complicating her development of a positive self-concept. Finally, impaired emotional development can affect a person with a mixed-race background who struggles to integrate their racial identity with societal expectations, leading to difficulties in achieving self-acceptance and self-worth.

These manifestations illustrate how deeply identity discrimination can affect both immediate well-being and long-term personal development, underscoring the importance of appropriate support and intervention.

Morgan's Story

Morgan, a 16-year-old second-generation Asian American from a Christian background, dealt with profound internal conflicts surrounding their gender identity amidst their affluent upbringing and lack of familial support. Raised in a community where adherence to traditional gender norms and evangelical beliefs was paramount, Morgan experienced a tumultuous time of self-discovery and acceptance.

At Morgan's prestigious private school, where conservative values prevailed, navigating their gender identity became an isolating experience. In the affluent social circles they moved in, discussions often revolved around conformity to gender roles and expectations that Morgan found stifling. Classmates, whose viewpoints were shaped by conservative religious teachings and affluent privilege, struggled to understand Morgan's gender fluidity, often dismissing it as a phase or an act of rebellion against their upbringing.

Within their own family, Morgan faced significant challenges. Their evangelical Protestant parents, deeply rooted in their faith and community, had difficulty reconciling Morgan's exploration of gender identity with their religious beliefs. This disconnect led to frequent disagreements and strained conversations at home, exacerbating Morgan's feelings of isolation and alienation.

Internally, Morgan battled conflicting emotions and self-doubt. They questioned whether their gender identity was valid within the context of their religious upbringing and affluent environment. The pressure to conform to societal and familial expectations weighed heavily on Morgan, contributing to anxiety and a sense of disconnection from their true self.

Despite these challenges, Morgan found moments of clarity and self-acceptance in online communities and smaller social circles where individuals with diverse gender identities shared similar experiences. These spaces offered a lifeline of support and understanding, helping Morgan navigate the complexities of adolescence and identity formation. However, when Morgan was unable to be online, they fantasized about moving away as far as possible from their home city, as this seemed like the only option left to them.

🔍 SELF-REFLECTION

Here are some self-reflection questions designed to help you navigate through experiences of identity discrimination and understand their impact on your personal growth and well-being:

* **Understanding Identity:** How do I see my identity beyond societal labels and stereotypes, and what parts of my cultural heritage, beliefs, or personal values are most important to me?

* **Impact of Discrimination:** How does discrimination affect my self-perception and sense of belonging, as well as my daily feelings and interactions with others, including family and authority figures?

* **Emotional Effects:** Have my experiences with discrimination changed my mood, energy, or motivation, and how do I feel daily because of it?

* **Current Coping Strategies:** What strategies do I use to handle discrimination, and do I have supportive people— friends, family, or mentors—who I can turn to for help?

⟨♀⟩ SELF-REGULATION STRATEGIES

If parts of Morgan's story resonate with you, especially if your identity feels at odds with what your family or society expects of you, I want you to know this: You deserve respect, just as you are. It's complicated, I know, to feel like you're constantly battling for understanding and acceptance. It can be exhausting, and it's easy to start doubting yourself when others don't seem to get you. You only have one life, and you owe it to yourself to live it authentically, without trying to fit into a mold that doesn't reflect who you truly are today.

Unfortunately, for many with marginalized identities— whether it's because of race, gender, sexual orientation, or any other aspect of self—there's a pervasive reality of xenophobia and systemic exclusionary practices that make it even harder to feel accepted. These larger forces often create barriers, making it feel like you're being pushed to the margins simply for being yourself. This can take an immense toll on your mental health, leaving you feeling isolated, misunderstood, or unwanted. Your identity is real and meaningful. You matter, and you deserve to be recognized, understood, and valued for who you truly are.

One of the most important steps you can take in these situations is to find people who *do* get you—whether that's through friendships, online communities, or even by reaching out to a teacher or neighbor who offers a safe space. We now know as general knowledge that connecting with a supportive community can make a huge difference in your mental health, offering a vital sense of belonging and connection. Even when your family or society doesn't fully understand, finding your people, your "tribe," can be a game-changer. That sense of belonging can help you counter the isolation imposed by systemic exclusion and keep you grounded when the world feels especially challenging.

You are growing, evolving, and becoming the person you're meant to be. And no matter how stifling it gets, celebrate your progress, no matter how small. Every step forward, even the ones that feel difficult or uncertain, are important. That's how resilience is built—by recognizing that each day, you're moving closer to the authentic life you deserve.

Here are some self-regulation strategies to help you gain greater self-compassion, and a future filled with acceptance, possibility, and joy.

Validation and Affirmation: It's crucial for you to validate your feelings and experiences of discrimination and being othered. Create a safe space where you can comfortably express yourself. Consider identifying the positive aspects of your identity and achievements that affirm your worth. Write and repeat affirmations daily, such as, *"I am proud of who I am, and my identity is beautiful."*

Psychoeducation: Learning about discrimination and identity development and their impacts on mental health can help you better understand your experiences. Attend workshops or webinars on these topics, and read books or articles by experts in fields related to your identity and experiences. See resources section at the end of this chapter.

Intersectional Approach: Recognize that your identity is multifaceted—encompassing race, gender, and sexual orientation—and understand how these intersecting aspects influence your experiences. Exploring these intersections can help you tailor support more effectively. Join support groups or online forums where individuals discuss similar intersections and share experiences.

Family and Community Involvement: There is strength and power in numbers. Engage your family and community in understanding discrimination by initiating conversations and sharing resources that highlight its impact. Connect with peers who share similar experiences for validation and support. Join a peer support group or find a mentor who has navigated similar challenges. Attend meetings or virtual sessions to share experiences and gain understanding. Build a group of friends who practice positive affirmations together, either in person or through text/social media. Affirming each other's identities with phrases like *"You are powerful"* or *"All the parts of you matter"* can strengthen your sense of belonging.

Advocacy and Activism: Channel your emotions into activism through social media, community organizing, or raising awareness. Advocating for others' rights can help you feel more in control and less isolated. Join advocacy groups focused on your identity for a sense of belonging and validation. Get involved in local social justice campaigns, take on leadership roles, and volunteer to address systemic discrimination. These actions build purpose, empower you to create change, and foster community connections.

Celebrate Cultural Heroes: Dive deeper into the stories of people from your cultural background who have faced identity-based challenges and emerged victorious. This can deepen your connection to your heritage and inspire pride in who you are.

Explore the Stories of Pioneers and Trailblazers: Many of your heroes may have faced similar struggles with identity discrimination and overcome them in extraordinary ways. Whether it's learning about civil rights leaders like Martin Luther King Jr. or 2SLGBTQ+ trailblazing activists like Marsha P. Johnson, their journeys can provide powerful lessons in resilience, courage, and self-empowerment. Their stories can remind you that even in the face of adversity, great things can be achieved.

Writing Letters (You Don't Have to Send): Write letters to yourself or to those who have discriminated against you (without necessarily sending them). This can be a cathartic way to release pent-up emotions, clarify your feelings, and reinforce your self-worth.

Storytelling and Narrative Building: Write your own life story or even fictionalize it in a way that reimagines a positive future where discrimination is no longer a factor. This exercise helps you reclaim control of your narrative and redefine how you see yourself.

Role-Playing: Practice role-playing scenarios in which you assert yourself or navigate microaggressions in a safe, controlled environment. This can help build confidence in standing up for yourself when discrimination occurs. Role-playing with a trusted friend or therapist can also provide feedback and emotional support.

Music and Sound Therapy: Curate playlists that elevate your mood and help you process emotions. Listen to music that resonates with your experiences or makes you feel empowered. Sound therapy, such as using singing bowls or binaural beats, can also be used to relax and manage emotional distress.

Dance Therapy or Movement Practices: Use dance or other movement practices to express emotions related to discrimination and reclaim control over your body. Dance can help release pent-up feelings and stress while allowing you to reconnect with yourself in an embodied way. You can create a dance routine to your favorite empowering song, or just free-style and let the music take you on a journey.

Poetry as Self-Expression: Write poems to express emotions related to your experiences with discrimination. Writing poetry gives you the freedom to explore your feelings in an abstract way, helping you process complex emotions and find beauty in your story.

Identity-Inspired Fashion or Styling: Express your identity through fashion by incorporating elements that celebrate who you are—whether it's wearing clothes that honor your cultural heritage or adopting a personal style that reflects your sense of self. This can be a fun, empowering way to make a statement without saying a word.

Create a Future Vision Board: Construct a vision board or digital collage of images, words, and symbols that represent the life you want to create for yourself—free from discrimination. Reflect on your dreams, aspirations, and what success looks like to you. This is a creative tool to reaffirm your identity and set intentions for the future.

✒ POSITIVE-CHANGE KICKSTARTER

Building Resilience: How can you build resilience and maintain a positive self-image despite the challenges you face related to discrimination?

Goals and Empowerment: How does discrimination shape your goals for education, career, and personal growth? Do you feel empowered to pursue your dreams despite these obstacles?

Advocacy and Celebration: What actions can you take to advocate for yourself and others facing similar challenges, and how can you celebrate and affirm your identity to counter negative stereotypes?

Cultural Pride: What activities or communities can help you strengthen your cultural pride and identity, and how can you educate others about the richness and diversity of your identity?

RESOURCES

WEBSITES

Calm Harm (calmharm.stem4.org.uk) and **MindShift** (www .anxietycanada.com/resources/mindshift-cbt): Apps designed to help manage stress and anxiety, particularly useful for dealing with the emotional impacts of discrimination.

Pride Foundation (pridefoundation.org) and **Human Rights Campaign** (www.hrc.org): Host educational events and workshops on identity, discrimination, and advocacy.

BOOKS

Disability Visibility: First-Person Stories from the Twenty-First Century, edited by Alice Wong (Vintage Books, 2020).

Intersectionality, by Patricia Hill Collins and Sirma Bilge (Polity Press, 2016).

So You Want to Talk About Race, by Ijeoma Oluo (Seal Press, 2018).

CHAPTER 12

RELATIONAL ABUSE

~~~~~

COMMONLY VOICED

✿ "I try to act like those nasty comments don't bother me, but honestly, they hurt way more than people realize. It's tough to feel good about myself when I'm always being put down by someone who's supposed to have my back."

✿ "I used to have friends, hobbies, and dreams, but it feels like they've all vanished because of this relationship. It's hard to remember who I am when I'm constantly being controlled and manipulated."

✿ "I'm totally on my own, like no one gets what I'm going through because everything looks perfect on the outside."

✿ "I know I should leave, but honestly, I'm terrified of what life would be like without them. I don't know if I'll ever be strong enough to walk away."

UNDERSTANDING RELATIONAL ABUSE

As you navigate the exciting yet complex world of relationships in your teens and twenties, it's crucial to understand that not all connections are healthy or fulfilling. While the media often portrays romance as a perfect blend of passion and drama, real-life relationships require more than just intense emotions—they need trust, respect, and clear communication.

To build and maintain these healthy connections, it's important to be aware of various forms of relational abuse that can undermine your well-being. Recognizing these different types can help you identify red flags and ensure that your relationships are truly supportive and positive.

Let's dive into the key forms of relational abuse and how they can impact your life.

PHYSICAL ABUSE

Physical abuse involves any form of violence or harm to your body, such as hitting, slapping, or pushing. It can also include threats that create fear. Even if the abuse isn't visible, it can still cause serious emotional trauma. For instance, imagine a partner who, during a heated argument, might slam doors or throw objects, creating an atmosphere of fear and tension. You might not have physical bruises, but the constant threat and aggressive gestures can leave you feeling anxious and on edge, constantly walking on eggshells.[57]

SEXUAL ABUSE

Sexual abuse includes any sexual activity without your clear and enthusiastic consent. This can range from unwanted touching to more severe acts like rape. It can also involve coercion, where someone pressures you into sexual activities you're uncomfortable with. For example, a partner might repeatedly insist on sex despite your reluctance, or use emotional manipulation to get you to agree. This undermines your autonomy and can leave deep emotional scars, affecting your sense of self and safety in intimate situations.[58]

DIGITAL ABUSE

Digital abuse happens when someone tries to control or harass you online. This might mean monitoring your texts, social media, or installing spyware on your devices. It can also involve sending threatening messages or controlling who you can interact with online. Imagine a partner who constantly checks your phone or social media accounts, demanding passwords and scrutinizing your interactions. This constant surveillance can lead to heightened anxiety and a pervasive sense of paranoia, making you feel trapped and isolated.[59]

EMOTIONAL AND PSYCHOLOGICAL ABUSE

Emotional abuse targets your self-worth and mental health, often through constant criticism, mocking, or put-downs. It can be as damaging as physical violence and lead to issues like anxiety and depression. Here are some behaviors to watch for in your relationships:[60]

❁ **Gaslighting:** This involves making you doubt your own memory or feelings. For instance, if your partner denies ever making a promise, even though you clearly remember it, you might start questioning your own sanity.

❁ **Breadcrumbing:** This is when someone gives you just enough attention to keep you hooked but rarely follows through. You might experience your partner disappearing for weeks, only to reappear with sweet messages, creating confusion of hope and disappointment.

* **Stonewalling:** When someone shuts down communication and avoids discussing issues, leaving you feeling frustrated and unheard. This might look like a partner who refuses to address problems, leaving you feeling invisible and neglected.

* **Love Bombing:** Overwhelming someone with gifts and compliments early in the relationship to manipulate them later. For example, a partner might shower you with affection and lavish gifts to win you over, only to use this affection as leverage for control.

* **Trauma Bonding:** Repeated breakups and reconciliations create a strong, unhealthy attachment, making it hard to leave the relationship. You might find yourself repeatedly returning to an abusive partner because the highs of reconciliation seem to overshadow the lows of abuse.

* **Microaggressions:** Small, offhand comments that might seem minor but accumulate to make you feel belittled. For example, repeated comments about your appearance or abilities can slowly erode your self-esteem.

* **Emotional Withholding:** When someone avoids comforting you or shows disinterest, leaving you feeling neglected. Imagine a partner who consistently fails to support you during harsh times, making you feel unimportant and unloved.

* **Projection:** Accusing you of behaviors they themselves are guilty of. For example, if your partner frequently calls you unreliable while they themselves are consistently late or forgetful.

* **Pathological Lying:** Making promises they don't keep and inventing elaborate excuses. This might manifest as a partner making grand promises about the future that are never fulfilled, and then coming up with complex stories to explain their broken commitments.
* **Blame Shifting:** Shifting the blame for a mistake onto you, even though it was their fault. If a partner messes up and then blames you for their failure, it can create confusion and self-doubt.
* **Conditional Love:** Affection given only if you meet certain expectations. You might feel that their love is dependent on you fulfilling specific conditions, making you feel like you're only valued for what you can provide.
* **Victim Blaming:** Suggesting you're partly to blame for abuse or harassment based on your behavior or appearance. For instance, an abuser might imply that your actions or clothing are the reasons for their abusive behavior, distorting the reality of the situation.

Abuse can start in small, subtle ways and gradually escalate. At first, it might seem like just a few minor issues or disagreements, but these can be early signs of something more serious. For example, a partner might begin by making negative comments about your friends or family, slowly isolating you from your support system. They might make you feel guilty for spending time with others or pursuing your own interests, leading to deep feelings of loneliness and helplessness.

The effects of relational abuse extend beyond immediate emotional pain. You might feel persistently sad or lose interest in activities you once enjoyed. Research shows a strong link between relationship abuse and a higher risk of mood disorders like depression.[61]

Anxiety is another common effect. Constant fear or uncertainty can impact various areas of your life, including school performance and friendships. The ongoing stress from abuse can lead to heightened anxiety, making even small tasks seem overwhelming.

Your self-esteem can also take a significant hit. Continuous emotional abuse can lead you to question your worth and abilities, causing you to doubt yourself and feel undeserving of respect and love. This negativity can make it difficult to believe in the possibility of healthy, positive relationships.

Past abuse can shape how you approach new relationships. You might struggle with trust or find it hard to believe in the potential for healthy relationships. The trauma from past abuse can lead to repeating unhealthy patterns or difficulties with communication and intimacy, making it challenging to build and maintain supportive connections.

Understanding these signs and their impact is key to creating the relationships you deserve—relationships that are safe, trusting, balanced, and fulfilling. Being aware of how relational abuse affects you can help you make better choices, seek the support you need, and build connections that truly enhance your well-being and happiness.

Learn about Skyler's experience with relational abuse, where they became increasingly withdrawn, confused, and isolated from their family, struggling to reclaim their sense of self and support system. This story highlights how challenging it can be to recognize the harm in an unhealthy relationship, especially when emotional manipulation clouds your perception.

Skyler's Story

Disclaimer: The following case example addresses emotional and psychological abuse, which may be destabilizing or distressing for some readers. If you find that this content brings up difficult feelings or memories, please be mindful of your comfort levels, and if need be, skip this section for now, prioritize your well-being, and seek support from a mental health professional, trusted friend, or family member.

Skyler is a senior in high school, eagerly anticipating graduation. A top student with a stellar academic record and active in several extracurriculars, Skyler's future seems bright. Recently, Skyler started dating Casey, a college student they met through a mutual friend. At first, the relationship appeared exciting and supportive, but it soon revealed disturbing patterns of emotional abuse and psychological control.

Skyler's background is grounded in a close-knit, modest family. They live with their parents—both hardworking professionals—and their older sibling, Alex, who is in their third year of college. Despite their busy careers, Skyler's parents have always prioritized their children's needs, attending important events and fostering a supportive family environment. Their mother works as a nurse, and their father is an IT consultant. Although the demands of their jobs sometimes limit their presence, they value open communication and mutual support.

Skyler's older sibling, Alex, has provided crucial guidance and advice throughout high school. Despite being occupied with their own college responsibilities, Alex has been a reliable source of support. However, their own commitments sometimes restrict how much support they can offer.

Skyler's relationship with Casey initially felt exhilarating. Casey was charming and attentive, but over time, their behavior became increasingly manipulative and controlling.

Casey started with subtle manipulations, often questioning Skyler's feelings and decisions. They would dismiss Skyler's concerns with statements like, "You're just being too sensitive," or "I don't know why you're making such a big deal out of this." When Skyler attempted to address these issues, Casey would accuse them of being overly dramatic or "not understanding how relationships work."

Casey's control tactics intensified. They frequently used gaslighting to erode Skyler's self-esteem. For instance, when Skyler mentioned Casey's broken promises, Casey would vehemently deny ever making them, insisting, "You're remembering it wrong," or "I never said that. You're imagining things."

One notable instance involved a planned family dinner, which was important to Skyler. Casey had promised to attend but failed to show up. When Skyler expressed their hurt and disappointment, Casey retaliated by accusing Skyler of being "clingy" and said, "You didn't make it clear how much this meant to you. It's your fault I forgot." This left Skyler feeling deeply invalidated and confused.

As time progressed, Casey's tactics became more severe. They began isolating Skyler from their support network, subtly undermining their relationships with friends and family. Casey would accuse Skyler's friends of being "bad influences" or "not understanding the relationship," pushing Skyler to spend less time with them. When Skyler tried to reach out to their family for support, Casey would criticize them for seeking external advice, implying that Skyler should only trust Casey's perspective.

Casey also used emotional manipulation to control Skyler's social life. They would insist on spending all their free time together, creating conflicts when Skyler wanted to engage in activities outside the relationship. Casey would often use guilt-tripping and fear tactics, like saying, "If you really loved me, you wouldn't need to hang out with anyone else," or, "You're making me feel insecure by spending time away from me."

Skyler's mental health began to deteriorate as Casey's behavior escalated. They felt increasingly isolated, struggling with declining academic performance and withdrawing from social activities. Friends noticed Skyler's changing demeanor, observing that they seemed more anxious, withdrawn, and less confident.

The impact of Casey's abuse began to strain Skyler's relationship with their family. Skyler spent less time with their parents and Alex, feeling guilty about their strained interactions and trying to avoid conflicts about their relationship. The psychological control and emotional abuse from Casey made Skyler feel disconnected from their once-supportive family environment, leaving them feeling alone and vulnerable.

🔍 SELF-REFLECTION

If it feels that you might be experiencing abuse in your relationship, asking yourself some key questions can help you gain clarity and determine the best steps forward. Here are some self-reflection questions to consider:

- ✿ **Emotional Impact:** How do I feel after spending time with my partner—anxious, unhappy, or drained? Am I questioning my own feelings and perceptions in this relationship?
- ✿ **Communication Dynamics:** How does my partner react to my concerns? Do they dismiss or belittle my emotions, and are my attempts to communicate met with anger or avoidance?
- ✿ **Isolation and Control:** Am I isolating myself from friends and family, and has my partner pressured me to cut ties with important people in my life? Do I feel controlled or manipulated, and does my partner use intimidation in our interactions?
- ✿ **Behavior Patterns:** Is my partner's behavior inconsistent, being kind in public but harsh privately?
- ✿ **Self-Esteem and Health:** Have I noticed changes in my self-esteem or health? Am I feeling more insecure or doubting my abilities?
- ✿ **Emotional Safety:** Do I feel like I'm walking on eggshells, constantly worried about setting my partner off?

⟨◉⟩ SELF-REGULATION STRATEGIES

Understanding how to love and be loved is essential for a fulfilling life, and much like financial literacy, it should be a part of every school curriculum. Now that you've gained a better understanding of what makes a relationship unhealthy—or if you can relate to Skyler's story—it's also crucial to know what a healthy relationship should be like.

In a healthy relationship, both partners support each other, communicate openly, and respect each other's boundaries and feelings. Imagine your relationship as a team where both of you are on the same side, cheering each other on and ensuring each other's well-being. Having worked with many young people navigating "relationship drama," I've put together a checklist of positive traits to look for in a great relationship. As you steer clear of unhealthy dynamics, aim to build relationships that embody as many of these characteristics as possible:

- ✿ **Open Communication:** Check if you and your partner talk honestly about your thoughts and feelings. Make sure you both listen to each other without judgment. If you can share what's on your mind and feel heard, that's a good sign.

- ✿ **Respect:** Notice if you both respect each other's boundaries and personal space. Respect means treating each other as equals and valuing each other's opinions. If decisions are made together and your boundaries are honored, you're on the right track.

- ✿ **Trust:** Look for reliability and honesty. Trust is built when both of you keep your promises and are transparent with each other. If you feel secure and believe in your partner's words and actions, that's a positive indicator.

- ✿ **Support:** Observe if your partner encourages your goals and is there for you during tough times. They should support your dreams and offer comfort when needed. A healthy relationship means both of you are each other's biggest cheerleaders.

* **Empathy:** Pay attention to how your partner reacts to your feelings. They should show understanding and compassion, trying to see things from your perspective. If they genuinely care about your emotions and experiences, that's a strong sign of a healthy relationship.
* **Conflict Resolution:** Watch how you handle disagreements. A healthy relationship involves discussing conflicts calmly and finding solutions together, without blaming or criticizing. If conflicts are resolved respectfully, it's a good sign.
* **Independence:** Notice if you both maintain your individual interests and space. It's important to have time for yourself and your own activities. If your partner supports your independence while also enjoying time together, that's a positive aspect.
* **Affection and Intimacy:** Check if there's a balance of physical affection and emotional closeness. If you both express love through gestures and share your feelings openly, it strengthens the bond.
* **Shared Goals and Values:** Look for common ground in your goals and values. Having similar beliefs and aspirations for the future helps you both work toward the same objectives.
* **Appreciation:** Notice if you regularly acknowledge and appreciate each other's efforts. Celebrating each other's achievements and expressing gratitude for the little things can enhance the relationship.
* **Joy and Humor:** Pay attention to how much fun you have together. Sharing laughter and enjoying each other's company makes the relationship more enjoyable and helps in overcoming demanding times.

✿ **Flexibility and Patience:** Look for how you both handle changes and growth. A healthy relationship involves being patient and adaptable as you both evolve.

Now, if you're feeling uncertain or anxious about your relationships, especially romantic ones, know that it's completely understandable to feel that way. Relationships can be confusing and challenging, and it's okay to have doubts. The key is to start by understanding and respecting yourself first—this is the foundation for any healthy relationship. As Fred Rogers, who truly understood people, once said, "The greatest gift you ever give is your honest self"—which means being real with each other and showing up as your true self.[62]

Contradictory ideas and facts can exist simultaneously. In DBT we learn that it's possible to love and still have doubts or frustrations. You can feel both supported and challenged in a relationship. The reality is that relationships are dynamic and imperfect, and that's okay. What matters most is that you're both actively working toward balance, respect, and emotional safety. Trust your instincts and take things at a pace that feels comfortable for you

If you're struggling with the effects of past relationships or feeling overwhelmed by your current ones, don't hesitate to seek support. Talk to trusted friends, family, or a counselor who can offer honest advice and help you navigate your feelings and situation safely.

Here are some self-regulation strategies to help you cope and regain a sense of control in your relationships, so that you may make the safest call for yourself if you are in an unhealthy relationship.

Safety Planning/Involve Trusted Individuals: Safety planning is creating a clear plan in case the situation gets dangerous or unsafe. This could include:

✣ **Making a list of emergency contacts:** Write down phone numbers of people you trust who can help in an emergency (parents, friends, mentors).

✣ **Having safe places to go:** Think of places where you can go if you need to leave your home or a dangerous situation (a friend's house, a community center, a neighbor).

✣ **Knowing how to leave safely:** Plan how you could exit a situation quietly if you're in danger (having your keys and phone nearby, knowing the quickest exit).

Involve trusted individuals by sharing your plan with people who care about you, like close friends, family members, or mentors. By talking about your plan, you ensure they can help you if needed, and you're not facing this alone.

Building Healthy Connections: Support from others is essential when you're going through a stressful time. Regularly check in with friends and family who you trust to understand your situation. These people can provide emotional support, offer advice, and just listen when you need it. You might also consider joining a support group. Support groups can be in-person or online, and they're filled with people who have gone through similar experiences. They offer a safe space where you can talk openly, receive validation, and learn helpful coping strategies.

Role-Play Boundary Setting: Boundaries are the limits you set to protect your emotional and physical space. Role-playing is practicing how to set and enforce these boundaries in real situations. For example: If someone disrespects your boundaries, you can practice saying "no" in different scenarios, like when someone asks for too much of your time or tries to pressure you. Role-play exercises with a trusted friend or therapist where you practice these situations can help reduce anxiety when it comes time to set boundaries in real life.

Boundary-Setting Art: Sometimes it can be hard to verbalize or think about your boundaries, so try creating a visual reminder. You can draw a picture that represents your boundaries, like a shield or a circle around yourself, symbolizing that your space and feelings are important. Also, try to create a list of things that feel okay in a relationship and things that don't, and keep this visual somewhere you can see it often.

Physical Boundaries Ritual: Creating physical reminders for your boundaries can be helpful when you're feeling stuck: Imagine an invisible shield around you when you feel threatened or uncomfortable. Use body language like crossing your arms, stepping back, or holding your hands in front of you to show you need space.

Create a Power Statement or Manifesto: Write a personal statement or manifesto that reminds you of your values and what you deserve. It could be a few sentences like: *"I am worthy of respect,"* or *"I stand for healthy relationships."* Keep it somewhere you can refer to regularly when you're feeling down or uncertain. This statement will help you shift your mindset from that of a victim to seeing yourself as a survivor of abuse, strong and capable of creating a better future.

Self-Reflection Prompts via Text: To challenge harmful beliefs and keep track of your growth, you can set up text reminders on your phone. For example: *"What's something positive that happened today?" "How did I assert my boundaries today?"* These texts will encourage you to reflect on your actions and remind you that you are taking steps toward healing and growth.

Social Justice or Advocacy Projects: Get involved in social justice or advocacy work that aligns with your values. This could mean volunteering for a cause related to domestic violence, or dating safety, or supporting campaigns that fight for the rights of marginalized communities. Being part of something bigger than yourself can help you reframe your pain into power and purpose. You'll meet others who care about similar issues and feel a sense of empowerment as you work toward making a positive change.

Adopt or Foster an Animal: Animals can offer unconditional love and companionship. If you can care for a pet, consider adopting or fostering one. Pets can: (a) Lower anxiety and stress with their calm presence; (b) Help combat loneliness by giving you someone to care for and love. If adopting isn't an option, look into pet therapy programs where trained therapy animals visit people to help them feel calm and supported.

⊘ POSITIVE-CHANGE KICKSTARTER

Desires for a Healthy Relationship: What do you want and need in a healthy relationship? Have you considered the qualities you value in a partner, and does your current relationship meet these needs?

Seeking Support: Have you sought support from friends, family, or a counselor about your concerns, and which resources are available to help you address and improve your situation?

# 🌐 RESOURCES

School counselors and **community social workers** are available in many schools for confidential support. **Legal aid organizations** offer help with legal issues related to abuse.

NATIONAL HELPLINES AND CRISIS SUPPORT

National Domestic Violence Hotline: 1-800-799-7233, Text "START" to 88788

Crisis Text Line: Text "HOME" to 741741

Rape, Abuse & Incest National Network (RAINN): 1-800-656-4673

ONLINE SUPPORT AND INFORMATION

Teen Line (www.teenline.org): 1-800-852-8336, Text "TEEN" to 839863

Love Is Respect (www.loveisrespect.org): 1-866-331-9474, Text "LOVEIS" to 22522

Break the Cycle (www.breakthecycle.org): Offers educational programs, advocacy, and legal services to help youth navigate relationships and recognize the signs of abuse.

BOOKS

100 Ways to Say No: How to Stop Saying Yes When You Mean No, by Nicole Monente (Spruce Books, 2023).

When Something Feels Wrong: A Survival Guide About Abuse for Young People, by Deanna S. Pledge (Free Spirit Pub, 2002).

The Will to Change: Men, Masculinity, and Love, by bell hooks (Washington Square Press, 2004).

CHAPTER 13

FAMILIAL DISCORD

~~~~

COMMONLY VOICED

* "I always thought my family would be my ride-or-die, but now I'm not so sure."
* "Sometimes it feels like I'm in a totally different universe from these people who are supposed to be my family. They just don't get me at all."
* "I used to be super close with my siblings, but now we're just drifting apart. All we do is argue, and it's hard to feel connected when we can't stop fighting."
* "I know I should probably try to fix things with my parents, but the thought of making the first move is really freaking me out. What if they don't respond well? I'm not sure I can handle that kind of rejection."

UNDERSTANDING FAMILIAL DISCORD

Navigating relationships is a big part of growing up, and from what I've seen in my practice, most of the relationship challenges people face in therapy are about family, not just friends or romantic partners. Family dynamics are crucial because they have such a big impact on our emotional health and personal growth.

A lot of issues can pop up—like disagreements with parents, conflicts over values, sibling rivalries, or tensions with extended family. Family conflict can really affect how young people develop. For example, when parents argue a lot, it can lead to long-term emotional and behavioral struggles. Conflicts with parents can shape how you see yourself and your overall well-being during these formative years. And let's not forget, sibling and extended family issues can also influence how you interact with others and how resilient you feel.

So, the following family dynamics, in the order of most prevalent to least, can really shape how you view yourself and navigate your world.

PARENTAL CONFLICT

Parental conflict means regular arguments or tension between your parents, whether they're married, separated, or divorced. For example, constant disputes over finances or parenting styles can make your home environment feel stressful and unpredictable. If you're witnessing these conflicts, it's natural to feel anxious and unsure about how to handle your own emotions while your parents are disagreeing. In fact, about 40% to 50% of kids and teens see frequent conflicts between their parents, which can lead to more emotional distress, behavioral issues, and higher rates of anxiety and depression.[63]

Additionally, ongoing parental conflict can impact how you feel about your family relationships. Seeing your parents argue a lot might lead to fears of abandonment and instability. You might feel caught in the middle, which can strain your relationships with both parents. This exposure to conflict can also affect how you handle relationships in your own life, potentially making it harder for you to form healthy connections.

The constant arguing can disrupt communication and erode trust within your family—key elements for strong, secure relationships. All these conflictual dynamics can lead to emotional instability and challenges in managing your emotions.

CONFLICTS WITH PARENTS

While it might seem like all teens are destined to rebel against their parents, research shows that your relationship with your parents can improve during adolescence. This time isn't just about conflict; it's also when you start to develop more mature and respectful relationships with them. Studies suggest that many teens feel closer to their parents as they get older, and conflicts often decrease as communication and understanding grow.[64] As you work toward independence, you might find that you increasingly value your parents' guidance and support, even if you express it differently at times. This phase can lead to deeper conversations and shared experiences that strengthen your relationship with your parents.

It's normal to have conflicts with your parents as you try to become more independent and figure out who you are. Disagreements often come up over things like curfews, school pressures, or your plans. These arguments can put a strain on your relationship at home and make you feel stressed and emotionally unsettled. Feeling annoyed or guilty during these clashes is common, especially as you're navigating your own identity while hoping your parents understand and support you.

SIBLING RIVALRY

Sibling rivalry is when you and your siblings compete for attention, approval, or resources from your parents. Lots of kids experience some form of rivalry with their siblings, which can lead to feelings of jealousy, resentment, and low self-esteem. These dynamics can significantly impact your social interactions and emotional well-being, shaping how you see yourself and your relationships with family members. Constant comparisons or perceived favoritism can heighten tensions, especially if you feel overshadowed by an older sibling's achievements or are trying to build your self-confidence in competitive situations.

EXTENDED FAMILY

Extended family tensions involve conflicts or disagreements with relatives like your grandparents, aunts, uncles, or cousins. While these issues might not come up as often as conflicts with your parents or siblings, they can still affect how you feel about belonging, your cultural identity, and your decision-making.

Cultural norms within extended family networks can sometimes make these conflicts even more intense, especially when it comes to traditions, values, or obligations. For example, if your family values stable careers like medicine but you're interested in pursuing a career in the arts, it can create stress and tension within the extended family. These disagreements can be tough to navigate, impacting your sense of connection and the choices you make.

~~~~~~

Angel's Story

Angel, a 14-year-old, has experienced significant upheaval in their family life. They live with their biological parent and stepparent, along with two stepsiblings from their stepparent's previous marriage. Angel's biological parent and stepparent married two years ago, blending their families together. Before this marriage, Angel witnessed their parents' divorce, which was marked by frequent arguments, emotional tension, and a prolonged custody dispute. This tumultuous period left a lasting impact on Angel's emotional well-being and their views on family relationships.

Angel's stepparent is warm and well-meaning but struggles to connect with Angel on a deeper level. They try to create a welcoming environment but often seem unsure about how to address Angel's feelings and needs. Despite their efforts, Angel sometimes perceives their stepparent's attempts as insincere or intrusive, which adds to their feelings of discomfort within the blended family.

The biological parent who lives with Angel seems to have moved on from their ex-partner, rarely mentioning their past marriage or family life. Angel feels like a discarded remnant from their parents' history, wondering if their very presence reminds the parent of the painful memories tied to their first marriage. This sense of being an unwelcome reminder makes Angel feel invisible and emotionally distant, as if they're a chapter long since closed rather than a valued member of the family. The lack of acknowledgment from their other parent only deepens Angel's sense of abandonment, leaving them to question their place in the family and whether they will ever truly be seen as more than a reminder of past hurt. Angel's biological parent, who is not living with them, is more distant and less involved in their daily life. This parent is supportive in terms of financial support and occasional visits but often seems preoccupied with their own life and commitments. The lack of consistent presence and emotional support from this parent has left Angel feeling neglected and struggling with unresolved feelings about the past.

Angel's stepsiblings, who are both older, were well-adjusted to each other and their previous family dynamics before Angel's parents entered the picture. The oldest stepsibling, at 17, is deeply involved in sports and is getting ready to go off to college, while the 15-year-old stepsibling is active in school clubs and has a close group of friends. Their established bond and shared experiences from before the marriage can make Angel feel like an outsider in their own home.

Due to their past experiences, Angel struggles to connect within their blended family. They often feel disconnected and misunderstood, especially with their stepparent and stepsiblings. For example, during family meals or outings, Angel finds it challenging to engage in conversations or activities that might foster a sense of belonging. The close bond between their stepsiblings, based on years of shared experiences, makes Angel feel like they're on the outside looking in.

Navigating the complexities of their blended family dynamics has been particularly hard for Angel. They harbor feelings of resentment and mistrust toward their stepparent due to unresolved emotions from their parents' divorce and custody battles. Additionally,

Angel often feels lonely and isolated during family gatherings, where their stepsiblings' preexisting bond makes it harder for Angel to fit in.

The emotional turmoil within Angel's family environment has affected their mental health and academic performance. For example, after family events where they feel excluded or overlooked, Angel tends to retreat to their room, struggling with feelings of sadness and alienation. This pattern has impacted their ability to concentrate on schoolwork and participate in social activities outside the home.

🔍 SELF-REFLECTION

Navigating conflicts with family can be incredibly challenging, and reflecting on these experiences can provide valuable insights into your emotional responses and communication patterns. To better understand how these dynamics affect you, consider the following questions.

- ✺ **Emotional Experience:** How do I typically feel during conflicts with family members (e.g., parents, siblings, extended relatives)? What emotions arise most often, such as anger, sadness, or guilt?

- ✺ **Communication and Expression:** How do I communicate my feelings and needs during family conflicts? Am I able to express myself effectively, or do I struggle to be heard?

- ✺ **Conflict-Resolution Strategies:** What strategies do I use to resolve conflicts with family members? Are these strategies constructive and respectful?

- ✺ **Triggers and Patterns:** What are my pain points during family conflicts? Are there specific topics or behaviors that consistently lead to tension? Do I notice recurring patterns or dynamics in conflicts with specific family members, and how do these patterns impact our relationship?

* **Impact on Well-Being:** How does ongoing familial conflict affect my overall well-being, including my emotional stability and mental health?

* **Role in Conflicts:** Reflecting on recent conflicts, what role do I typically play (e.g., mediator, instigator, peacekeeper)? How does this role affect the outcome of the conflict?

* **Post-Conflict Feelings:** How do I feel after conflicts are resolved (or not resolved)? Do I experience closure, or do lingering feelings continue to affect me?

🧠 SELF-REGULATION STRATEGIES

The holidays, or culturally endorsed "family time," are one of the busiest times of the year for mental health professionals, and it's no surprise why. The holiday season often amplifies the larger struggles we face in life—a time when the push for harmony, togetherness, and joy collides with the underlying stress, unresolved conflicts, and the endless drama that seems to surface. It's like being thrown into a pressure cooker of social expectations: Everyone's supposed to come together and celebrate, but for many, it feels more like trying to fit a square peg into a round hole.

When there's ongoing family tension, holiday gatherings—despite the twinkling lights, cheerful music, and Instagram-worthy moments—can feel more like a performance to create harmony than an opportunity to experience it. Have you ever had to smile through the awkwardness while ignoring the elephant in the room? (The one who's probably wearing a festive sweater and gripping their drink a little too tightly.) The emotional weight of unresolved issues can feel even heavier during this time, making it even harder to pretend everything is perfect when it's clearly not.

You want to celebrate, but the smallest thing—a comment, an awkward silence, or someone mentioning the one person you've been avoiding for good reason—can activate old resentments or even spark a full-blown argument. It's intense trying to juggle all those mixed emotions while keeping the peace, especially when there's so much unspoken hurt just beneath the surface. It's like walking on eggshells...but with fruitcake everywhere.

What can really help in these situations is leaning into social support—resisting the urge to isolate yourself. It might seem easier to retreat and avoid the drama, but sometimes just talking things out with a trusted friend or family member can provide a huge sense of relief. You'd be surprised how much lighter it feels to share your frustrations with someone who won't judge you. They can help you gain perspective, offer emotional support, and—most impor-tantly—remind you that you're not alone in feeling this way. Having a support network outside of the family can really help you stay grounded when everything feels just a little *too* festive.

Here are some self-regulation strategies to help maintain emotional balance and resilience when family dynamics are challenging.

Understanding Your Role: Acknowledge that while it's natural to care for those around you, you are not responsible for solving everyone's problems. By detaching from conflicts that don't directly involve you, you protect your emotional well-being. This allows you to focus on maintaining your peace and balance, rather than absorbing the stress of others.

Protect Your Energy: Family conflicts can be emotionally draining. Practice emotional self-care by setting boundaries and deciding not to absorb the negativity of situations you can't control. Redirect your focus to activities that nurture your mental health, such as hobbies, relaxation, or connecting with supportive people. This helps keep your emotional energy intact.

Identify Patterns: Take time to reflect on recurring patterns in family conflicts and your role within them. Becoming aware of these patterns helps you break negative cycles and approach future conflicts more thoughtfully. You can anticipate potential flashpoints and prepare yourself emotionally to handle them more effectively.

Collaborative Problem-Solving: Encourage open discussions with family members about ongoing issues, and brainstorm solutions together. Involving everyone in the resolution process helps create a sense of shared responsibility and fosters mutual respect. A cooperative approach reduces resentment and increases the likelihood of finding lasting solutions.

Time-Out Technique: Establish a "time-out" rule during heated arguments. If a conflict escalates, anyone involved can call for a brief break to cool off and reflect. This prevents saying hurtful things in the heat of the moment and provides everyone with the space to return to the discussion with a calmer mindset.

Proactive Communication: Set aside regular times for family check-ins to discuss how everyone is feeling and address potential issues before they escalate into full-blown conflicts. Proactive communication helps create an environment where everyone feels heard and understood, preventing minor frustrations from becoming larger problems.

Invest in Family Relationships: Establish shared family routines, such as regular family meals or meetings, to create a sense of stability and mutual respect. Routines promote healthy communication and help create moments of connection, which are vital during times of family discord.

Shared Positive Experiences: Strengthen family bonds by engaging in non-conflict-related activities together, such as cooking, playing games, or volunteering. Positive interactions help counterbalance tensions and build trust, creating a foundation for healthier relationships.

Active Appreciation: Regularly show appreciation for your family members by acknowledging their efforts, contributions, and positive actions. Verbal appreciation fosters a supportive and nurturing environment where family members feel valued and respected.

Nonverbal Communication: During conflict, be mindful of your body language. Use calm, open gestures, maintain eye contact, and speak in a calm tone to avoid adding unnecessary tension. Nonthreatening body language can help deescalate emotions and make the conversation feel more constructive.

Empathetic Rephrasing: When tensions are high, rephrase what the other person is saying with empathy. For example, *"I hear that you're frustrated because you feel unheard."* Rephrasing helps clarify understanding, shows empathy, and helps prevent the conversation from escalating further.

Avoid Blame: Use "I" statements to express your feelings without placing blame. For example, instead of saying, *"You always ignore me,"* say, *"I feel hurt when I don't feel heard."* Focusing on your own feelings helps prevent defensiveness and keeps the conversation more productive.

Address Behaviors, Not Character: During disagreements, focus on specific behaviors that are problematic rather than making personal attacks. For instance, instead of saying *"You're selfish,"* say, *"I feel upset when my needs are overlooked."* This keeps the conversation solution-oriented rather than hurtful.

Active Listening: Take time to listen fully to the other person's side before reacting. Show you're engaged by nodding, summarizing what they've said, or asking follow-up questions. Active listening fosters mutual respect and empathy, which are essential for resolving conflicts.

Reflect and Validate: Even if you don't agree with someone's point of view, acknowledge their feelings and let them know you understand. For example, saying, *"I see that you're really annoyed right now"* helps the other person feel heard and can defuse tension.

Compromise and Find Solutions: Shift your focus from winning the argument to finding a resolution that works for both parties. Be open to compromise and focus on solutions that satisfy both you and the other person. This creates a more cooperative atmosphere and encourages problem-solving rather than conflict.

Respect Differences of Opinion: Not all disagreements have to be resolved in one conversation, and sometimes agreeing to disagree is the healthiest outcome. Respecting differing opinions allows space for each person's perspective without escalating conflict.

Apologize and Own Your Part: Take responsibility if you've contributed to the conflict. Offer a sincere apology that addresses specific actions, such as *"I'm sorry for interrupting you earlier."* Owning your mistakes promotes a healthier environment and encourages others to do the same.

Lighten the Mood: If appropriate, use humor to relieve tension and create a more relaxed atmosphere. However, make sure the humor is not sarcastic or passive-aggressive. Lighthearted humor can help both parties feel less defensive and more open to resolution.

No Yelling or Insults: Establish ground rules for communication during arguments, including no yelling, name-calling, or personal attacks. By setting boundaries for respectful conversation, you create a more constructive environment where both parties feel safe to express themselves.

Using a Safety Phrase to Deescalate Tensions: A safety phrase is a pre-agreed word or phrase that signals when a conflict is getting too heated and a break is needed. It helps prevent escalation. Examples like *"Let's take a breath"* or *"banana split sundae"* remind everyone to step back, cool off, and return with a clearer mindset. To establish one, discuss with family members to choose a phrase everyone feels comfortable using, and agree on its purpose and use to ensure clarity during tense moments.

⟡ POSITIVE-CHANGE KICKSTARTER

Lessons Learned: What lessons have you learned from past conflicts with family members? How can you apply these lessons to improve current familial conflicts? Which skill from the suggested options will you use at the next family conflict?

_____

_____

_____

Seeking Support: Are you comfortable seeking support or advice from others (friends, mentors, professionals) when navigating familial conflicts? If not, how can you remove the perceived barriers today?

_____

_____

_____

🖐 RESOURCES

MOBILE APPS

Making Conflict Work App (www.makingconflictwork.com /app-iphone-android): Designed to help users effectively navigate conflicts in both personal and professional settings.

BOOKS

But What Will People Say?: Navigating Mental Health, Identity, Love, and Family Between Cultures, by Sahaj Kaur Kohli (Penguin Life, 2024).

Fault Lines: Fractured Families and How to Mend Them, by Karl Pillemer (Avery, 2020).

How to Survive Your Parents: A Teen's Guide to Thriving in a Difficult Family, by Shawn Goodman (Rocky Pond Books, 2024).

It Didn't Start with You: How Inherited Family Trauma Shapes Who We Are and How to End the Cycle, by Mark Wolynn (Penguin Life, 2017).

CHAPTER 14

GRIEF AND LOSS

~~~~

COMMONLY VOICED

* ❋ "I feel so alone in this. Will this grief ever end?"
* ❋ "I'm trying to stay strong for everyone else, but I'm falling apart inside. I wish people would just stop asking if I'm okay."
* ❋ "I used to look forward to growing up, but now I'm paralyzed by fear. It's hard to face the unknown when all I want is to stay in my comfort zone."
* ❋ "I should accept what happened and move on, but letting go feels terrifying. I don't know if I can ever truly say goodbye."

UNDERSTANDING GRIEF AND LOSS

When you go through a big loss—whether it's losing someone you care about, moving away from a place you love, or even just something that's really important to you—it can feel like the ground is shaking beneath you. It's like everything you know is suddenly different, and the emotions can be all over the place. Sam Smith really nails this feeling in their song

"Love Goes," even though they were the one to initiate the goodbye: "Say one day I'll be back / Don't hold your breath / Just know I hold a place / For you always."[65]

So, why does grief hit so hard when you're your age? Well, it's partly because your brain is still developing, especially the parts that handle emotions. This means you might feel things more intensely and unpredictably compared to younger kids or older adults, who might deal with loss differently.[66]

Grief can look different depending on what you've lost. Here's how the many kinds of loss can mess with you.

DEALING WITH A SIGNIFICANT DEATH

Losing someone close to you, such as a beloved family member or a long-time friend, can be overwhelming and profoundly impactful. Undoubtedly, the death of a parent or sibling can create a deep void in your daily life, leaving you to grapple with a new reality where their presence is no longer felt. This type of grief fills life with a deep sadness that can permeate every aspect of your day.

You might experience a sense of emptiness and question how you can move forward without them by your side. Behaviorally, grief may lead you to withdraw from the world, avoiding friends and family as you contend with the weight of your emotions. For example, you might find it hard to engage in social activities or hobbies that you once enjoyed.

Sleep patterns might become erratic, with either sleepless nights filled with thoughts of your loved one or excessive sleep as a way to escape the pain. These disruptions can affect your concentration on daily tasks, impacting your performance at school, work, or in personal responsibilities. Additionally, the physical toll of grief can manifest as fatigue, changes in appetite, or frequent illnesses, reflecting how your body reacts to the stress and emotional strain.

NAVIGATING A BREAKUP

Similarly, experiencing a breakup can stir up deep emotions such as sadness, anger, and confusion, often leaving you feeling adrift. For example, the end of a long-term relationship can lead to a profound sense of loss and uncertainty about the future. During this time, you might find yourself withdrawing from friends, isolating yourself, or struggling to enjoy activities you once loved. Trouble sleeping is common, whether due to worrying about what went wrong or sleeping too much to avoid facing reality. This disruption can also impact your concentration, affecting your performance in school or at work.

Additionally, you might become preoccupied with thoughts of your ex, obsessively checking their social media or replaying conversations in your mind. This mental fixation can hinder your ability to move on and adjust to life without them, with emotional ups and downs straining your daily life and relationships. For instance, you might experience frequent mood swings that affect your interactions with friends and family, causing additional stress and conflict.

COPING WITH BIG LIFE CHANGES

Similarly, significant life changes such as moving to a new city or changing schools can cause a profound sense of loss and grief. Although these changes do not involve the loss of a person, they can still feel intensely disorienting. For example, relocating to a new city might bring feelings of sadness about leaving behind close friends and familiar routines, coupled with the uncertainty of starting over in an unfamiliar place. You may struggle to form new connections or feel disconnected from your previous life, leading to social withdrawal, feelings of overwhelm, or difficulty sleeping as you adjust to your new surroundings.

Likewise, starting at a new school can evoke grief over leaving behind familiar faces and routines. You might feel anxious about fitting in, managing new expectations, and establishing a place for yourself. These emotions can impact your academic performance and social life, making it harder to concentrate or engage fully. For instance, you might find it challenging to focus on your studies or participate in extracurricular activities that were previously a source of joy.

THE IMPACT OF UNPROCESSED GRIEF

When grief remains unaddressed or unresolved, it can complicate your emotional life. Persistent sadness, anxiety, or emptiness can result from unprocessed grief. For example, unresolved grief from a past loss might cause ongoing difficulties in forming new relationships or finding joy in everyday activities. Mood swings and intense emotional responses may become frequent, potentially leading to conditions such as depression or anxiety. Behaviorally, unresolved grief often manifests as withdrawal from social interactions, changes in sleep patterns, or unhealthy coping mechanisms like substance use. Academically and professionally, it can impair concentration, memory, and motivation, making it challenging to meet responsibilities and perform well. Moreover, unresolved grief can strain relationships, making it difficult to trust or connect with others. The ongoing stress can weaken your immune system and contribute to other health issues, such as chronic illnesses or frequent infections, adding to the overall challenges you face. Over the long term, failing to resolve grief can hinder your ability to find closure and move forward, impacting your overall well-being and development.[67]

Meet Drew, who's navigating their own grief while also caring for their father, who is grieving in his own way. Grief can feel incredibly personal and unique to each person. Take a moment to reflect on how deeply loss can affect not just you, but also those around you, like with Drew and their family.

Drew's Story

Drew, a 20-year-old psychology major in college, lives with their widowed father and has a close-knit family, including their grandmother, Rose, who played a significant role in their upbringing. Drew's father works full-time and became a widower when Drew was seven, following their mother's death from cancer.

Rose, aged 70, passed away unexpectedly due to complications from a stroke. Drew, who was away at college when they received the news, felt profound grief despite being surrounded by friends. Rose had been a constant presence, attending school events, offering advice, and providing emotional support.

Drew's relationship with Rose was exceptionally close. They shared hobbies like gardening and baking, and Rose often shared cherished stories from their youth. Drew saw Rose not only as a grandmother but also as a friend and mentor.

Since Rose's passing, Drew has experienced shock, disbelief, and intense sadness. After the funeral, they returned to college but struggled with loneliness and difficulty concentrating on their studies, missing Rose's comforting presence and guidance.

Drew's father, still grieving the loss of Drew's mother, has struggled emotionally and relies on sleeping pills, which worries Drew. Despite their own grief, Drew often suppresses their emotions to support their father, fearing that expressing their pain might add to their burden. Drew encourages their father to seek counseling or support groups but is unsure how to effectively manage their own grieving process while prioritizing their well-being.

🔍 SELF-REFLECTION

Based on the experiences of grief and loss, such as those faced by someone like Drew, please take a few moments to reflect on how loss has touched your own life. Use the following self-reflection questions to guide your thoughts:

* **Emotional Experience and Responses:** What emotions am I experiencing most intensely right now, and do they fluctuate throughout the day?
* **Impact on Daily Life:** How has this loss affected my daily routines and tasks? Have my routines (e.g., getting up, eating, work/school, hygiene) changed? What tasks or responsibilities have become harder, such as focusing, managing time, or completing daily activities?
* **Support Needs:** What support do I need right now, and where do I feel unsupported (e.g., emotional, practical, or professional counseling)? Are there specific areas in my life where I lack support?

* **Relationships:** How are my emotions affecting my relationships and behavior? Am I more withdrawn, irritable, or seeking comfort from others? Have I noticed changes in how I communicate or engage with others?
* **Future Outlook:** How has this loss shifted my perspective on the future, including my goals and dreams? Have they changed in importance or direction?
* **Future Concerns:** What worries or uncertainties do I have about moving forward? Are there aspects of the future that feel particularly daunting?
* **Personal Growth:** What lessons or insights have I gained from this experience about my resilience, coping abilities, and personal strengths? Have I discovered new coping skills or strategies?
* **Insights into Self:** How has this loss influenced my values or beliefs? Have my views on life, relationships, or personal values shifted?

⚇ SELF-REGULATION STRATEGIES

Poet and philosopher John O'Donohue once said, "Grief is the price we pay for love," reminding us that whatever we feel in times of loss—whether sadness, anger, or even moments of unexpected peace—is a natural part of life.[68] Grief isn't something we simply "get over"; it's something we move through, gently, at our own pace.

Creating a safe space to express your emotions is essential. It can help to try different coping strategies and see what resonates with you, whether that's sharing memories, finding comfort in rituals, or exploring mindfulness practices. If cultural or spiritual traditions are important to you, weaving them into your routine can offer a sense of connection and healing.

I remember a deeply moving moment at my paternal grandfather's funeral, when the Taoist priest offered us a piece of candy in a red envelope after we placed flowers in his grave. At the time, I didn't understand the ritual, but the sense of peace I felt when I tasted the candy was profound— it literally felt like I was receiving a tender and secure hug from my grandfather. Later, I learned that in Taoist and broader Chinese traditions, offering candy symbolizes a wish for the deceased's smooth, "sweet" transition to the afterlife, filled with goodwill, nourishment, and—most importantly— freedom from suffering and any form of debt. The offering also serves to counterbalance grief, bringing lightness and positivity, restoring harmony between yin and yang. For those of us still living, it provides a brief respite from sorrow and a reminder of life's joys, which was exactly how I experienced it—and how I continue to feel when I think of my grandfather.

In every experience of loss—whether of people, places, or things—stay open to discovering what helps you honor your own path to healing. This process is deeply personal, but it is worth finding the strength to move forward with purpose, even on the hardest days.

Here are some specific self-regulation strategies that could support you in processing your grief and nurturing your emotional well-being.

Acknowledge and Express Grief: It's important to give yourself permission to feel everything you're going through, whether it's sadness, anger, confusion, or guilt. You might feel pressure to stop being sad quickly, but grief has its own timeline. If you feel angry or upset, it's okay. Let yourself cry, journal, or talk to someone who listens without judgment.

Stick to What You Know: Keeping a schedule can provide comfort when everything else feels chaotic. You could stick to regular sleep patterns, set aside time each day for schoolwork or activities you enjoy, and include self-care routines like skincare or reading in your day to maintain a sense of normalcy.

Set Small Goals: When grieving, the thought of accomplishing big tasks can feel overwhelming. Break down your day into smaller steps and celebrate small victories. For example, *"I'll finish my homework before dinner," "I'll go for a walk today,"* or *"I'll call a friend for a chat."* These small wins remind you that you still have control over aspects of your life.

Reach Out to Others: Grief can be isolating, but reaching out for support is essential. Whether it's a close friend, family member, or even someone in a similar situation, having people who understand your experience can help you feel less alone. Sometimes your friends might not know how to help, but simply being there to listen can make a big difference. You might find online communities, like grief forums or subreddits (e.g., r/grief), where other teens or young adults can share their stories and offer support. Talking to people who get it can be incredibly validating and comforting.

Create a Memory Container: A memory box is a personal, physical way to keep your loved one's memory alive. It allows you to preserve things that represent them and the loss you're experiencing. Collect photos, letters, or items that remind you of the person, event, or phase of life you're grieving. You might put in a ticket from an event you attended together, their favorite book, or a handwritten letter. Whenever you're feeling down or need comfort, open the box and take a moment to reflect on the positive memories and moments of joy you shared.

Create a Memorial: Creating a memorial can provide a way to honor the memory of someone you've lost or the end of a chapter in your life. It's an act of remembering and celebrating their significance. If you've lost a loved one, plant a tree, flower, or a small garden as a living tribute. If you're grieving the end of a friendship or phase in life, write a letter to that chapter. For example, write to your high school years or the friendship you've outgrown, expressing gratitude and saying goodbye.

Celebrate Milestones and Traditions: Honor the anniversaries or dates that feel significant. Maybe on their birthday, you could watch a favorite movie you both loved, visit a special place or activity that they enjoyed, or share a meal or dessert they loved. If you're mourning a life change, like graduating or leaving home, create a personal ritual to say goodbye to that phase, such as writing a list of things you're thankful for and things you want to leave behind.

Cultivate Gratitude: Even when it's hard, practicing gratitude can help shift your focus. Keep a gratitude journal, where you write three things you're thankful for each day. This can help remind you that even in grief, there's still positivity around you. Perhaps before bed, take a moment to say thanks for something in your day, no matter how small. Saying something like, *"I'm thankful for today's rain... it made me feel calm"* can refocus your mind and help you feel more grounded.

Meditate or Pray: If you are spiritually inclined, prayer or meditation can be a grounding way to process loss. Even just sitting in silence, focusing on your breath, and reflecting on your feelings can help you feel more at peace.

Engage in Mindful Distractions: Distractions, when done mindfully, can help shift your focus. Watch a favorite show or movie that brings comfort or familiarity. Read a book or start a new TV series that helps you get lost in a different world.

◎ POSITIVE-CHANGE KICKSTARTER

Coping Strategies: What specific coping methods are you using right now, and how can you apply them today? Do you need to reach out to a friend, jot down your thoughts in a journal, or take a break from social situations?

_____

_____

_____

Healing Steps: What concrete actions can you take right now to start your healing process? Maybe schedule a regular check-in with a therapist or look for a support group to join.

_____

_____

_____

Honoring the Memory: What specific ways can you honor and recall the person or situation you've lost? Think of one ritual or personal project that feels meaningful and start planning it today. Consider creating a memory scrapbook or looking for a charity event that reflects their values, and take a step toward making it happen.

 RESOURCES

Grief support apps and sites offer tools, resources, and community support for those grieving. Take a look at these:

MOBILE APPS

GoodGrief (goodgriefapp.com)

Untangle available on Google and Apple app stores

WEBSITES

What's Your Grief (whatsyourgrief.com)

BOOKS

Bearing the Unbearable: Love, Loss, and the Heartbreaking Path of Grief, by Joanne Cacciatore (Wisdom Publications, 2017).

The Grieving Brain: The Surprising Science of How We Learn from Love and Loss, by Mary-Frances O'Connor (HarperOne, 2022).

How to Survive Change... You Didn't Ask for: Bounce Back, Find Calm in Chaos, and Reinvent Yourself, by M. J. Ryan (Conari Press, 2014).

It Won't Ever Be the Same: A Teen's Guide to Grief and Grieving, by Korie Leigh (Free Spirit Publishing, 2024).

Life Is in the Transitions: Mastering Change at Any Age, by Bruce Feiler (Penguin Books, 2021).

PART III

THRIVING IN A TURBULENT WORLD

*"It's not the size of the dog in the fight,
it's the size of the fight in the dog."*

—**Mark Twain**

CHAPTER 15

CLIMATE CHANGE ANXIETY

~~~~~

COMMONLY VOICED

✿ "I try to keep up on what's happening with the environment, but the more I know, the more terrified I become."

✿ "I know climate change is real, but it's hard to understand all the science and what exactly I should be doing."

✿ "I'm trying to do my part, like eating less meat and buying from brands that actually care about sustainability, but I'm only one person."

✿ "I believe I should try to take action and make a difference, but it's overwhelming to think about the scale of the problem and where to start."

UNDERSTANDING CLIMATE CHANGE ANXIETY

Feeling anxious lately but not sure why? You're not alone. Many of my clients are reporting feeling overwhelmed by environmental issues—in fact, what once felt like distant concerns are now front and center in their minds. Many describe a constant unease, particularly with threats like hurricanes, earthquakes, and extreme temperatures. We're all noticing these changes, and they're having a real impact. Not long ago, during a routine teletherapy session, an earthquake actually hit my client's location in-real-life, briefly rattling the desk her laptop was on. I found myself quickly applying self-regulation techniques to manage the stress for both of us. While this felt like a rare experience, I'm certain it won't be the last time I'm called upon to provide psychological first aid in the face of extreme weather and environmental challenges.

I want to make it clear that I'm not here to push any political agenda or change anyone's mind about climate change. However, it's evident that many people are concerned about the state of the environment. Reports from the Intergovernmental Panel on Climate Change (IPCC) and the National Oceanic and Atmospheric Administration (NOAA) highlight the increasing frequency of extreme weather events, such as stronger hurricanes and more intense heatwaves. The American South is still recovering from the devastation caused by back-to-back hurricanes, Helene and Milton, which struck in the fall of 2024. Just days into 2025, seven large fires swept through California, destroying entire communities, displacing tens of thousands of residents, and claiming dozens of lives. On a global scale, we're witnessing the melting of ice caps, coral bleaching, and shifts in animal habitats—changes that affect not only nature but also agriculture, as well as animal and human health.[69]

In my practice alone, I'm seeing more and more young people voice their concerns about climate change. A 2019 study found that many are dealing with eco-anxiety, which leads to feelings of helplessness and despair.[70] This anxiety can really shape how they see their lives and future. In fact, some young people are even choosing to opt out of parenthood altogether due to worries about the world their children would inherit. It's heartbreaking that the fear of what's to come is affecting such a fundamental choice.

I often tell my clients to "dress for the weather, not just fret about it." But let's be real—how do you prepare for catastrophic weather? Do you need emotional insulation or a raincoat for tears of frustration?

The concept of climate grief has existed prior to 2020, but it became a more widely recognized phenomenon around that time, highlighting the sadness many young people feel over the loss of natural environments and species due to climate change.[71] You might find yourself worrying about the Earth's future or feeling anxious about environmental disasters— even if you haven't experienced them directly. This worry often comes from seeing others suffer or hearing about disasters, which can shake your sense of safety. For instance, the decline of the Great Barrier Reef due to coral bleaching has left many feeling profound grief. Given that the reef supports both marine life and coastal communities who rely on it for food, tourism, and livelihood, witnessing such a vital system deteriorate can feel like a personal loss—especially for those with a strong emotional or spiritual connection to it.

This grief can blend with existential anxiety. A 2021 study found that young people are increasingly worried about humanity's long-term survival, creating a sense of hopelessness.[72] You might even experience survivor's guilt if you're safe while others are affected by climate events. During the

2023 wildfires in Hawaii and 2025 wildfires in Los Angeles, California, many who escaped felt deep remorse for their neighbors who didn't.

Eco-trauma is another heavy response, especially for those directly impacted by disasters. After Hurricane Katrina, many survivors dealt with PTSD-like symptoms from the destruction.[73] Then there's climate paralysis, where the overwhelming nature of the climate crisis makes it feel impossible to act. It's like being so aware of the crisis that you freeze up, even if you want to help.

Lastly, moral injury can happen when your values clash with society's inaction. For environmental advocates, watching policy delays can feel disheartening. This disconnect adds emotional strain to an already heavy load.

Explore the effects of eco-anxiety through River's experience, a young person who became overwhelmed by the stark contrast between the serene natural world and the escalating environmental challenges we all face.

River's Story

River grew up in a major city, where their daily life was devoid of nature unless they went to the city's major park. During the COVID-19 pandemic, River had the opportunity to spend close to a year in a rural area with extended relatives when the world went on lockdown. This time away from the cement jungle and immersed in nature was transformative for River. They developed a deep appreciation for the natural world that had previously been overshadowed by city life. The tranquility of the countryside gave rise to a strong connection to nature that River had never known better.

However, this newfound awareness brought a significant emotional burden too. The obvious contrast between the tranquil natural environment they experienced and the constant reports about climate change, biodiversity loss, and pollution brought about a severe form of eco-anxiety. This appreciation for nature was marred by a growing sense of sadness and helplessness about the state of the planet, further intensified by their frustration with the political system. River, who had always been interested in politics, became increasingly disheartened by the lack of substantial action from government officials to address climate change. Despite their passion for political engagement and a strong desire to see effective policies, River felt that the pace of governmental action was too slow to counteract the rapid progression of environmental degradation. This sense of political stagnation only amplified their eco-anxiety, as they grappled with the disconnect between the urgent need for change and the insufficient responses from those in power.

Adding to River's emotional burden was their struggle to communicate their eco-anxiety to others. They often felt that expressing their concerns about the environment led to misunderstandings. River worried that people would label them as a "tree-hugger" or overly sensitive, dismissing their genuine feelings as extreme or irrational. This fear of being misunderstood further isolated River, making it difficult to find supportive spaces where they could discuss their stress and anxiety openly without feeling judged.

Moreover, River felt profoundly alone because their emotional pain did not align with a clear, clinically diagnosable mental health challenge. Despite their distress, River's overall functioning in other areas of life seemed unaffected; they continued to perform well at school and work, and maintain relationships. This discrepancy made it challenging for them to seek help or validate their feelings, as their internal struggles did not disrupt their external functioning. River's sense of isolation, furthered by the difficulty of finding a framework or language to articulate their eco-anxiety, left them feeling unsupported and disconnected from others who might share their concerns.

Q SELF-REFLECTION

Does any of River's story resonate with your experiences? Here are some self-reflection questions that you can use to explore your experiences with climate change–related stress and anxiety and its impact on your life:

* **Patterns and Triggers:** What climate change events or issues contribute to my anxiety or stress, and how do I typically react? How do local environmental changes, such as less wildlife or more extreme weather, contribute to my anxiety?

* **Emotional Reactions:** Do I feel emotions like crying, anger, guilt, fear, sadness, existential dread, or hopelessness when I hear about environmental disasters? How do these emotions manifest in my daily life, and do they affect my focus, relationships, or ability to enjoy activities?

* **Sources of Anxiety:** What sources of information heighten my climate anxiety, and how does the scale of the crisis overwhelm me? Which news outlets, social media platforms, or types of content make me feel stressed?

- ✿ **Future Outlook:** How has my perspective on the future changed due to climate concerns, and do I feel more pessimistic or hopeful about what lies ahead?
- ✿ **Personal Impact:** Do I believe my actions, like recycling or reducing plastic use, make a meaningful impact on the environment? How much time do I spend on these behaviors?
- ✿ **Social and Relational Impact:** How do my feelings about climate change affect my relationships with others? Do I find it hard to connect with friends who don't share my concerns, or do I bond over these issues?

⟨♡⟩ SELF-REGULATION STRATEGIES

If you're feeling eco-anxiety like River, know that your feelings are utterly valid and understandable. It's overwhelming to watch our planet face so many challenges, and it can feel burdensome. More often than I'm willing to admit, I find myself googling where in the continental US would be the safest from natural disasters.

We don't have any other means but to embrace uncertainty, as it's okay not to have all the answers, and it's common to feel unsure about the future. The world's problems can feel so big, and trying to figure out how to help can leave you feeling exhausted and unsure. In moments like these, taking a pause to breathe deeply or spending some time in nature—whether it's a walk in the park or just sitting outside for a bit (yes, touching grass)—can be incredibly grounding. It's a small reminder that the planet still holds beauty, even amid all the stress.

Caring for yourself is just as crucial as acting for the planet. You don't have to do everything at once, and you don't have to carry the weight of it all by yourself. Reaching out to friends, family, or even a counselor who understands can really help lighten the load. Talking about your worries and having someone listen can be cathartic. It's a sign of strength to seek support when you need it, and it doesn't diminish your care for the planet. Every step you take to process these emotions and understand them is valuable.

Here are some self-regulation strategies that might help you build resilience against eco-anxiety.

Forest Therapy (Shinrin-yoku): Forest therapy involves walking slowly through a forest while paying deep attention to sensory experiences: the feel of the ground beneath your feet, the smell of trees, the sound of rustling leaves. This process can significantly reduce stress and foster a healing bond with nature.

Breathing with Nature Visualization: While doing deep breathing exercises, imagine inhaling the fresh air of forests, oceans, or mountaintops. Visualize each breath filling you with strength and calm, while you exhale the anxiety about environmental threats.

Planting for the Future Ceremony: Participating in global initiatives like "One Tree Planted" or local Earth Day events where your community gathers to plant trees can offer both a tangible act of environmental healing and an emotional release. Each tree planted represents hope for the future and the personal commitment to nurturing life. The Arbor Day Foundation organizes annual events where you can plant trees locally to help mitigate environmental damage while symbolizing positive environmental action.

Eco-Grief Letter Writing: Write a letter to your future self, expressing your hopes for the world in the face of climate change. The act of writing letters of hope or sadness can be deeply therapeutic as you confront your grief while simultaneously expressing what you want the future to hold.

Reframing Eco-Anxiety with Action: Challenge negative thoughts by reframing them. For instance, if you're feeling anxious about environmental issues, write down practical actions you can take—like reducing waste or supporting green initiatives—that shift the focus from worry to action. When intrusive thoughts about the planet's future overwhelm you, try saying *"Stop!"* out loud or in your mind, then immediately follow with an affirmation like, *"I am part of the solution,"* or *"I can take action, no matter how small."*

DIY Environmental Solutions: Engage in do-it-yourself projects that promote sustainability—like creating a homemade compost bin, building a rain garden, or making eco-friendly cleaning products. The act of creating something with your hands fosters a sense of agency and control over environmental impact.

Climate Conversations: Organize or participate in community conversation circles focused on eco-anxiety, grief, or trauma. These spaces provide an opportunity to share feelings, validate each other's experiences, and brainstorm collective solutions. Attend or create eco-focused gatherings, such as a "green gathering" in a local park, where people come together to share stories, engage in collective environmental action, and practice mindfulness. These events foster a sense of togetherness and community healing.

Environmental Advocacy Projects: Channel your eco-anxiety into advocacy by researching and supporting policy changes related to environmental protection. This can include drafting letters to lawmakers, signing petitions, or participating in campaigns that call for stronger environmental regulations.

Policy Research and Presentations: Research environmental policies that align with your values, such as carbon reduction initiatives or sustainable agriculture practices. Create presentations or reports that you can share with local community groups, schools, or even elected officials to advocate for change.

Youth-Led Activism: Get involved in youth-led environmental movements or start your own, such as organizing school walkouts or rallies for climate action. Being part of a collective effort amplifies your voice and provides a sense of solidarity and empowerment, reducing feelings of helplessness in the face of environmental crises.

Social Media Campaigns: Use your social media platforms to advocate for policy change by creating or sharing posts, infographics, or videos that educate others about environmental protection and the importance of policy reform. This can create a ripple effect of awareness and action, while also offering a platform for your voice to be heard on a greater scale.

Local Government Engagement: Attend town hall meetings or community forums to speak directly with local policymakers about pressing environmental concerns, like waste management, clean energy, or pollution. Engaging in local government offers tangible ways for you to make a difference and feel involved in direct change-making efforts.

☺ POSITIVE-CHANGE KICKSTARTER

Staying Informed vs. Mental Well-Being: What one strategy can you implement today to balance staying informed about climate issues with maintaining your mental well-being? For example, can you set a timer for your news consumption?

Support and Resources: What specific support or resource can you explore today to help manage your eco-anxiety? Maybe look up a local support group or workshop you can attend this week.

Coping Strategies and Empowerment: Is there an activity you can engage in right now that empowers you or reduces your anxiety about environmental issues? For instance, can you start a small garden or participate in a community clean-up this weekend? Consider taking a few minutes for mindfulness or a quick workout.

Finding Hope: Can you find one positive change or success in environmental efforts to celebrate today? Perhaps research a local initiative or share a success story on social media to inspire others.

RESOURCES

WEBSITES

Writing for Earth (www.letterstotheearth.com): Offers an online platform where you can join letter-writing workshops to express personal experiences and hopes about the future of the planet.

Youth Climate Action Team Inc. (www.ycatinc.com): An international nonprofit organization that offers online courses and webinars teaching young people how to advocate for policies that address climate change. Participants are encouraged to start campaigns and engage with legislators for policy reforms.

Youth for Policy (www.youthforpolicy.org): Participants can research and advocate for policies on sustainable energy or carbon reduction, culminating in presentations to local government bodies and schools.

BOOKS

The Climate Book, by Greta Thunberg (Penguin Books, 2024).

Climate Optimism: Celebrating Systemic Change Around the World, by Zahra Biabani (Mango, 2023).

Field Guide to Climate Anxiety: How to Keep Your Cool on a Warming Planet, by Sarah Jaquette Ray (University of California Press, 2020).

Generation Dread: Finding Purpose in an Age of Climate Crisis, by Britt Wray (Knopf Canada, 2022).

The Great Displacement: Climate Change and the Next American Migration, by Jake Bittle (Simon & Schuster, 2023).

CHAPTER 16

ECONOMIC STRESS

~~~~

COMMONLY VOICED

✢ "I'm always stressing about money—it seems like there's never enough. I'm just stuck in this constant anxiety, wondering if we can even cover the basics."

✢ "I try to play it cool and act like everything's fine, but the stress is always there, just under the surface. It's tough to keep up appearances when we're barely scraping by."

✢ "I feel like I'm missing out on so much because of our money situation. Watching my friends enjoy stuff I can't afford? So frustrating."

✢ "I used to be super hopeful about my future and all the dreams I had, but now it's hard to think big when money is such a huge barrier."

UNDERSTANDING ECONOMIC STRESS

Navigating this phase of life is demanding enough with all the pressures of growing up and figuring out your path, but toss in financial stress and it can feel like everything's spiraling. With rising tuition, unpredictable job markets, and skyrocketing living costs (think of the record cost of eggs in 2025!), your financial situation can become a major source of anxiety.

There are a ton of factors that make this stress worse. Working a part-time job while studying is demanding enough, but when your paycheck barely covers rent and essentials like food and textbooks, it's a serious struggle. If you live in a city, the high cost of living can add even more stress, leaving you to choose between a doctor's appointment or buying books for class. And while you're dealing with your own struggles, it's hard not to feel FOMO (fear of missing out) when you see friends or influencers posting about their vacations or new gadgets. It's frustrating to feel like you're falling behind, especially when you're doing your best to manage.

Let's be real: Not having enough money can make everything feel ten times harder. While we hear that "money can't buy happiness," financial stability does provide the resources and opportunities that can really help reduce stress. Constantly worrying about money—whether it's dealing with student loans, low-paying jobs, or unexpected expenses—can make it tough to focus on other important parts of your life.

Financial stress impacts way more than just your wallet—it can mess with almost every aspect of your life.[74] Here's how:

- **Emotional:** You might feel anxious, irritable, or overwhelmed. Worrying about bills can lead to mood swings or sadness, making it hard to enjoy life.
- **Social:** Financial strain can push you away from friends or make you skip outings because you're worried about spending money. This can lead to feelings of isolation, and money issues can cause tension with family or friends.

* **Behavioral:** You might cope with stress in unhealthy ways, like overspending to feel better or avoiding financial issues altogether, which only leads to bigger problems.
* **Cognitive:** Financial worries can distract you from school or work. If you're stressed about money, it's harder to focus on homework or projects, which can hurt your grades and productivity.
* **Physical:** Stress can show up in your body—think headaches, trouble sleeping, or feeling drained. Constantly worrying about money might even affect your eating habits, making it hard to stay healthy.

Notably, financial stress often feels like a never-ending progression, and here's why:

* **Too Much on Your Plate:** You're juggling school, work, friends, and maybe even trying to handle money stuff like saving, budgeting, or paying for your phone or apps. It can feel like your brain is on overload. When you're already trying to keep everything else together, adding bills and budgeting can make it hard to think clearly or stay on top of things.
* **An Insecurity You Can't Shake Off:** When you're always thinking about money (or stressing about not having enough), it can feel like it never leaves your mind. You might try to push it away, but it keeps popping up, making it hard to focus on anything else. Whether it's worrying about rent, saving for something big, or not having enough for emergencies, that constant stress can wear you down.
* **Feeling Late to the Party:** Sometimes, when money problems hit, it's easy to start thinking, *"I'll never get ahead"* or *"I always mess this up."* It's like your brain starts

focusing on the worst-case scenarios, and that makes it harder to see a way out. If something goes wrong, like missing a payment or not saving enough, it might feel like you've ruined everything, even though that's not the case.

✴ **Pretending Like It's Not Happening:** A lot of people try to avoid dealing with money stuff because it's just too stressful. Maybe you avoid checking your bank account, skip looking at your bills, or even try to ignore those money talks with your parents. It might feel like you're giving yourself a break, but avoiding it only makes the problem worse in the long run.

✴ **Feeling Behind When Everyone Else Seems Fine:** Social media can make things feel even worse. You scroll through Instagram, and everyone else seems to be living the dream—vacations, cool clothes, eating out all the time. But when you're stuck trying to save or cut back, it can make you feel like you're doing something wrong or falling behind. This can lead to the pressure to spend on things you can't really afford, just to "keep up" or because it looks like everyone else has it all figured out.

✴ **Tying Your Worth to What You Can Buy:** It's easy to tie your self-worth to money—like thinking that the more money you have or the more stuff you can buy, the more "successful" you are. But when you're struggling financially, it can feel like you're not measuring up. Maybe you feel embarrassed to talk about your finances with others or feel like you've failed when you can't buy what you want or need. These thoughts can affect your self-esteem and make you feel worse about your situation.

❈ **Stress Taking a Toll on Your Body:** The constant worry about money doesn't just affect your mind; it can affect your body too. Stress about finances can lead to sleepless nights, feeling drained, or even health issues like headaches or stomach problems. And when you're physically worn out, it becomes even harder to focus or deal with your financial situation.

❈ **Money Stress Affecting Relationships:** Money issues can also spill into your relationships. Whether it's with family, friends, or a significant other, money stress can create tension and lead to arguments. Maybe you don't feel comfortable asking your parents for help, or maybe you're fighting about shared expenses. This extra strain can impact your overall happiness and sense of connection with others.

Take a look at France's story to learn more about how financial stress affected them. Pay attention to how their experiences are similar or different from your own.

Frances's Story

Frances, a 22-year-old fine arts graduate, faced unemployment and struggled to find a full-time job. To make ends meet, they juggled several part-time jobs, including freelance art projects and retail work, while living with multiple roommates to share rent costs.

Frances's financial situation was precarious. Their modest income barely covered essentials like rent, utilities, and groceries, leaving little room for savings or unexpected expenses. On top of that, significant student loan debt from their degree added to the strain.

This instability caused Frances frequent anxiety and frustration, affecting their mood and overall well-being. They often avoided social activities that involved spending, leading to feelings of isolation, especially compared to friends who could afford leisure and travel. Social media exposing Frances to friends and influencers showcasing luxurious lifestyles exacerbated their financial anxiety. This created feelings of inadequacy and pressure to keep up with trends, prompting unnecessary spending that deepened their financial strain.

Reluctant to move back home and be labeled a "boomerang kid," Frances was determined to maintain their independence, despite mounting financial pressures. They regretted their choice of major, wishing for a more lucrative career, yet had no real interest in pursuing alternatives. This created a conflict between their passion for art and their financial reality, adding to their stress. Additionally, family expectations added pressure; Frances sometimes felt the need to contribute to household expenses or support younger siblings, further stretching their already tight budget and increasing stress.

Managing multiple jobs hindered Frances's concentration, as worries about unpaid bills distracted them at work. The exhaustion from juggling these responsibilities diminished their productivity. Physically, the financial stress manifested in frequent headaches and sleep issues. To save money, Frances cut back on meals, neglecting their nutrition, and delayed medical appointments, further impacting their health.

Frances also avoided financial discussions and was uncomfortable seeking help. They often postponed budgeting, leading to increased reliance on credit cards and worsening their debt situation.

🔍 SELF-REFLECTION

Reflecting on financial or economic stress can help you gain insight into your situation and identify ways to manage it better. Here are some self-reflection questions that can guide you in understanding and addressing your financial stress:

* **Recognizing Financial Stress:** How does financial stress show up in my life? Am I constantly worried about bills, or do I find it hard to enjoy social activities because of money concerns?

* **Emotional Response:** What thoughts or feelings come to mind when I think about my finances? Am I experiencing anxiety, frustration, shame, or other feelings? Are there specific situations—like receiving a bill or seeing friends on social media—that incite anxiety?

* **The Impact on My Well-Being:** Am I feeling more anxious or irritable lately?

* **Social Impact:** Am I avoiding friends or events because of money? What's the impact of money stress on my relationships and overall happiness?

* **Maladaptive Coping Habits:** Have I noticed any changes in my habits? For instance, do I tend to shop impulsively when stressed? What are a few examples of these maladaptive behaviors?

* **Recognizing Patterns:** What coping strategies am I currently using? What is more effective and less effective in bringing down my stress levels?

✴ **Cultural and Intergenerational Beliefs:** What are some beliefs about money that I have inherited from my culture and family? How do these beliefs contribute to my financial stress?

⟨💡⟩ SELF-REGULATION STRATEGIES

When I was in high school, I went over to a friend's house to work on a shared project. While I was there, I observed something that totally blew my mind at the time. I noticed that there were random $20 bills sitting on the kitchen counter and side tables. Not a lot of money, just a few bills here and there, almost like they were inconsequential.

In my own house, even the smallest bills had a clear purpose before I even saw them on the kitchen table. They were meant for groceries, bus fares, bills—anything that was part of keeping our lives running. I remember thinking at the time that it would be nice to one day have money sitting around like that—unassigned, unspoken for, just hanging out casually on the counter, like it was too relaxed to care about anything else. I call this phenomenon "money on vacation," and it felt like a symbol of financial freedom, or at least of not having to constantly worry about where the money needed to go next.

This memory stuck with me, especially as I grew older and began to face my own financial worries in high tuition and board, and low earnings during the Great Recession. It made me realize how much financial stress can affect how we see our own worth and potential. The truth is, many of us are in survival mode—every dollar is assigned a specific task, and that's okay. What I've learned is that it's important to take a step back and know that you're not failing when you feel overwhelmed. Many of the pressures you're facing are bigger than you and are part of systemic issues—things that aren't your fault. So, be kind to yourself, take a break when you need it, and do not feel discouraged when you can't yet afford the types of vacations or things your friends are having. I believe that so long as you keep up with your mental and physical wellness, live in the service of your core values, and build a healthy relationship to money, you will have a rich life.

Look at these practical, low-cost, or free techniques that are supported by research to help you regain a sense of control of your financial stress and overall well-being.

Money Stories: Take a moment to think about how you view money. Do you tell yourself things like, *"I'll never be good with money"* or *"I'll always rely on my parents"*? If so, try rewriting these thoughts. Instead of thinking you're stuck, tell yourself, *"I can learn how to manage my money better"* or *"I can take small steps toward financial independence."* Rewriting your money story helps you build confidence and feel more empowered about your financial future.

Increase Your Money-Talk Comfort: Money conversations don't have to be awkward. If you rely on your parents for financial support, talk to them about your goals, what you're learning, or any worries you have. Being open and honest about money can reduce any stress or guilt you might feel. Plus, having these conversations will help you learn more about managing money and prepare you for when you take on more responsibility.

Create a Personal Budget That Fits Your Lifestyle: Even if you're not fully responsible for your finances yet, budgeting is still important. Start by tracking how much money you get from your parents, part-time jobs, or birthdays, and how you spend it. This will help you become more aware of where your money goes and how you can plan for your goals, whether that's saving for something special like a concert, a trip, or a car, or just managing the money you receive. Budgeting now helps you set a solid foundation for when you're managing your own money.

Set Realistic Financial Goals: Setting financial goals is important, even if you rely on your family for money. You can still set goals like saving a certain amount from your allowance, paying for your personal items, or budgeting for things you want. Break these goals into smaller steps that you can manage. Achieving small goals builds confidence and helps you feel more prepared for when you have full control over your finances.

Practice Thoughtful Money Decisions: Even if your parents help with your money, treat their money as though you went to work for it every day. It's important, therefore, to think carefully about how you spend. Before making any purchase, pause and ask yourself: *"Is this something I really need or can't live without?"* or *"Does this fit with my values or long-term goals?"* Practicing mindful spending helps you make smarter decisions and ensures that you're not just buying things on impulse, whether or not you're fully independent.

Differentiate Wants vs. Needs: When you're spending money, it's easy to mix up wants and needs. Start paying attention to whether you really need something or just want it. Needs are things like food, transportation, and school supplies. Wants are things like new clothes or the latest gadgets. By understanding the difference, you can prioritize your money for the things that matter most to you and avoid overspending on things that won't make a big difference in your life.

Current-Self, Meet Future-Self: Regularly talk to your future self. Imagine how your future self would feel and think about the financial decisions you're making now. Purchasing all the things that your friends have right now may seem nice now, but will you actually care about their approval six months or a year from now? Having a conversation with your future self, who's financially stable, can help you take more positive actions today and feel more hopeful about the future.

Manage Debt: If you don't have debt yet, it's never too early to learn how to manage it. Whether it's a student loan you might take on in the future or credit card debt, understanding how to approach debt responsibly is key. Start by learning how interest works and how to make payments on time. Having a plan for managing debt early on will help prevent stress and set you up for success later when you have more financial independence.

Build Your Financial Identity: Even if you're not financially independent yet, think about the kind of financial person you want to be. Do you want to be able to save for your future? Do you want to avoid debt? Start creating your financial identity now by defining your values. This will help guide you when you make decisions and give you a clear idea of what kind of financial future you're working toward.

Mindful Tracking of Expenses: Tracking your spending will help you become more aware of how you're using your money. Write down what you spend, even if it's just the allowance or money your parents give you. This helps you see where your money is going and allows you to make smarter choices when you're ready to take control of your own finances.

Visualize Your Financial Goals: You can use visualization to help you focus on your financial goals. Take a few minutes to close your eyes and picture what you want your financial future to look like. Maybe you're debt-free, saving for a big purchase, or even financially independent. Imagine how good it will feel to achieve those things. The more clearly you can picture your future success, the more motivated you'll be to take steps toward it. To make this even more effective, write down your goals and visualize yourself making progress each day. The more you picture your goals coming to life, the more confident you'll feel in working toward them.

Identify Financial Strengths: Identify your strengths and areas where you are already doing well with money. Reflect on past financial successes, even small ones, such as saving a bit of money or avoiding debt. Remind yourself of the steps you're already taking to build a positive financial future, which can boost your confidence.

Up Your DIY Life Skills: Learning to do things yourself, like cooking at home, mending your clothes, or tinkering with things if broken instead of replacing right away, can save money and bring a sense of accomplishment. It can also become a form of self-care, allowing you to feel empowered and capable. In the age of YouTube university, you are just a few videos away to being a beginner in lots of helpful life skills.

☯ POSITIVE-CHANGE KICKSTARTER

Seeking Support: What resources can you tap into right now? Consider options like financial workshops, counseling services, or online communities focused on financial literacy. Look up at least one resource to explore further.

_____

_____

_____

Concrete Steps You Can Take: Can you schedule a regular check-in with a friend or counselor? Talking about your financial situation can lighten the load and give you fresh perspectives. Go ahead and send that text or email to set up a time!

_____

_____

_____

Prioritizing Your Well-Being: How can you celebrate small wins? Take a moment to recognize your progress—no matter how small. Write down one thing you're proud of, like sticking to a budget or having an honest conversation about money. Celebrate that achievement!

_____

_____

_____

Reflecting on Your Growth: What have you learned about your relationship with money? Are there any beliefs or patterns you want to change? Take a few minutes to reflect and jot down your thoughts.

Finding Balance: How can you honor your financial struggles while still enjoying life? Consider setting aside specific times for reflection, but also make time for activities that bring you joy. Schedule at least one enjoyable activity for this week.

 RESOURCES

FINANCIAL LITERACY PROGRAMS AND BUDGETING

National Endowment for Financial Education (www.nefe .org): Offers free online courses and helps to build financial literacy.

Khan Academy–Personal Finance (www.khanacademy.org /college-careers-more/personal-finance): Provides free video tutorials and articles on budgeting, saving, and investing.

Smart About Money (www.smartaboutmoney.org): Offers free courses, tools, and resources for managing money and building financial plans.

National Foundation for Credit Counseling (www.nfcc.org): Offers free or low-cost financial counseling and education.

GoodBudget (goodbudget.com): An envelope-based budgeting app that helps you manage your money and track your spending.

BOOKS

Inherited Trauma and Family Wealth: A Guide to Heal Your Relationships and Build a Lasting Legacy, by Ruschelle Khanna (Echo Legacy Press, 2024).

Money: A User's Guide, by Laura Whateley (Fourth Estate, 2020).

A Money Mindset for Teens and Young Adults, by Sydney Sheppard (Sonia Pace, 2023).

CHAPTER 17

MASS TRAUMA

~~~~~

COMMONLY VOICED

✿ "I'm living in a state of perpetual fear, wondering if something terrible is going to happen at any moment."
✿ "I try to go about my day like everything's normal, but events of that day [trauma] keep replaying in my mind, and I don't know how to make them stop."
✿ "I've long lost my innocence and sense of safety. Is the world as safe as I once thought it was?"
✿ "I know I should try to move on and find a sense of normalcy again, but what is normal anymore?"

UNDERSTANDING MASS TRAUMA

Mass trauma, or collective trauma, happens when large groups of people experience catastrophic events, like natural disasters, terrorist attacks, or pandemics. Unlike individual trauma, which impacts just one person, mass trauma affects entire communities. Think of it like a shared nightmare that everyone wakes up from together, creating a collective sense of vulnerability and grief. This shared experience reshapes how people see themselves and the world around them.

At your age, you've already witnessed how deeply mass trauma can affect us. The COVID-19 pandemic, for example, felt like a plot twist for the world. It didn't just bring illness; it led to economic struggles and social isolation while also fueling hate crimes against Asian Americans. Research shows that the pandemic significantly increased anxiety, depression, and PTSD across various age groups, including teens and young adults.[75]

Another significant event was the killing of George Floyd in 2020, which ignited nationwide protests and important conversations about racial injustice. This tragedy heightened emotional distress, especially for those directly affected by racism. Then there was the January 6 Capitol riot—this chaos resulted in not just physical harm but also widespread psychological distress, deepening feelings of insecurity and political anxiety across the nation.

The Uvalde school shooting in 2022 was another devastating moment, claiming the lives of 19 children and two teachers. It left shockwaves of grief and a surge in PTSD and anxiety within the community and beyond. The ongoing Russia-Ukraine conflict, starting with Russia's invasion in 2022, has led to significant violence and displacement, causing trauma for civilians facing constant threats. More recently, the Gaza-Israel conflict in 2024 has added yet another layer of trauma, resulting in immediate stress responses and long-term mental health issues like PTSD and depression. Each of these events highlights the profound impact of mass trauma on entire populations.

IMMEDIATE EFFECTS

After a mass trauma event, you might find yourself dealing with intense stress reactions that can throw your life off balance. It's completely normal to feel anxiety, shock, or disbelief after events like the pandemic or the Uvalde shooting. These acute stress reactions can lead to trouble sleeping, irritability, and intrusive thoughts. Your daily routine might get disrupted—think about how the Capitol riot impacted school or work, increasing overall stress and anxiety. If you've experienced a traumatic event, you might be more vulnerable to psychological distress. Studies show that young people affected by conflicts or school shootings are particularly at risk for trauma-related symptoms. These immediate reactions are a natural response, and acknowledging them is crucial for managing the broader impacts of mass trauma.

LONG-TERM EFFECTS

The long-term effects of mass trauma can shape your life in profound ways. For instance, Holocaust survivors carried psychological baggage—flashbacks and severe anxiety that lingered for decades after World War II. Similarly, survivors of the atomic bombings of Hiroshima and Nagasaki faced long-lasting trauma, impacting their mental health and relationships for years.

Trauma can disrupt your development and academic performance, often in ways that go beyond mental health. Children who lived through the Vietnam War didn't just deal with emotional fallout; they faced challenges concentrating and succeeding academically. Imagine a brilliant young person with the potential to make groundbreaking discoveries, whose focus was hindered by trauma. Society might have missed out on innovations that could have changed fields like the humanities, medicine, or technology. The cognitive effects of mass trauma can stifle personal growth and rob society of crucial advancements.

Socially and emotionally, mass trauma can create serious challenges. After the Rwandan Genocide, many survivors struggled to rebuild relationships and regain a sense of normalcy. The pervasive isolation and emotional distance led to long-term issues like depression and anxiety.[76] Displacement due to conflict adds another layer of difficulty. For example, the Kurdish population displaced by conflicts in the Middle East faces ongoing psychological challenges, including PTSD and anxiety, due to loss of homes and forced migration.[77] This loss of stability makes recovery even harder.

The effects of mass trauma can ripple through generations. The children of Holocaust survivors, known as the second generation, often deal with intergenerational trauma, facing developmental and mental health challenges linked to their parents' experiences.[78] Similarly, economic hardships from traumatic events, such as job loss during the Great Depression, worsened mental health issues and limited access to support services.

Despite these challenges, many people demonstrate incredible resilience. History shows that with the right support—strong social networks, therapy, and mental health resources—you can develop effective coping strategies and work toward recovery from trauma.

Learn more about the effects of collective trauma through the experiences of Avery, a student who attended a middle school where a mass shooting occurred and continues to see similar events in the news. You may find yourself relating to Avery's fears and concerns, so please remember to take a break if you feel overwhelmed while reading their story.

Avery's Story

High school student Avery, a 17-year-old junior, had grown up in an era characterized by frequent mass shootings and heightened security measures in schools. As a member of the "mass shooting generation," Avery was accustomed to regular safety drills, including active shooter exercises, which were intended to prepare students for emergencies but also contributed to a pervasive sense of vulnerability. Avery had previously attended a middle school where a recent mass shooting occurred and had relatives, including cousins and neighbors, still attending the same school. The trauma of the shooting had profound implications for Avery and the broader community connected to the school.

Last year, Avery learned of another mass shooting that had taken place at a high school in a bordering city. The news, confirmed to involve a person armed with an automatic rifle who had entered the school, led to multiple casualties and injuries. The details were extensively covered in the media, increasing the community's sense of distress. Avery's immediate reaction was one of shock and disbelief, intensified by the realization that the shooting had affected a place and people closely connected to them. The fact that Avery's cousins and friends were directly impacted made the news particularly distressing.

The mass shooting had a significant and multifaceted impact on Avery, shaped by their personal connection to the event and the broader context of growing up amidst frequent mass violence. Avery experienced heightened anxiety and hypervigilance, characterized by an increased state of alertness and worry. This anxiety led to constant checking of news updates and a heightened concern about potential threats, severely shaking their previous sense of security.

Avery's daily functioning was disrupted, as they struggled to concentrate on academic work and daily activities. The emotional burden of the trauma led to difficulties in maintaining performance in school and changes in routine, including alterations in sleep patterns, appetite, and engagement in previously enjoyed activities. Emotional distress was compounded by psychosomatic symptoms such as headaches, stomachaches, and fatigue.

The trauma also led to increased fear and distrust. Avery developed a pervasive fear of future incidents, with a constant worry about similar violence occurring again. This fear was accompanied by skepticism regarding the effectiveness of school safety measures and drills, which, despite previous familiarity, seemed inadequate in preventing or mitigating such tragedies.

Relationships and social interactions were affected as well. Avery experienced difficulties in maintaining relationships with peers and family, leading to withdrawal and isolation. The process of seeking and accepting support was challenging, and there were instances of tension and misunderstanding as Avery navigated their emotions and the responses of those around them.

In terms of psychological processing and coping, Avery engaged in frequent rumination about the traumatic event, which led to intrusive thoughts and flashbacks. This ongoing mental processing was emotionally taxing and interfered with their ability to move forward.

🔍 SELF-REFLECTION

Experiencing a mass trauma can be deeply unsettling, and self-reflection can be a valuable tool for understanding and processing those experiences. Here are some self-reflection questions to ask of yourself or those around you:

- ✿ **Safety and Security:** In what ways has the traumatic event changed how safe and secure I feel in my daily life? What specific moments have I felt more anxious or on edge? Are there places I avoid now, or situations that activate that feeling?
- ✿ **Emotional Awareness:** What emotions am I experiencing right now, and how are they affecting my mood and actions? Taking a moment to identify my feelings— am I angry, sad, confused? How have these emotions influenced my interactions or energy levels each day?
- ✿ **Relationships and Connections:** How has this trauma shifted my relationships with family and friends? Have I distanced myself from certain people or leaned more on others? Are there conversations I've been avoiding or ones I wish I could have?
- ✿ **Behavioral Changes:** What changes in my behavior or daily habits have I noticed since the event? Considering aspects like my sleep patterns, eating habits, and how often I've reached out to friends, have I developed any new coping mechanisms, whether positive or negative?

* **Identity and Self-Worth:** How do I currently see my identity and self-worth after this experience? Has this event altered how I view myself? Am I more resilient, or do I feel diminished in some way?
* **Stress and Anxiety Management:** What specific sources of stress or anxiety are weighing on me right now, and how am I managing them? What would make the list of my biggest stressors—school, work, social pressures? What am I doing to cope with this stress, whether it's healthy or not?
* **Support Systems:** Who are the key people I can turn to for support, and how comfortable do I feel reaching out to them? Who would be on a list of friends, family, or professionals I can talk to? Are there barriers stopping me from reaching out, like fear or uncertainty?
* **Coping Strategies:** What coping strategies am I using, and are they helping or hurting me? What are my go-to methods for dealing with stress—like scrolling on my phone, binge-watching shows, or exercising? Are these strategies giving me relief or adding to my anxiety?
* **Future Goals and Aspirations:** How has this trauma shifted my goals or dreams for the future? Have I adjusted my aspirations—am I more motivated to make a change, or do I feel discouraged? What new goals have I formed?

⊙ SELF-REGULATION STRATEGIES

The push and pull between control and safety is something many of us feel, especially in a world that often seems unpredictable and out of our hands. On one side, we crave control—the ability to shape our circumstances and influence outcomes. On the other, we long for safety—the assurance that we are secure, that everything will be okay, or that we can avoid harm. These desires often clash, leaving us feeling overwhelmed, stuck, or anxious.

This tension becomes even more pronounced in the aftermath of mass trauma, like a school shooting, natural disaster, or any event that deeply shakes us. In the wake of such events, we instinctively try to regain control, hoping that by managing our routines, environments, or responses, we can restore some sense of safety to a world that now feels chaotic and unsafe. This need to regain control is crucial during times of acute stress, as it's a human instinct to seek stability when everything feels uncertain. I know I felt a deep sense of relief when classes resumed after 9/11. Despite the heartbreak, it was comforting to see my classmates—especially those who had lost loved ones—sitting in their usual spots, as though some semblance of normalcy had returned.

But here's the paradox: While control and safety offer comfort, they are often not permanent. Life is unpredictable, and no matter how much we try to plan, we can't control everything. Whether it's a sudden change, a tragedy, or the constant flux of events, some things will always be beyond our reach. Think of "entropy"—the principle that systems tend toward greater disorder and chaos over time. The more we try to control or predict outcomes, the more anxious we may feel when things don't go as planned. We want life to be clear, manageable, and understandable, but it doesn't always work that way.

The irony is that the more we chase safety, the more stressed we may become. Clinging to the idea of perfect safety can leave us feeling unsettled when things go wrong, caught in a pattern of trying to control the uncontrollable. This frustration is natural, but it's also a sign that we need to rethink our relationship with control.

Here's the freeing part: When we accept that we can't have total control or perfect safety, we begin to let go of the pressure to make everything predictable. Acknowledging that life is uncertain shifts our focus from controlling every outcome to embracing the unpredictability. It means being proactive or preparing for the future, while also accepting that uncertainty is part of the package deal. And when we make peace with that, we often feel more empowered to handle whatever comes our way.

Especially after trauma, letting go of the need for total control helps us focus on what we *can* control—our responses, self-care, and how we support others. While we can't guarantee safety or predict the future, we can show up, be present, and take things one step at a time. When we stop demanding absolute safety from every situation, we often find we are more capable of adapting and moving forward, even without all the answers.

Life will always have its uncertainties, and that's okay. Embracing uncertainty can make us more resilient, flexible, and at peace. It's a challenge, but one that ultimately involves trusting ourselves to navigate the unknown.

Here are some other trauma-informed approaches you might find helpful during times of chaos and uncertainty.

Reestablish a Daily Routine: Establishing a daily routine can provide a sense of normalcy and control, which is essential after a crisis. Plan simple activities that can help you feel anchored, such as waking up at the same time, eating regular meals, exercising, and setting time aside for self-care (like reading, relaxing, or hobbies). If routines are difficult, try using a whiteboard, planner or calendar to break your day into manageable parts. It can also help you visualize your goals and create stability. When those foundations are in place, returning to school or work, and surrounding yourself with things that bring you joy again is important.

Designate a Safe Space: This can be a physical space (like a corner of your room) or a mental one (like a place you can visualize in your mind). Fill this space with comforting objects (a favorite blanket, comforting photos, or calming scents). Whenever you're feeling unsafe or uncomfortable, spend time in that space to help regain your sense of security.

Create an Emergency Plan: In case of future distress, having a plan in place can give you a sense of security. This can include a list of people to contact for help, places you can go to feel safe, and coping strategies to use in the moment. Likewise, write down various coping techniques that help you feel calm and safe, so you can reference them whenever needed.

Develop Long-Term Healing Goals: In the face of social crises, it's easy to get consumed by the immediate aftermath. However, setting long-term recovery goals can help you find purpose and hope. These goals might involve furthering your education, traveling, starting a creative project, or getting involved in causes that matter to you. Having something to look forward to can provide a sense of direction and motivate you to continue working toward positive change, both personally and within your community.

Media Critique and Empowerment for Teens and Young Adults: Instead of simply scrolling through traumatic news stories, take an active role in understanding how media outlets frame crises. Recognize how sensational headlines or biased reporting can amplify feelings of fear and helplessness. Learn to differentiate between responsible journalism and clickbait. Being able to assess media critically helps you feel more in control of your emotions, reducing the overwhelming effect that constant exposure to crisis news can have. You can also start conversations with peers about how the media portrays social issues, and raise awareness about the impact of misinformation.

Engage in Peer Counseling or Support Groups: Sometimes, talking to someone who understands your experience is the best way to process difficult emotions. Peer counseling programs or support groups are an excellent resource, as they offer a safe space to share your feelings with others who have lived through similar challenges. Many organizations run peer counseling services or group therapy specifically for teens and young adults. Not only can you find support for yourself, but you can also become a support system for others in your community who are struggling. For instance, in the aftermath of the Boston Marathon Bombing in 2013, the Boston Strong Foundation was created to support the victims, including offering peer support groups for survivors, first responders, and their families. These groups helped survivors cope with grief, PTSD, and other emotional struggles in the wake of the bombing. These groups also allowed them to share their stories, raise awareness about the emotional impacts of terrorism, and help others who were also struggling.

Support Crisis Relief: Get involved with organizations that provide direct assistance to individuals and communities affected by crises. This could involve helping organize food drives, volunteering at shelters, or supporting mental health services. By donating your time or skills, you contribute to the recovery and well-being of others while also gaining a sense of purpose and empowerment from the work you're doing. Fundraising or volunteering for these causes gives you a direct way to help in the aftermath of crises. Examples of reputable organizations who work in crisis relief include Doctors Without Borders, UNICEF, International Committee of the Red Cross, Amnesty International, International Rescue Committee, World Central Kitchen, and Human Rights Watch.

Get Involved with Local Youth Organizations: Look for local youth organizations or create one that is led by young people, specifically designed to address social crises or injustices. By working alongside peers who share your commitment, you can contribute to initiatives that actively support those affected by crises. Volunteering with mental health organizations, helping rebuild communities, or supporting organizations helps combat feelings of powerlessness and gives you the tools to create tangible change. For instance, Youth United for Change (YUC), focuses on social justice activism, particularly related to issues like violence, trauma recovery, and education reform. YUC works on local and national campaigns, supporting youth-led initiatives. Join or create a YUC chapter in your area to lead campaigns focused on trauma prevention and healing. This can include working on anti-violence initiatives or supporting victims of mass trauma.

Participate in Civic Education: Take the time to learn how social systems and institutions work, particularly in times of crisis. Understanding how crises are managed and how social systems can be changed helps you feel less helpless and more confident in your ability to influence real change. You might join workshops or community meetings about policymaking, social services, or youth leadership. Being educated empowers you to act, whether that's through voting, advocacy, or influencing policies that directly affect you and your peers.

Advocate for Improved Crisis Management in Your School or Community: Use your voice to push for better mental health resources and trauma-informed practices within your school or community. This could involve working with administrators, counselors, or local government officials to ensure that schools and communities are equipped to handle crises effectively. Advocating for change can help rebuild trust and create a safer environment for everyone, while showing others that their voices matter in times of crisis. One powerful example of a youth who has engaged in safety initiatives and crisis prevention is Emma Gonzalez, a survivor of the 2018 school shooting at Marjory Stoneman Douglas High School in Parkland, Florida. After the tragedy, Emma became one of the most prominent youth voices advocating for safer schools and stronger gun control policies.

⊘ POSITIVE-CHANGE KICKSTARTER

Self-Care Actions: Can you identify a small action to integrate into your daily routine today? Whether it's a few minutes of stretching or listening to your favorite song, pick something you can do immediately to feel better.

Personal Discoveries: What's one thing you've discovered about yourself through this experience that you can reflect on today? Take a moment to write down any strengths or weaknesses you've noticed.

Engaging with Everyday Life: How can you honor your feelings while still engaging in everyday life starting today? Think of one activity you love and allow yourself to enjoy it, even if it feels hard.

RESOURCES

WEBSITES

The Resilience Project (theresilienceproject.com.au): An initiative that focuses on building mental well-being and emotional resilience, particularly through programs that teach individuals practical strategies for coping with adversity and stress. It emphasizes the development of emotional intelligence, mindfulness, and gratitude, all key elements of strengthening resilience to manage the effects of mass trauma.

BOOKS

The Trauma of Everyday Life, by Mark Epstein (Penguin Books, 2014).

Trauma Recovery Workbook for Teens: Exercises to Process Emotions, Manage Symptoms and Promote Healing, by Deborah Vinall (Callisto Teen, 2022).

The Unspeakable: And Other Subjects of Discussion, by Meghan Daum (Farrar, Straus, and Giroux, 2014).

CHAPTER 18

POLITICAL FATIGUE

~~~~

COMMONLY VOICED

❂ "I'm really feeling overwhelmed by the constant negativity in the news and online—scandals, controversies, and endless debates that never seem to lead anywhere. I'm not even eligible to vote yet, and honestly, I'm starting to wonder if I ever will want to when the time comes."

❂ "I don't know if I've ever been hopeful about social change, since we're in a constant nightmare of division and dysfunction."

❂ "Despite voting, staying informed, and engaging in discussions, I often feel powerless and exhausted, like my efforts don't make a difference."

❂ "Sometimes I want to disconnect for my own sanity but feel guilty about neglecting my civic duty or my community.

UNDERSTANDING POLITICAL FATIGUE

Your political views and engagement—whether you're part of Generation Z, Millennials, Generation X, or Baby Boomers— are shaped by a unique combination of historical events, technological advancements, and evolving social norms. Each generation's experiences contribute to its distinct political perspectives and behaviors. And what an exciting, yet perplexing, time it is to be part of a younger generation like yours. Growing up immersed in the internet and social media, these platforms have become powerful tools for organizing and advocating for important causes like climate change, racial justice, and 2SLGBTQ+ rights. A prime example is the #FridaysForFuture movement, led by Gen Z activist Greta Thunberg, which demonstrates how social media can spark meaningful, real-world change. This highlights how your generation is revolutionizing sociopolitical engagement and advocacy.[79]

Even more encouraging, research shows that participating in civic activities can have a positive impact on mental health. Volunteering, campaigning, or taking part in community projects can provide a sense of purpose and accomplishment, boosting self-esteem and helping to counter feelings of helplessness and uncertainty. This kind of engagement also fosters connections with others who share your values, reducing isolation and creating a supportive network. Working toward—and achieving—goals through these activities enhances your sense of control and effectiveness, offering a productive way to manage stress. Instead of letting personal challenges weigh you down, you can channel your energy into meaningful action and change.[80]

My first experience with political campaigning during my first summer in college really demonstrated the benefits of community involvement for me. I had stumbled upon a Craigslist ad (back when Craigslist was less sketchy for job postings) for political canvassing work with an ultra-progressive political party. At 19, with minimum opinions or knowledge of social policies or politics, I thought it would be an interesting summer gig—certainly more engaging than making dumplings at our family business or doing retail work at the mall (yes, this was before the days of online shopping). As a canvasser, I recall how intimidating it was to knock on doors in the Bronx, talking to people about the grassroots causes the party supported. I was trained by a hipster graduate student who also worked part-time as a DJ—he wore a beanie in the summer before it was cool. I had my first exposure to political jargon like left-leaning, right-leaning, redlining, constituencies, and coalition-building.

I ended up quitting after about five weeks. It was nerve wracking for me to talk to strangers about impactful issues I didn't fully understand at the time, the commute from Queens to the Bronx was exhausting, and I wasn't a fan of the peer pressure to party hard after work. But despite these challenges, it turned out to be one of the most eye-opening experiences of my late teens. It gave me a deep appreciation for local politics and the importance of engaging with a community—having open, thoughtful conversations and taking action to influence social policies that matter. I learned so much about advocating for marginalized communities and thinking beyond myself, and these values have remained with me to the present day.

While grassroots organizing can be rewarding for some, it's not for everyone—including my 19-year-old self. Passionate engagement in political causes can sometimes lead to political fatigue, a form of emotional and mental exhaustion that comes from constant exposure to high-stress situations, overwhelming information, or persistent conflict. This kind of continuous engagement can drain your energy, diminish your motivation, and lead to burnout, making it difficult to maintain activism and preserve your mental well-being.

Here's how various psychological factors can contribute to this fatigue:

※ **Cognitive Dissonance:** This theory explains how feeling conflicted between your beliefs and your actions can be draining. For example, if you're passionate about climate action but find that debates on the Green New Deal seem more about arguing than solving problems, you might feel frustrated and exhausted.

※ **Information Overload:** The sheer volume of news and social media updates can be overwhelming when scrolling through endless reports on scandals, protests, and policy debates. This flood of often negative or sensationalized information can be exhausting and lead to burnout.

※ **Social Comparison:** Seeing others who are highly engaged or seem to have all the answers can make you feel inadequate if you don't measure up. If you're involved in a cause but notice others organizing big events or creating viral content, you might feel discouraged and disconnected.

✻ **Learned Helplessness:** Repeated failures or lack of visible results can lead to feelings of powerlessness. If you've participated in many protests or advocated for change but haven't seen significant outcomes, you might start to feel like your efforts are in vain.

✻ **Stress and Coping:** Constant exposure to stressful issues, especially without good coping strategies, can cause significant anxiety. For instance, following news about police brutality or student loan debt without strong coping methods can impact your mental health.

✻ **Affective Forecasting:** This theory suggests we often poorly predict how future events will affect us emotionally. For example, you might expect to feel great after voting in a key election, but if the result is disappointing, you might feel even more disillusioned than anticipated.

✻ **Cultivation and Desensitization:** Regular exposure to negative media portrayals can make you see politics as inherently corrupt or ineffective, which become normalized over time. If the media constantly shows political leaders as corrupt or debates as polarized, you might start to believe that politics is fundamentally broken, leading to more disengagement.

Recent events, like the Israel-Gaza conflict and student protests, illustrate the psychological effects of political fatigue. These events, filled with intense activism and heated debates, can heighten stress and anxiety. For instance, if you're deeply involved in these discussions and constantly exposed to conflicts or distressing updates, it can take a toll on your outlook.[81]

In the short term, the emotional intensity of political debates might lead you to withdraw and view potential change more cynically. Over time, ongoing disillusionment and burnout might reduce your political participation and make it harder to stay informed or advocate for the causes you care about. This chronic stress could even lead to more serious mental health issues, like anxiety or depression.

Take a look at Vic's story of political involvement, and how political fatigue is real and challenging to work through.

Vic's Story

Vic, a high school student living near a major railroad line, faced a significant challenge when a train carrying dangerous chemicals derailed in their community. The spill created an environmental emergency, and Vic, passionate about environmental issues, decided to contribute to the response efforts. While direct cleanup was not feasible and left to professionals, Vic took on roles such as organizing community support, participating in awareness campaigns, and helping with educational outreach.

As Vic immersed themself in these activities, they began to experience political fatigue, which became increasingly evident in their daily life. Vic was actively involved in managing social media updates and coordinating information for local community groups. At first, they were enthusiastic about keeping everyone informed about the derailment and response efforts. However, as the situation progressed, the volume of information became overwhelming. Vic received constant alerts about the spill's impact, updates on the cleanup progress, and media reports filled with alarming details. This incessant flow of information led to mental fatigue. Vic felt constantly stressed trying to keep up with new developments, leading to difficulty focusing on schoolwork and personal life.

The endless barrage of updates created a sense of overload, where Vic struggled to process the information and felt emotionally drained. This flood of often distressing news made it hard for them to engage with the issues effectively and led to a feeling of being trapped in continuous stress.

Vic also felt a significant disconnect between their efforts and the actual progress being made in the cleanup. Despite their advocacy and hard work, they observed that the bureaucratic red tape and delays were hindering effective action. For instance, while they pushed for more immediate measures to address the chemical spill, local authorities seemed slow to act. Vic found themself increasingly frustrated by meetings that seemed more focused on finger-pointing than on actionable solutions. This clash between Vic's ideals and the slow pace of progress led to growing frustration and a sense of futility.

While working on community support, Vic frequently saw posts from other activists who appeared to have more influence or were involved in high-profile efforts. For example, a peer from a nearby school was featured in local news for organizing a major rally, which seemed to draw significant attention and recall. In contrast, Vic's role, though important, was less visible and did not receive the same level of recognition. Vic's exposure to these more prominent efforts made them feel inadequate. They began to compare their own contributions unfavorably against those of their peers, leading to feelings of self-doubt and discouragement. This comparison created a sense of inadequacy and disconnection, further fueling their disengagement and contributing to their overall sense of political fatigue.

The combination of information overload, cognitive dissonance, and social comparison led to significant impacts on Vic's well-being. They started to withdraw from their activism, feeling overwhelmed and increasingly disillusioned by the response efforts. Their academic performance suffered as they struggled to balance their schoolwork with the stress of their involvement. Social relationships also felt strained as Vic's engagement with the response efforts became a source of tension and frustration.

🔍 SELF-REFLECTION

Vic's experience underscores the importance of understanding and managing the psychological toll of activism, particularly for young activists. Also, political fatigue can be overwhelming, especially in a rapidly changing and intense sociopolitical landscape. Self-reflection can help you process your feelings and find a constructive way forward. Here are some questions to consider:

* **Identifying Stressors:** What specific aspects of politics or current events are causing me the most stress or fatigue? How do these issues manifest in my daily life?
* **Values and Goals Alignment:** How does my current level of political engagement reflect my personal values and long-term goals? In what ways does it align or conflict with what I truly believe in?
* **Balanced Information Consumption:** Am I consuming news and information from a variety of sources? How

can I ensure that my consumption is balanced and not overwhelming?

* **Emotional Impact of Engagement:** How do I feel after engaging in political discussions or consuming political content? Do these interactions energize or drain me, and why?

* **Role of Social Media:** How do social media and digital platforms influence my political engagement? Are they a source of stress or empowerment for me?

SELF-REGULATION STRATEGIES

For those from marginalized or minority groups, the political climate can feel indifferent—or even outright hostile—toward your identities, beliefs, and struggles. The fight for rights, dignity, and visibility can be draining, emotionally, mentally, and physically. When it's as though society is dismissing or overlooking your existence, it's easy to become overwhelmed by political fatigue. But even in those uncertain moments, remember: Your voice is powerful and part of a larger story of resistance, persistence, resilience, insistence, and eventual change.

I want to remind you that, while your experiences are uniquely yours, you are not alone. It's isolating, I know, to be part of a group whose rights and identities seem to be constantly under attack—but presence is revolutionary. Your identity is your strength, and the more you embrace who you are and live in alignment with your social justice values, the more resilient you'll become in the face of adversity. There will be moments of doubt, and it won't always be easy, but trust that your existence and triumphs are making a difference.

And don't forget: You are not fighting alone. There are allies and fellow activists out there, waiting to link arms with you. The work you do, no matter how big or small, is part of a larger movement—a movement built by countless others who've faced similar struggles and are working to rebuild and strengthen our communities. Change has always come when people dared to speak up, and your participation, in whatever way you can, is contributing to that ongoing effort.

In a world where political polarization, tribalism, the 24/7 news cycle, social media, and constant controversies can leave you mentally and emotionally drained, understand that you don't have to sacrifice your peace to be effective. It's okay to take a step back. Limit your news consumption, take breaks from social media, and disconnect when things feel overwhelming. By being mindful of your capacity to engage, you ensure that your activism remains sustainable and grounded in what truly matters to you. Embrace doing what you can, when you can, and staying true to your purpose.

So, in the face of political fatigue, lean on others, take care of yourself, and allow space for rest. It's completely understandable to feel frustrated or disheartened, but above all, keep your head up. Your perspectives are precious, your struggles are valid, and your mission is worth it. Keep fighting for what's right, stay rooted in your values, and trust that your efforts—no matter how small they may seem in the moment—are shaping a better world for those who come after you.

Here are some specific self-regulation strategies to help with political fatigue:

You Have Friends: In times when human rights are under threat, having a safe space to discuss these issues is crucial. Set up or join a local support group where you can engage with others in a civil, open dialogue. These groups can be held in person or online. Platforms like Discord or Zoom can host safe spaces to talk about current events and social justice without fear of judgment or retribution.

Digital Force Field: Create boundaries around your social media usage to protect your mental health. For example, limit your scrolling to certain times of the day, and use apps to block certain sites or time spent on social media. Reducing constant exposure to distressing news can help you process everything more mindfully. Limit your social media use to 30 minutes in the morning and 30 minutes in the early evening. Choose specific times—like 8:00 a.m. for catching up on news and 8:00 p.m. for updates or messages. This way, you avoid being constantly exposed to distressing news throughout the day. Consider using a phone app that tracks and limits your screen time to help stick to this schedule.

Media Literacy Workshops: Attend or organize a media literacy workshop that focuses on identifying misinformation or biased reporting in the media. This is particularly useful when political narratives are intentionally manipulated to incite fear or confusion. You can learn how to spot fake news, fact-check sources, and become more critical of the media you consume.

Join or Start a Local Fact-Checking Group: With the rapid spread of disinformation, you might want to join or create a group dedicated to fact-checking news and raising awareness of misinformation. You can use tools like Snopes or Media Bias/Fact Check to educate yourself and your peers on what's real and what's not, empowering you to engage in a healthier, more informed way.

Solution-Focused Journaling: When you're feeling disillusioned, try writing about solutions. What would a better world look like? What changes do you want to see in your community, and how can you contribute? Focusing on solutions can help combat feelings of helplessness and rekindle hope for the future.

Discussion Group with Friends: Start a weekly discussion group with your friends to talk about current events and political issues in a supportive environment. Focus on sharing perspectives and solutions rather than dwelling on negativity. This will help you feel more connected and less isolated.

Family Conversation Nights: Set aside time each week for open conversations with your family about various social and political topics. Ensure that these discussions are respectful and constructive. This allows you to express your concerns and gain new insights, helping you manage stress and feel more supported.

Role-Reversal Exercises: Try engaging in role-playing where you argue for a perspective you don't necessarily agree with. It can help you understand different viewpoints and feel less polarized. It's also an effective way to build empathy and reduce anger.

Perspective-Expanding Exercises: Consider researching and reflecting on the different sides of political issues. This helps build empathy for others who may be affected by policies, and it can help you step away from believing it's all about your viewpoint.

Political or Social Justice Internships: Consider taking internships with organizations working on issues that matter to you, such as voting rights, climate justice, racial equality, or refugee support. Interning can provide hands-on experience, networking opportunities, and a deeper understanding of how to advocate for systemic change.

Activism Through Art: Create political art to channel your frustration, confusion, or hope. Many teens have turned to creating murals, posters, or digital art to express their stance on human rights, democracy, and justice. For example, in the aftermath of the #MeToo and Black Lives Matter movements, artists used murals and graffiti to demand justice and accountability. You could also participate in or start an art-based protest, like creating posters for rallies, creating online campaigns, or holding your own virtual gallery.

Digital Storytelling: Use platforms like YouTube, TikTok, or a podcast to create short videos or audio content about political issues that matter to you. For example, create a series explaining why specific rights are under threat, or use video interviews to showcase voices from marginalized groups. These platforms provide an immediate way to amplify voices and connect with others who share similar concerns.

Social Media Activism: With so many feeling the urgency of the erosion of rights, starting or supporting online petitions is a practical way to take action. Platforms like Change .org and Care2 make it easy to create petitions on important issues like voting rights, freedom of speech, and human rights. By sharing these petitions with your peers, you can help raise awareness and get others involved in the cause. You can even post about the issues that matter to you, tag your local elected representatives, and use relevant hashtags to amplify your message. Politicians are often responsive to public comments on platforms. Likewise, follow your representatives' social media accounts to stay updated on their work, and engage with their posts by commenting, sharing, or starting conversations about the issues you care about.

Youth-Led Movements: Get involved in youth-led movements that fight for democracy, human rights, or specific causes (e.g., climate justice, immigration reform, gender equality, voting rights). For example, the Sunrise Movement, which advocates for climate change policy, is led by young activists and provides platforms for youth to take part in political action. These groups offer training, support, and a sense of purpose to combat political disillusionment.

Human Rights Fundraisers: Raise funds for organizations that protect and fight for human rights in your community or globally. Platforms like GoFundMe or Kickstarter make it easy to start fundraising efforts. Support groups like Amnesty International or the American Civil Liberties Union (ACLU) often have youth volunteer programs or offer ways to contribute financially to campaigns that fight back against rights violations.

⊘ POSITIVE-CHANGE KICKSTARTER

Self-Care Strategies: What self-care practices can you implement while still staying informed and involved in political matters? How can you create boundaries to protect your mental health?

_____

_____

_____

Reconnecting with Passions: How can you reconnect with your personal motivations and passions outside of politics? What activities bring you joy and fulfillment?

Building Resilience: What strategies can you adopt to cultivate resilience and adaptability in the face of political challenges?

Long-Term Goals: What are your long-term goals, and how does your current level of civic or political engagement fit into those goals? Are there adjustments you need to make to align your actions with your aspirations?

 # RESOURCES

WEBSITES

CommonCause (www.commoncause.org): Nonprofit organization that advocates for reforms to ensure a more transparent, accountable, and inclusive government. They focus on campaign finance reform, voting rights, and protecting democracy.

GovTrack (www.govtrack.us): Tracks the activities of the US Congress, including bills, resolutions, votes, and information about individual members of Congress.

The Lit (thelit.org): Youth-run newsletter that simplifies current events and politics for younger audiences, encouraging critical thinking.

BOOKS

Micro Activism: How You Can Make a Difference in the World without a Bullhorn, by Omkari L. Williams (Storey Publishing, LLC, 2023).

The Righteous Mind: Why Good People Are Divided by Politics and Religion, by Jonathan Haidt (Vintage, 2013).

Run for Something: A Real-Talk Guide to Fixing the System Yourself, by Amanda Litman (Atria Books, 2017).

Social Justice for the Sensitive Soul: How to Change the World in Quiet Ways, by Dorcas Cheng-Tozun (Broadleaf Books, 2023).

CHAPTER 19

TECHNOLOGICAL WOES

COMMONLY VOICED

- "I know I'm constantly glued to my phone, but I just can't resist the notifications and alerts that force me to pay attention to my screen."
- "I try to stay connected with my friends and stay up to date with everything online, but I end up leaving them 'on read' all the time because the pressure of sounding clever or responding timely is unnerving. They must all hate me."
- "The person I appear online isn't the real me."
- "My parents don't think I can communicate in real life, but I see them on their devices all the time too, so we just have lots of silent meals together."

UNDERSTANDING TECHNOLOGICAL WOES

Technology has profoundly reshaped our lives, offering opportunities and tools that once seemed unimaginable.

Social media platforms like Instagram, TikTok, YouTube, and Snapchat help us stay connected with friends and family around the world, enabling us to build and maintain relationships, share experiences, and engage in global conversations. The internet provides an endless supply of information, making research for school projects or exploring new interests incredibly accessible. The idea that information is always at our fingertips has been ingrained from an early age, with even *Sesame Street* introducing a talking smartphone character named "Smartie," whose catchphrase is "Look it up!" Whether diving into the latest scientific discoveries or mastering new skills through online tutorials, technology has become an invaluable educational and social resource.

During the pandemic, technology proved to be a lifeline, fundamentally changing how we function in society. With schools facing unprecedented challenges, virtual learning platforms like Zoom, Google Classroom, and Microsoft Teams became essential for continuing education remotely. This shift allowed students and teachers to maintain routines, engage in live discussions, and access resources from the safety of their homes, ensuring that learning continued despite widespread school closures.[82]

Similarly, technology revolutionized healthcare. The rise of telemedicine enabled patients to consult healthcare providers without needing to visit a clinic, breaking down barriers to access and ensuring continuity of care. Personally, I transitioned my therapy practice entirely online during the pandemic and can't imagine going back to exclusively in-person sessions. Digital health records, remote monitoring, and virtual consultations have made healthcare more accessible and effective, paving the way for improvements in patient care and medical research.[83]

However, as with any powerful tool, technology's impact is not entirely positive. The Disney movie *WALL-E* serves as a poignant reminder of the potential downsides of excessive reliance on technology. In the film, Earth becomes a desolate wasteland due to environmental neglect, and humanity, living in space, has become completely absorbed by screens and automated systems. The film underscores how overreliance on technology can lead to disconnection from real-life experiences, physical health, and meaningful relationships. This dystopian vision serves as a cautionary tale, reminding us of the importance of finding a balance in our use of technology to avoid becoming too detached from the non-digital world around us.[84]

On an individual behavioral level, technology-related challenges can intersect and compound each other, impacting your mental health and well-being. Common issues include:

* ✷ **Cyberbullying:** The anonymity of digital spaces can intensify harassment, leading to significant emotional trauma and a heightened risk of mental health issues such as depression, anxiety, and suicidal ideation.

* ✷ **Addiction and Overuse:** Excessive use of technology, particularly social media and gaming, can lead to addiction-like behaviors that interfere with daily responsibilities and social interactions, contributing to social isolation and poor mental health outcomes.

* ✷ **Sleep Disruption:** Screen time, especially before bed, can interfere with melatonin production and disrupt sleep patterns, leading to poorer sleep quality, which is linked to various mental health issues, including depression

and anxiety. One common behavior contributing to this disruption is "revenge procrastination," where you use technology to avoid responsibilities or stressors. This behavior often stems from a desire to reclaim personal time and autonomy after feeling overwhelmed or constrained by obligations during the day. While this form of procrastination might offer temporary relief or distraction, it often exacerbates sleep problems. The blue light emitted by screens can further interfere with melatonin production, making it harder to fall asleep and maintain restful sleep. This cycle of inadequate sleep and extended screen time can significantly impact your overall well-being, leading to increased stress, anxiety, and diminished cognitive function.

* **Privacy Concerns:** Breaches of privacy and data exploitation can lead to heightened stress and anxiety, as individuals feel vulnerable and lose control over their personal information.
* **Toxic Social Comparisons:** Constant updates from friends and influencers can create anxiety about missing out on social events or experiences, increasing feelings of loneliness and dissatisfaction.
* **Body Image Issues:** Idealized body images on social media can significantly impact body satisfaction, contributing to low self-esteem and an increased risk of eating disorders.
* **Information Overload:** The vast amount of information available online can be overwhelming, particularly when it includes negative news or unrealistic expectations, leading to increased stress and anxiety.
* **Online Dating Challenges:** Experiences such as rejection and ghosting on dating platforms can negatively impact

self-esteem and mental health, affecting one's ability to form meaningful connections.

✥ **Lack of Boundaries:** Difficulty in setting boundaries between online and offline life can lead to significant stress and burnout, affecting work-life balance and overall quality of life.

The individual challenges associated with technology also have broader societal implications, straining social systems and public health in several ways. Firstly, the rise of technology-related mental health issues, such as anxiety and depression linked to social media, creates an increased demand for mental health services. This surge can strain public health systems, leading to longer wait times for treatment and higher costs for mental health care. As technology's impact on well-being grows, the need for more comprehensive mental health support becomes critical. Additionally, technology addiction and overuse can contribute to social isolation, reducing face-to-face interactions and weakening community bonds. This erosion of social capital can have wide-reaching effects, including diminished community support systems and increased loneliness, which can exacerbate mental health issues and lead to societal disconnection.

Furthermore, while technology has enabled remote learning, it has also highlighted and sometimes widened educational disparities. Students without reliable internet access or necessary devices face significant barriers to learning, exacerbating inequalities in education. This digital divide can perpetuate socioeconomic disparities and limit opportunities for disadvantaged students.[85] The difficulty in setting boundaries between work and personal life due to constant connectivity can lead to burnout and decreased productivity, affecting not only individuals but also organizations. This strain can result in higher turnover rates, increased absenteeism, and reduced overall efficiency in the workplace.

Privacy and security concerns also come into play, as the prevalence of data breaches affects not just individuals but also organizations and governments. The financial and reputational costs of managing and mitigating these breaches can be substantial, impacting trust in digital systems and requiring increased investment in cybersecurity measures. Lastly, online dating challenges and the superficial nature of digital interactions can alter societal norms around relationships and intimacy. Issues such as ghosting and rejection can contribute to a decline in trust and satisfaction in personal relationships, affecting broader social dynamics.

Learn more about the impact of technology on individuals like Kai, whom you may share characteristics with.

Kai's Story

Kai, a 20-year-old who recently left college, embarked on a new career as a social influencer specializing in gaming. Initially, Kai's enthusiasm and dedication to gaming led to rapid success, turning them into an internet sensation. This early achievement enabled Kai to move out of their family home and live independently. However, this initial triumph has been marred by unforeseen challenges within the online world, emphasizing the emotional toll of dealing with toxic online communities and its impact on Kai's well-being, productivity, and financial stability.

Kai's daily routine has been increasingly affected by the negative aspects of their online presence. They became entangled in a toxic environment characterized by harassment, negative comments, and persistent criticism. Despite their early success, the constant exposure to hostility has led to escalating feelings of anxiety and stress.

The stress from dealing with relentless negativity has adversely affected Kai's content creation process. They have struggled with procrastination and maintaining a consistent content schedule. The burden of addressing and mitigating negative feedback has contributed to burnout, undermining their initial productivity and creativity.

The emotional strain has had severe consequences for Kai's financial stability. Although their initial success allowed them to move out and enjoy a degree of independence, the current instability of their income stream is jeopardizing their ability to sustain their new lifestyle. The fluctuating nature of online revenue—affected by viewer engagement, sponsorship deals, and platform algorithms—has made it difficult for Kai to secure a steady income. This financial uncertainty adds to their stress and complicates their career decision-making process.

Kai's online experiences have also led to significant social isolation. They began to withdraw from friends and family, feeling increasingly disconnected despite ongoing virtual interactions. This withdrawal has strained personal relationships and diminished their ability to engage meaningfully with those around them. The emotional toll has impacted Kai's ability to manage their feelings effectively, further isolating them from their support network.

Faced with mounting stress, decreased productivity, and financial instability, Kai is contemplating a career change. However, exploring alternate career paths is challenging without a college degree. The lack of a formal educational credential complicates their job search and limits their options, making it difficult to transition into more stable fields. The prospect of returning to college or pursuing other qualifications adds another layer of complexity to their situation.

The combined effects of online harassment, reduced productivity, social isolation, and financial instability have significantly impacted Kai's overall well-being. They are experiencing self-doubt and frustration, struggling to reconcile their early success with current difficulties. To address these challenges, Kai would benefit from supportive measures focusing on mental health and financial planning. Professional guidance and a strengthened support system could help Kai navigate their emotional struggles and explore new opportunities aligned with their interests and aspirations.

🔍 SELF-REFLECTION

Take a moment to reflect on your own relationship with technology:

* **Time and Goals:** How much time do I spend on technology each day, and how does this compare to my goals or expectations? How well do I manage my time when using technology, and do I often spend more time online than intended?
* **Online Activities and Feelings:** What are the primary activities I engage in online (e.g., social media, gaming, research), and how do these activities make me feel? Do

I feel that technology enhances or detracts from my daily life and overall well-being?

☼ **Impact of Social Media:** How do I feel after spending time on social media platforms? Do I usually feel better or worse, and how often do I compare myself to others online? What impact does this comparison have on my self-esteem and mental health?

☼ **Privacy and Sharing:** Am I comfortable sharing personal information online, and how aware am I of the privacy settings on my social media accounts? Have I ever experienced a data breach, and how did I respond?

☼ **Mood and Mental Health:** Have I noticed any changes in my mood or mental health related to my technology use, such as increased anxiety or depression? How does screen time affect my sleep patterns, and do I find it difficult to fall asleep after using technology?

⟨♀⟩ SELF-REGULATION STRATEGIES

As someone who studies human behavior for a living, I've learned to use a variety of self-regulation techniques on myself to help maintain a healthy relationship with technology. Most days, I manage to avoid obsessing over things like being "left on read" or falling into the trap of doom-scrolling. But some days, I find myself down a wormhole of information I have no real need for. For example, when will I ever need to know that, in Victorian times, chairs called "fainting chairs" were placed in hallways or other strategic spots so women could rest if they felt faint from the physical strain of wearing tight corsets and heavy hoop skirts? At the time, I told myself it was just an interesting historical tidbit (though, now I do feel somewhat redeemed to have included this nugget here). But when I should be finishing this book, I can see how easily these technological advantages can turn into distractions.

Another issue that many of us struggle with is the pressure of social etiquette in the digital age. Some report feeling an overwhelming sense of obligation to respond quickly to text messages, and others report constant worry about whether their tone comes across as appropriate or accurate. The anxiety doesn't stop there—there's also the pressure to keep the conversation going or, if they don't reply in time, they start feeling guilty about being unresponsive or even uninteresting. This can leave them wondering if their relationships will suffer as a result. To complicate matters further, many clients find that the simple act of talking on the phone has become a nerve-wracking ordeal. It's not that they don't want to talk to loved ones, like their grandparents; it's just that the direct connection through voice feels so unfamiliar or awkward compared to texting. It's as if the very act of picking up the phone has become anxiety-inducing.

This shift in how we communicate has created new challenges in our relationships and mental well-being, but the good news is that we can learn to manage it. Finding balance is key, and being aware of these patterns can help us regain control over how we interact with technology.

Fortunately, there are things we can all do to protect ourselves from technology's negative effects. Setting boundaries around screen time, being more intentional with your social media use, and taking time to unplug when you need to are all ways to help reduce the stress that technology can sometimes create.

Our ideal is not to abandon tech altogether, but to create a healthier relationship with it. You're not alone in feeling the pressure, but by being mindful and proactive, you can make tech work for you, not the other way around. You deserve to feel connected, but also to have space for yourself. It's about finding that sweet spot that supports your mental health and helps you thrive. Here are more specific strategies to self-regulate when dealing with your technological challenges:

Protect Yourself from Cyberbullying: Learning how to protect yourself online can help you avoid toxic situations. Here are some helpful tips:

✲ Block and report harmful accounts. Most social media platforms allow you to protect your space by reporting and blocking bullies.

✲ Don't engage with online bullies. If you receive hurtful messages, try not to respond. Responding can often escalate the situation. Instead, report them and save any screenshots or messages.

✲ Educate yourself on how to handle cyberbullying. Many online platforms and organizations provide resources to help you navigate these situations, giving you the tools to protect yourself.

Use Technology, Don't Let It Use You: Instead of believing you have to check social media every 10 minutes, think of your phone as a tool for specific tasks. Use it for quick check-ins with friends or organizing your schedule, but try to avoid aimless scrolling. When you use your phone, have a clear reason—like listening to a podcast or checking in on a specific goal—rather than just browsing without purpose.

Try Going Tech-Free During Key Moments: It's easy to think you have to be on your phone 24/7, but consider leaving it in another room during meals, study time, or when hanging out with friends. Try having a "no-phone" dinner, so you can reconnect and enjoy the moment without distractions.

Reclaim Your Time from the Screen: Ask yourself if your time online is really fulfilling you. If you're using your phone because you're bored, try doing something active instead, like going for a walk, swimming, or biking. These small changes help you take back time for activities that are more meaningful and provide a break from constant digital pressure. Try setting a digital curfew—like no screens after 9 p.m.—to improve sleep quality and create space for relaxation.

Check How Technology Affects Your Mood: Notice how you feel after spending an hour scrolling through social media— do you feel more anxious or drained? Take a moment to check in with yourself. If the time spent online leaves you feeling exhausted, try limiting it and focus on activities that leave you feeling better, like discovering a new cuisine, spending time with an animal, or gardening.

Use Technology with Purpose, Not Just for Distraction: If you're using your phone to discover new music, look for inspiration, or complete school projects, set an intention for each session. Ask yourself, *"What do I hope to achieve from this?"* If you get distracted, put the phone down and switch to something that aligns with your goals, like journaling or sketching out ideas for a project. Practicing this kind of mindfulness makes your tech use more productive and less overwhelming.

Imagine Life with Less Tech: Picture spending an afternoon without your phone—maybe hanging out with friends, taking a road trip, or diving into a hobby you've been meaning to start, like learning an instrument or painting. Imagining these moments helps you see that the world outside your phone can feel just as exciting and fulfilling.

Question the Need for Instant Gratification: In today's world, we're used to instant replies, likes, and quick entertainment. Test out what it's like to delay gratification. For example, instead of checking your phone every time you're waiting for a reply, try reading a chapter of a book or journaling. Look for ways to balance the instant gratification with more meaningful activities that take time to enjoy.

Create Tech-Free Rituals: Build small habits into your day that don't require screens. Start your mornings with a 10-minute stretch or meditation session without your phone. You can also dedicate time in the evening to read a book or listen to music without your device. These rituals help you unwind and take a break from the constant pull of your devices.

Appreciate Offline Moments: When you're hanging out with friends, take a moment to notice how it feels to spend time together without phones. It's easier to connect when there are no distractions. You could even jot down these moments in a journal to reflect on how valuable "phone-free" time can be. It'll help you realize that some of life's best experiences don't need a screen to be enjoyable.

⊘ POSITIVE-CHANGE KICKSTARTER

Coping with Online Issues: How do you handle online conflicts or cyberbullying? What coping strategies can you use to address bullying head on?

Physical Symptoms and Breaks: Do you notice any physical symptoms related to your technology use, such as eye strain or headaches? How can you take breaks from screens today?

Personal Goals and Values: What role does technology play in helping you achieve your personal goals and aspirations? How do you better use technology to support your learning and personal development?

Aligning with Values: What values are important to you in your technology use, and how can you ensure that your habits align with these values?

 # RESOURCES

BOOKS

The Anxious Generation: How the Great Rewiring of Childhood is Causing an Epidemic of Mental Illness, by Jonathan Haidt (Penguin Press, 2024).

Digital Minimalism: Choosing a Focused Life in a Noisy World, by Cal Newport (Penguin Press, 2019).

CONCLUSION

~~~~

As we approach the end of our time together, exploring and developing self-regulation skills to navigate the personal, social, and societal challenges you may be facing, I'd like to share a well-known Chinese tale that offers valuable insight into moving *through*, rather than over, adversity. This is a story I often share with my clients when they feel stuck, and it consistently brings them a sense of relief by the time we reach its end.

The story begins with a poor farmer whose prized horse runs away. When the neighbors hear the news, they offer their sympathy, saying, "How unfortunate!" But the farmer simply replies, "Maybe so, maybe not. We'll see." The next day, the horse returns, bringing with it three wild horses. The neighbors, now impressed, say, "What good luck!" To which the farmer responds, "Maybe so, maybe not. We'll see." Later, the farmer's son attempts to ride one of the wild horses, is thrown off, and breaks his leg. The neighbors, eager to offer their opinion, say, "How terrible!" Once again, the farmer replies, "Maybe so, maybe not. We'll see." The next day, the king's army arrives to draft young men for war—but because of his broken leg, the farmer's son is exempted.

There are many ways to connect with this story, but to me, it offers a profound reflection on the unpredictable nature of life. What initially seems like a setback may eventually lead to an unexpected benefit, and conversely, what appears to be good fortune can quickly turn into a complication. This lesson is particularly relevant in the context of self-regulation, where challenges can take many forms—mental health struggles, such as overwhelming anxiety or depression; interpersonal challenges with family, friends, or partners; or macro issues, like economic instability, political unrest, or environmental crises, which often feel beyond our understanding and influence. In each of these situations, what matters most is not the event itself, but how we choose to respond.

As you may recall, a key aspect of self-regulation is recognizing the limits of our control and accepting that not all circumstances are within our power to change. By learning to fully engage with each moment and the emotions it brings, we empower ourselves to respond thoughtfully rather than react impulsively. Life will inevitably present challenges, big and small, but like the farmer, we have the power to determine how we engage with each situation. His calm, measured response to uncertainty (and strong public opinion) serves as an exemplary model of self-regulation in action.

By maintaining self-compassion and composure and staying grounded, we can better navigate both personal struggles and larger societal shifts. This allows us to cultivate a trauma-informed mindset that promotes clarity, resilience, and adaptability. The farmer's repeated refrain, "Maybe so, maybe not. We'll see," illustrates a cognition that relieves the pressure of needing to predict or control every circumstance, creating space for patience, understanding, and openness to whatever comes next. In doing so, we can develop a more balanced approach to growth and well-being. So, with that, I leave you with this: Remain open to the possibility of trans-formation, knowing that every experience, whether planned or unexpected, contributes to your growth and resilience. Therefore, let's boldly say to adulthood, *"Bring it on!"*

ENDNOTES

~~~~~~

1 Daniel G. Whitney and Mark D. Peterson, "US National and State-Level Prevalence of Mental Health Disorders and Disparities of Mental Health Care Use in Children," *JAMA Pediatrics* 173, no. 4 (2019): 389–91, https://doi.org/10.1001/jamapediatrics.2018.5399.

2 National Institute of Mental Health, "Major Depression," NIH.gov, last updated July 2023, https://www.nimh.nih.gov/health/statistics /major-depression.

3 National Institute of Mental Health, "Any Anxiety Disorder," NIH.gov, accessed February 11, 2024, https://www.nimh.nih.gov/health /statistics/any-anxiety-disorder.

4 National Institute of Mental Health, "Suicide," NIH.gov, last updated February 2025, https://www.nimh.nih.gov/health/statistics/suicide.

5 National Institute on Drug Abuse, "Reported Drug Use Among Adolescents Continued to Hold Below Pre-Pandemic Levels in 2023," NIH.gov. December 13, 2023, https://nida.nih.gov/news-events /news-releases/2023/12/reported-drug-use-among-adolescents -continued-to-hold-below-pre-pandemic-levels-in-2023.

6 Jerica Radez , Tessa Reardon, Cathy Creswell, Peter J. Lawrence, Georgina Evdoka-Burton, and Polly Waite, "Why Do Children and Adolescents (Not) Seek and Access Professional Help for Their Mental Health Problems? A Systematic Review of Quantitative and Qualitative Studies," *European Child & Adolescent Psychiatry* 30 (February 2021): 183–211, https://doi.org/10.1007/s00787-019-01469-4.

7 Vincent J. Felitti , Robert F. Anda, Dale Nordenberg, David F. Williamson, Alison M. Spitz, Valerie Edwards, et al., "The Adverse Childhood Experiences (ACE) Study: Relationship of Childhood Abuse and Household Dysfunction to Many of the Leading Causes of Death in Adults," *American Journal of Preventive Medicine* 14, no. 4 (1998): 245–58, https://doi.org/10.1016/s0749-3797(98)00017-8.

8 Nadine Burke Harris, *The Deepest Well: Healing the Long-Term Effects of Childhood Adversity* (Houghton Mifflin Harcourt, 2018).

9 Abraham H. Maslow, "A Theory of Human Motivation," *Psychological Review* 50, no. 4 (1943): 370–96, https://doi.org/10.1037/h0054346.

10 Mary A. Carskadon, "Sleep in Adolescents: The Perfect Storm," *Pediatric Clinics of North America* 58, no. 3 (2011): 637–47, https://doi.org/10.1016/j.pcl.2011.03.003.

11 Anne G. Wheaton, Sherry Everett Jones, Adina C. Cooper, and Janet B. Croft, "Short Sleep Duration Among Middle School and High School Students—United States, 2015," *Morbidity and Mortality Weekly Report* 67, no. 3 (2018): 85–90, https://doi.org/ 10.15585/mmwr.mm6703a1.

12 Seithikurippu R. Pandi-Perumal, "Why We Sleep: The New Science of Sleep and Dreams by Matthew Walker, Ph.D," *Sleep and Vigilance* 2, (2018): 93–94, https://doi.org/10.1007/s41782-018-0034-0.

13 Barbara L. Fredrickson, "The Role of Positive Emotions in Positive Psychology: The Broaden-and-Build Theory of Positive Emotions," *American Psychologist* 56, no. 3 (2001): 218–26, https://doi.org /10.1037//0003-066x.56.3.218.

14 Daniel Carvalho, Carlos Sequeira, Ana Querido, Catarina Tomás, Tânia Morgado, and Olga Valentim, et al., "Positive Mental Health Literacy: A Concept Analysis," *Frontiers in Psychology* 13 (April 2022), https://doi.org/10.3389/fpsyg.2022.877611.

15 Kristen P. Morie, Michael J. Crowley, Linda C. Mayes, and Marc N. Potenza, "The Process of Emotion Identification: Considerations for Psychiatric Disorders," *Journal of Psychiatric Research* 148 (April 2022): 264–74, https://doi.org/10.1016/j.jpsychires.2022.01.053; Alessandra D'Agostino, Raffaele Pepi, Mario Rossi Monti, and Vladan Starcevic, "The Feeling of Emptiness: A Review of a Complex Subjective Experience," *Harvard Review of Psychiatry* 28, no. 5 (2020): 287–95, https://doi .org/10.1097/HRP.0000000000000269.

16 Cara C. Young and Mary S. Dietrich, "Stressful Life Events, Worry, and Rumination Predict Depressive and Anxiety Symptoms in Young Adolescents," *Journal of Child and Adolescent Psychiatric Nursing* 28, no. 1 (2015): 35–42, https://doi.org/10.1111/jcap.12102.

17 Aastha Singh, Ravindra Singh, and Ajay Kumar Singh, "A Review -Based Theoretical Analysis on Somatization of Psychological Symptoms and Physical Manifestation of Trauma in Youths," in *Exploring Cognitive and Psychosocial Dynamics Across Childhood and Adolescence*, ed. Maria Sofologi, Dimitra Katsarou, and Efthymia Efthymiou (IGI Global, 2025), 273–94, https://doi.org/10.4018/979-8-3693-4022-6.ch014.

18 Steven C. Hayes, Kirk D. Strosahl, and Kelly G. Wilson, *Acceptance and Commitment Therapy: The Process and Practice of Mindful Change. 2nd ed.* (Guilford Press, 2011).

19 Dan-Feng Tang, Li-Qiong Mo, Xin-Chu Zhou, Jun-Hong Shu, Lei Wu, Dong Wang, et al., "Effects of Mindfulness-Based Intervention on Adolescents Emotional Disorders: A Protocol for Systematic Review and Meta-Analysis," *Medicine* 100 no. 51 (2021): e28295, https://doi .org/10.1097/MD.0000000000028295.

20 American Psychiatric Association, *Diagnostic and Statistical Manual of Mental Disorders: Fifth Edition* (*DSM-5*) (American Psychiatric Association, 2013), 165–68.

21 Billie Eilish, "Bellyache," *Don't Smile at Me* (EP), Darkroom / Interscope Records, 2017, https://www.youtube.com/watch?v =gBRi6aZJGj4.

22 Margaretha Wilhelmina Laurence Morssinkhof, "Waves of Change: Sex Hormones, Depression and Sleep" (PhD thesis, Vrije Universiteit Amsterdam, 2024), https://doi.org/10.5463/thesis.676; Eric R. Lewandowski, Mary C. Acri, Kimberly E. Hoagwood, Mark Olfson, Greg Clarke, William Gardner, et al., "Evidence for the Management of Adolescent Depression," *PEDIATRICS* 132, no.4 (2013): e996–1009, https://doi.org/10.1542/peds.2013-0600.

23 Natalie L. Colich, Margaret A. Sheridan, Kathryn L. Humphreys, Mark Wade, Florin Tibu, Charles A. Nelson, et al., "Heightened Sensitivity to the Caregiving Environment During Adolescence: Implications for Recovery Following Early-Life Adversity," *Journal of Child Psychology and Psychiatry* 62, no. 8 (2020), https://doi.org/ 10.1111/jcpp.13347; Lidia Piccerillo and Simone Digennaro, "Adolescent

Social Media Use and Emotional Intelligence: A Systematic Review," *Adolescent Research Review* , July 21, 2024, https://doi.org/10.1007 /s40894-024-00245-z.

24 *Black Panther*, directed by Ryan Coogler (Burbank, CA: Walt Disney Studios Motion Pictures, 2018).

25 Daniel Goleman, *Emotional Intelligence: Why It Can Matter More Than IQ* (Bantam, 1995), 34–35; Antonio Damasio, *The Feeling of What Happens: Body and Emotion in the Making of Consciousness* (Harcourt, 1999), 110–12.

26 Jerry Suls, "Anger and the Heart: Perspectives on Cardiac Risk, Mechanisms and Interventions," *Progress in Cardiovascular Diseases* 55, no.6 (2013): 538–47, https://doi.org/10.1016/j.pcad.2013.03.002.

27 Laura K. Guerrero, "'I'm So Mad I Could Scream:' The Effects of Anger Expression on Relational Satisfaction and Communication Competence," *Southern Communication Journal* 59, no. 2 (1994): 125–41, https://doi.org/10.1080/10417949409372931.

28 Richard M. Ryan and Edward L. Deci, "Intrinsic and Extrinsic Motivation from a Self-Determination Theory Perspective: Definitions, Theory, Practices, and Future Directions," *Contemporary Educational Psychology* 61 (April 2020): 1–11, https://doi.org/10.1016/j.cedpsych .2020.101860.

29 Alanna McCrory, Paul Best, and Alan Maddock, "'It's Just One Big Vicious Circle': Young People's Experiences of Highly Visual Social Media and Their Mental Health," *Health Education Research* 37, no. 3 (2022): 167–84, https://doi.org/10.1093/her/cyac010.

30 Hahna Patterson , Casey Mace Firebaugh, Tara Rava Zolnikov, Rebecca Wardlow, Stephanie M. Morgan, and Brett Gordon, "A Systematic Review on the Psychological Effects of Perfectionism and Accompanying Treatment," *Psychology* 12, no. 1 (2021): 1–24, https:// doi.org/10.4236/psych.2021.121001.

31 Xinhang Gao, "Academic Stress and Academic Burnout in Adolescents: A Moderated Mediating Model," *Frontiers in Psychology* 14 (June 2023): 1133706, https://doi.org/10.3389/fpsyg.2023.1133706; Daniel J. Madigan, Lisa E. Kim, and Hanna L. Glandorf, "Interventions to Reduce Burnout in Students: A Systematic Review and Meta-Analysis," *European Journal of Psychology of Education* 39 (June 2024): 931–57, https://doi.org/10.1007/s10212-023-00731-3.

32 Tricia Hersey, *Rest is Resistance: A Manifesto* (Hachette UK, 2022), 141.

33 Reef Karim and Priya Chaudhri, "Behavioral Addictions: An Overview," *Journal of Psychoactive Drugs* 44, no.1 (2012): 5–17, https://doi.org/10.1080/02791072.2012.662859.

34 Corrado Villella, Giovanni Martinotti, Marco Di Nicola, Maria Cassano, Giuseppe La Torre, Maria Daniela Gliubizzi, et al., "Behavioural Addictions in Adolescents and Young Adults: Results from a Prevalence Study." *Journal of Gambling Studies* 27, no. 2 (2010): 203–14, https://doi.org/10.1007/s10899-010-9206-0.

35 Minji Kim and Susanna Lee, "The Effects of Autonomous Sensory Meridian Response (ASMR) on Modality, Mood, and Mindfulness (3Ms)," *Psychology of Popular Media* 13, no. 3 (2024): 313–23, https://doi.org/10.1037/ppm0000488.

36 Eric H. Chudler and Kelly S. Chudler, *Neuropedia: A Brief Compendium of Brain Phenomena* (Princeton University Press, 2022).

37 Nancy Doyle, Lorraine Hough, Karen Thorne, and Tanya Banfield, "Neurodiversity," in *Challenging Bias in Forensic Psychological Assessment and Testing*, ed. Glenda C. Liell, Martin J. Fisher, and Lawrence F. Jones (Routledge, 2022): 329–57.

38 Meng-Chuan Lai, "Mental Health Challenges Faced by Autistic People," *Nature Human Behaviour* 7 (October 2023): 1620–37, https://doi.org/10.1038/s41562-023-01718-2.

39 Erin E. McKenney, Jared K. Richards, Talena C. Day, Steven M. Brunwasser, Claudia L. Cucchiara, Bella Kofner, et al., "Satisfaction with Social Connectedness Is Associated with Depression and Anxiety Symptoms in Neurodiverse First-Semester College Students," *Autism* 28, no. 8 (2024): 1972–84, https://doi.org/10.1177/13623613231216879.

40 Valeria Khudiakova, Joel M. Le, and Alison L. Chasteen, "To Mask or Not to Mask: The Role of Concealment Behavior, Stigma Experience, and Community Connectedness in Autistic People's Mental Health," *Neurodiversity* 2 (May 2024), https://doi.org/10.1177/2754633024 1255121.

41 Heidi Morgan, "Connections between Sensory Sensitivities in Autism; the Importance of Sensory Friendly Environments for Accessibility and Increased Quality of Life for the Neurodivergent

Autistic Minority," *PSU McNair Scholars Online Journal* 13, no. 1 (2019), https://doi.org/10.15760/mcnair.2019.13.1.11.

42 Juliana L. Vanderburg, Antonio F. Pagán, and Deborah A. Pearson, "Neurodiversity Framework: Model, Tenets, and Critiques," in *The Palgrave Encyclopedia of Disability* (Macmillan, 2025), 1–6, https://doi.org/10.1007/978-3-031-40858-8_65-1.

43 John Green, *The Fault in Our Stars* (Dutton Books, 2012), 133.

44 John T. Cacioppo and William Patrick, *Loneliness: Human Nature and the Need for Social Connection* (Norton, 2008).

45 Jean-Paul Sartre, *Being and Nothingness: An Essay on Phenomenological Ontology* (Washington Square Press, 1992), 374.

46 Martin Heidegger, *Being and Time* (Harper & Row, 1962), 219.

47 Sue E. Williams and Bonnie Braun, "Loneliness and Social Isolation—A Private Problem, a Public Issue," *Journal of Family & Consumer Sciences* 111, no.1 (2019): 7–14, https://doi.org/10.14307/JFCS111.1.7.

48 Segun Kehinde, "The Loneliness Epidemic: Exploring Its Impact on Mental Health and Social Well-Being in Modern Society," Qeios, March 25, 2024, https://doi.org/10.32388/8ped34.

49 Silva Junior, Silva Sales, Souza Monteiro, Cardoso Costa, Braga Campos, Gomes Miranda, et al., "Impact of COVID-19 Pandemic on Mental Health of Young People and Adults: A Systematic Review Protocol of Observational Studies," *BMJ Open* 10, no. 7 (2020): e039426, https://doi.org/10.1136/bmjopen-2020-039426.

50 Gaia Sampogna, Vincenzo Giallonardo, Valeria Del Vecchio, Mario Luciano, Umberto Albert, Claudia Carmassi, et al., "Loneliness in Young Adults During the First Wave of COVID-19 Lockdown: Results from the Multicentric COMET Study," *Frontiers in Psychiatry* 12 (December 2021), https://doi.org/10.3389/fpsyt.2021.788139.

51 Maya Angelou, *I Know Why the Caged Bird Sings* (Random House, 1969).

52 Yael Gross, "Erikson's Stages of Psychosocial Development," in *The Wiley Encyclopedia of Personality and Individual Differences*: *Volume 1* (Wiley, 2020), 179–84, https://doi.org/10.1002/9781118970843.ch31.

53 Bojana Marinković and Luka Borović, "Personality Traits and Identity Status of Adolescents: A Person-Centered Approach," *Godišnjak*

za Psihologiju 19 (2022): 101–16, https://doi.org/10.46630/gpsi.19
.2022.06

54 Jan E. Stets and Peter J. Burke, "Identity Theory and Social Identity Theory," *Social Psychology Quarterly* 63, no. 3 (2000): 224–37, https://doi.org/10.2307/2695870.

55 Kanchana N. Ruwanpura, "Multiple Identities, Multiple-Discrimination: A Critical Review," *Feminist Economics* 14, no. 3 (2008): 77–105, https://doi.org/10.1080/13545700802035659.

56 Jessica P. Montoro, Jessica E. Kilday, Deborah Rivas-Drake, Allison M. Ryan, and Adriana J. Umaña-Taylor, "Coping with Discrimination from Peers and Adults: Implications for Adolescents' School Belonging," *Journal of Youth and Adolescence* 50 (January 2021): 126–43, https://doi.org/10.1007/s10964-020-01360-5.

57 Antonio Piolanti and Heather M. Foran, "Efficacy of Interventions to Prevent Physical and Sexual Dating Violence Among Adolescents: A Systematic Review and Meta-Analysis," *JAMA Pediatrics* 176, no. 2 (2022): 142–49, https://doi.org/10.1001/jamapediatrics.2021.4829.

58 Molly J. Richards, Amanda Bogart, and Jeanelle Sheeder, "Communication and Interpretation of Sexual Consent and Refusal in Adolescents and Young Adults," *Journal of Adolescent Health* 70, no. 6 (2022): 915–21, https://doi.org/10.1016/j.jadohealth.2021.12.013.

59 Yok-Fong Paat and Christine Markham, "Digital Crime, Trauma, and Abuse: Internet Safety and Cyber Risks for Adolescents and Emerging Adults in the 21st Century," *Social Work in Mental Health* 19, no. 1 (2021): 18–40, https://doi.org/10.1080/15332985.2020.1845281.

60 Lauren Francis and Dominic Pearson, "The Recognition of Emotional Abuse: Adolescents' Responses to Warning Signs in Romantic Relationships," *Journal of Interpersonal Violence* 36, no. 17–18 (2021): 8289–313, https://doi.org/10.1177/0886260519850537.

61 Marta Ciabatti, Amanda Nerini, and Camilla Matera, "Gaslighting Experience, Psychological Health, and Well-Being: The Role of Self-Compassion and Social Support," *Journal of Interpersonal Violence*, ahead of print, December 27, 2024, https://doi.org/10.1177/08862605241307232.

62 Fred Rogers, *The World According to Mister Rogers: Important Things to Remember* (Hyperion, 2003), 21.

63 Jesús Maya, Isabel Fuentes, Ana Isabel Arcos-Romero, and Lucía Jiménez, "Parental Attachment and Psychosocial Adjustment in Adolescents Exposed to Marital Conflict," *Children* 11, no. 3 (2024): 291, https://doi.org/10.3390/children11030291.

64 Francesca Lionetti, Benedetta Emanuela Palladino, Christina Moses Passini, Marta Casonato, Oriola Hamzallari, Mette Ranta, et al., "The Development of Parental Monitoring During Adolescence: A Meta-Analysis," *European Journal of Developmental Psychology* 16, no. 5 (2019): 552–80, https://doi.org/10.1080/17405629.2018.1476233.

65 Sam Smith, "Love Goes," *Love Goes* (LP), Capitol Records, 2020.

66 Charles A. Corr and David E. Balk, eds., *Adolescent Encounters with Death, Bereavement, and Coping* (Springer Publishing Company, 2009).

67 Katherine M. Shear, "Grief and Mourning Gone Awry: Pathway and Course of Complicated Grief," *Dialogues in Clinical Neuroscience* 14, no. 2 (2012): 119–28, https://doi.org/10.31887/DCNS.2012.14.2/mshear.

68 John O'Donohue, *To Bless the Space Between Us: A Book of Blessings* (Harmony Books, 2008).

69 World Health Organization, "Climate Change," October 12, 2023, https://www.who.int/news-room/fact-sheets/detail/climate-change -and-health; Ehsan Eyshi Rezaei, Heidi Webber, Senthold Asseng, et al., "Climate Change Impacts on Crop Yields," *Nature Reviews Earth & Environment* 4 (2023): 831–46, https://doi.org/10.1038/s43017-023 -00491-0; Tianyi Ma, Jane Moore, and Anne Cleary, "Climate Change Impacts on the Mental Health and Wellbeing of Young People: A Scoping Review of Risk and Protective Factors," *Social Science & Medicine* 301, (May 2022): 114888, https://doi.org/10.1016/j.socscimed.2022.114888.

70 Linda Goldman, "Climate Change and Youth: Grief, Loss, Trauma, and Action 1," in *The Routledge International Handbook of Child and Adolescent Grief in Contemporary Contexts* (Routledge, 2023), 321–34.

71 Emma L. Lawrance, Rhiannon Thompson, Jessica Newberry Le Vay, Lisa Page, and Neil Jennings, "The Impact of Climate Change on Mental Health and Emotional Wellbeing: A Narrative Review of Current Evidence, and Its Implications," *International Review of Psychiatry* 34, no. 5 (2022): 443–98, https://doi.org/10.1080/09540261.2022.2128725.

72 Larissa Dooley, Jylana Sheats, Olivia Hamilton, Dan Chapman, and Beth Karlin, *Climate Change and Youth Mental Health: Psychological Impacts, Resilience Resources, and Future Directions* (See Change

Institute, 2021), https://seechangeinstitute.com/wp-content/uploads /2022/03/Climate-Change-and-Youth-Mental-Health-Report.pdf.

73 Csilla Ágoston, Benedek Csaba, Bence Nagy, Zoltán Kőváry, Andrea Dúll, József Rácz, et al., "Identifying Types of Eco-Anxiety, Eco-Guilt, Eco-Grief, and Eco-Coping in a Climate-Sensitive Population: A Qualitative Study," *International Journal of Environmental Research and Public Health* 19, no. 4 (2022): 2461, https://doi.org/10.3390/ijerph 19042461.

74 Jack S. Peltz, Jamie S. Bodenlos, Julie N. Kingery, and Ronald D. Rogge, "The Role of Financial Strain in College Students' Work Hours, Sleep, and Mental Health," *Journal of American College Health* 69, no. 6 (2021): 577–84, https://doi.org/10.1080/07448481.2019.1705306.

75 Feng Li, "Impact of COVID-19 on the Lives and Mental Health of Children and Adolescents," *Frontiers in Public Health* 10 (October 2022): 925213, https://doi.org/10.3389/fpubh.2022.925213.

76 Megha Jacob, "Forgiveness and Reconciliation: The Rwandan Genocide and Implications for Mental Health," *Journal of Theta Alpha Kappa* 46, no. 2 (2022): 39–52, https://jtak.scholasticahq.com /article/37425-forgiveness-and-reconciliation-the-rwandan-genocide -and-implications-for-mental-health.

77 Jasmin Wittmann, Hawkar Ibrahim, Frank Neuner, and Claudia Catani, "Fleeing the War: A Socio-Ecological Perspective on the Mental Health of Internally Displaced and Refugee Children and Adolescents Living in the Kurdistan Region of Iraq," *PLOS Mental Health* 2, no. 1 (2025): e0000170, https://doi.org/10.1371/journal.pmen.0000170.

78 Irene Esther Krauskopf, Glen William Bates, and Roger Cook, "Children of Holocaust Survivors: The Experience of Engaging with a Traumatic Family History," *Genealogy* 7, no. 1 (2023): 20, https://doi .org/10.3390/genealogy7010020.

79 Paul Beckh and Agnes Limmer. "The Fridays for Future Phenomenon." Strategies for Sustainability, September 21, 2021, 427–32. https://doi.org/10.1007/978-3-030-74458-8_28.

80 Julianne Holt-Lunstad, "The Major Health Implications of Social Connection," *Current Directions in Psychological Science* 30, no. 3 (2021): 251–59, https://doi.org/10.1177/0963721421999630.

81 Carola Cerami, "A Reflection on Global Protests over Gaza: The Role of Universities in the Public Debate," *Nuovi Autoritarismi e Democrazie:*

Diritto, Istituzioni, Società (NAD-DIS) 6, no. 2 (2024), https://doi
.org/10.54103/2612-6672/27754.

82 Maya E. Rao and Dhananjai M. Rao, "The Mental Health of High
School Students During the COVID-19 Pandemic," *Frontiers in Education*
6 (July 2021): 719539, https://doi.org/10.3389/feduc.2021.719539.

83 Sonu Bhaskar, Alma Nurtazina, Shikha Mittoo, Maciej Banach,
and Robert Weissert, "Telemedicine During and Beyond COVID-19,"
Frontiers in Public Health 9 (March 2021): 662617, https://doi.org
/10.3389/fpubh.2021.662617.

84 Moh Faidurrohman, "Exploration of Human Degradation as
Depicted in Wall-E 2008," *Elite Journal: International Journal of
Education, Language, and Literature* 3, no. 3 (2023): 121–35, https://
journal.unesa.ac.id/index.php/elite/article/view/33719.

85 Alexandrea R. Golden, Emily N. Srisarajivakul, Amanda J. Hasselle,
Rory A. Pfund, and Jerica Knox, "What Was a Gap Is Now a Chasm:
Remote Schooling, the Digital Divide, and Educational Inequities
Resulting from the COVID-19 Pandemic," *Current Opinion in Psychology*
52 (August 2023): 101632, https://doi.org/10.1016/j.copsyc.2023
.101632.

ACKNOWLEDGMENTS

~~~~~~

I am deeply thankful to all my past, present, and future clients who have and will entrust me with their stories of both pain and triumph. Through you, I am continuously inspired to reflect and evolve—not only as a psychologist, but as a mother, partner, daughter, sister, friend, and community member. Your experiences shape who I am and the work I do, and for that, I am profoundly grounded in gratitude.

ABOUT THE AUTHOR

~~~~~

Dr. Kathy P. Wu is a first-generation psychologist who once considered a wide range of career paths, including toy maker, anesthesiologist, publisher, journalist, lawyer, civic leader, sociologist, and guidance counselor. It wasn't until someone recognized her natural ability to find the silver lining in any situation that she realized her true calling was to be a professional helper. With a deep love for people, Dr. Wu thrives in environments where she can empathize, actively listen, educate, creatively problem-solve, and cheer others on. Her career spans across corporations, educational institutions at all levels, hospitals, and community health centers. Now in private practice, Dr. Wu is constantly devising new therapeutic strategies to help young people flourish in our frustratingly beautiful world.